Eisenhower Center Studies on War and Peace
Douglas Brinkley, Editor

TIBURCIO CARÍAS

Portrait of a Honduran Political Leader

Thomas J. Dodd

With a Foreword by Douglas Brinkley

Louisiana State University Press

Baton Rouge

Designer: Barbara Neely Bourgoyne
Typeface: Quadraat
Typesetter: The Composing Room of Michigan, Inc.
Printer and binder: Thomson-Shore, Inc.

Library of Congress Cataloging-in-Publication Data

Dodd, Thomas J.
    Tiburcio Carías : portrait of a Honduran political leader / Thomas J. Dodd.
        p. cm. — (Eisenhower Center studies on war and peace)
    Includes bibliographical references and index.
    ISBN 0-8071-3037-0 (cloth : alk. paper)
    1. Carías Andino, Tiburcio, 1876– 2. Honduras—Politics and govern-
ment—1838–1933. 3. Honduras—Politics and government—1933–1982.
4. Caudillos—Honduras. I. Title. II. Series.
F1508.22.C37D63 2005
972.8305′1—dc22
                                                            2004029982

Frontispiece photograph courtesy of Rafael Bardales Bueso

To my children Abaigeal, Alison, and Justin

Contents

Illustrations

Foreword

How the wit brightens! How the style refines!
Before his sacred name flies ev'ry fault,
And each exalted stanza teems with thought.

— EDWARD LONG (1774)

Living for the past decade in New Orleans, I've gotten to know a few Honduran exiles who still maintain a fervent interest in their tropical homeland. We've spoken about the Bananalands in the northern lowlands along the Caribbean Sea and the Cerros de Calaque interior mountains where high-altitude coffee growing is the way out of grim poverty. All of my friends—by virtue of their entrepreneurial bent—are ardent CAFTA (Central American Free Trade Agreement) devotees. Although these recent immigrants still speak Spanish at home, and read La Prensa, the local Hispanic newspaper, they're fully Americanized in vision; they believe in the Algerian dream of hard work equaling monetary rewards.

And, it turns out, they have much in common with many Louisiana natives. Because 90 percent of all Hondurans are mestizos (a combination of white and Indian ancestry), they share a mixed ethnic legacy as so many Creoles in Louisiana do. Occasionally, Honduras is featured in the Times-Picayune—like when Hurricane Mitch nailed the Caribbean nation in 1998, killing thousands and causing nearly two billion dollars of damage—but not often. Seldom, in fact, is Honduran politics ever discussed in a Louisiana newspaper. The exiles put dictatorship—and even burgeoning democracy—behind them when they migrated to metro New Orleans. They focused on the future. They are rooting for the Saints to win an NFL Championship and the Mississippi River not to flood. The bloody decades of the twentieth century were left back home in Honduran towns like Comayagua and San Pedro Sula and Choluteca. America is for them the Land of New Beginnings.

That does not mean, however, that Honduran Americans have completely forgotten their political past. On the contrary, after reading this well-researched biography of Tiburcio Carías—written by Professor Thomas Dodd of Georgetown University School of Foreign Service (and a former U.S. Ambassador to Costa Rica and Uruguay)—in galley, I decided to ask my Honduran friends what they thought of the famed caudillo who became president in 1933—the same year as Franklin D. Roosevelt—and stayed in power until the late 1940s. Their reaction was emotional and mixed. They all described him as larger-than-life, a tall, imposing figure whose fanciful mustache and Grover Cleveland-like girth are as symbolic in Central American culture as Castro's beard or Guevara's beret or Ortega's shaggy hair. He was a populist, they all said. When pressed to elaborate, they added, "Well, he was a dictator, but a pretty good one."

As Americans we don't ever really think of dictators as being "pretty good." But Carías—perhaps like the colorful demagogue Huey Long in Louisiana during the Great Depression years—had a devoted following. And he made it a point not to cross the United States. He fancied himself not as a strong-armed bully but as a legitimate tribune of the people. Slapping backs and staring down his enemies was part of his inherent DNA. Even a passing glance at his résumé will tell you that he held just about every Honduran government post imaginable, including governor and legislator. As you'll learn when reading this informed biography, it's difficult to fully dislike Carías. For in the final analysis, he was a masterful politician, perhaps, along with Ramon Villeda Morales, the best natural-born pol Honduras has ever produced. (He is certainly the most remembered.) Cleverly, Carías manipulated the governmental bureaucracy in Tegucigalpa like a master puppeteer. He navigated his way through civil wars and coup attempts and economic woes of the most severe kind. His genius was that he also had an ear tilted to what the *people* wanted from government. He was not stone deaf to suffering or despair. Informed by the Honduran Revolution of the 1920s, Carías was able to govern because he had created a vast network of people—friends and surrogates—who saw in him political greatness. They tended, however, to overlook, which Professor Dodd doesn't, the cruel, inhuman aspects of his unflinching leadership. It's been said that Carías crushed dissidents as if they were cockroaches. If pressed against the glass, he could become an exterminator. You could count on it. Yet he also brought Honduras into the modern age.

Understanding Latin American history is, after all, a difficult and always paradoxical proposition. That's why Borges and Marquez and Cortázar became magic realists. You learn that Columbus arrived in 1502, for example, and shortly thereafter the 42,277-mile land parcel was named "Honduras," the Spanish word for *depths*. But was Columbus's arrival a positive development?

Did the European invasion better the lives of the indigenous peoples? Sometimes it seems that one is better off reading *One Thousand Years of Solitude* or Ruden Dario's "Poetry of Pain" than biographies of Carías-like caudillos to get answers. Yet this book is different. Professor Dodd has thought about Carías for so long, has ferreted out every document the Honduran leader ever stamped or signed, that the reader gets a real, fair-minded understanding of the *people* rising from revolution to create a quasi-democracy on his long coattails. Whether he used clever mediation or backroom favoritism or vicious threats to accomplish his political goals, nobody ever accused Carías of not being in charge. "As Latin American dictators go," Dodd writes, "President Carías is fairly good, far better than most, perhaps less enlightening than some." That is precisely what my Honduran friends say about him.

As a trained academic historian, an Americanist with a Central American history minor, I'm obviously aware that talking about Carías with a few random exiled Hondurans in a French Quarter café or Garden District cocktail party is an unscientific endeavor. Yet sometimes such random sampling engenders ripe results. One of my friends, a former reporter for *La Tribuna* (Tegucigalpa), now into the coffee import-export business via the Gulf of Mexico, summed up Carías very succinctly: "He was tough," he said. "But in a good, old-fashioned Honduran way."

As you learn from this book, Carías, through all of his *caudillo* tactics, remains admired in 2005 Honduras. Admired but not venerated. He is considered a thoughtful leader worthy of exalting. But he is *not* an exemplar of Jeffersonian-Hamiltonian democracy. He is, you might say, their tame "Kingfish," a populist politician who's become something of a folk legend, and this is his true story.

Douglas Brinkley
New Orleans
May 2005

Acknowledgments

Although my name appears on the cover of this book, there are many who helped in its preparation. Fulbright and Organization of American States grants provided the financial assistance needed for work in the Republic of Honduras. I am particularly grateful to numerous archivists and librarians in Tegucigalpa and San Pedro Sula for guiding me through the vast resources of their institutions. Dr. Julio Ponce Leon and Hector Roberto Luna of the National Archives and Library were particularly helpful during the year researching in Honduras. Maria Edith Fernandez in the Archives of the National Palace assisted in the search for records of particular ministries. Dr. Ramon Valladares of the Commission on Sovereignty and Fronteras in the Ministry of Foreign Affairs in Comayaguela directed me to the diplomatic resources during the entire Carías era. Carlos Cáceres Castillo of the archives in the Ministry of War, Navy, and Aviation provided records on the initial departmental organization at the start of the Carías presidency in 1933. The staff of the Library and Military Training School provided records on Carías's administrative duties in the northern departments during the first decade of the twentieth century. Victor Meza, director of the Honduran Document Center, constantly offered a wide array of official published records on the later Carías era.

I could not possibly count the days and hours spent with Honduran historians at the National University. But a few who have spent years researching and writing on the country's mid-twentieth century deserve particular thanks. Professor Ramón Oquelí, Laura Gálvez, Alejandro Solomon Sagastumé, and Vicente Cáceres Lara offered advice on the use of primary and secondary materials. Dr. Orfila Piñel, director of the University Library, directed me to Carías's academic records.

Numerous Hondurans, foes and admirers of Carías, shared stories of their experiences during the dictatorship. Political associates, exiles, and incarcerated opponents described their many experiences too. Some offered not only stories but also correspondence and papers from family archives. Rudolfo Velásquez of Intibucá, Gabriel Mejía of San Pedro Sula, and Tomás Martínez spent hours of their time reconstructing events, particularly those in which they were involved. The late Jorge Fidel Durón and Rafael Bardales Bueso, National Party loyalists, provided materials covering their work during the Carías era. Oscar Guerrero, a longtime opponent of Carías and a leader of the July 4, 1944, demonstration, gave me access to valuable personal correspondence and letters from other exiles in Guatemala, El Salvador, and Costa Rica.

Francisca Antunes, Presentación Rivera, José Antonio Barahona, and Gonzalo "Chalo" Luque—Carías's personal secretary (1954–1963), telegraph operator, Presidential Guard member, and militia leader, respectively—offered invaluable insights into the life of the president's "inner circle," those who closely observed his work habits and political skills.

The last bastion of Carías's political career, the PPP (the Popular Progressive Party)—based more on personal loyalty than on ideology—included Raul Barnica, Eliseo Lizardo, and Luís M. Coello Ramos, each of whom recalled his efforts to continue political support for Carías after the National Party looked elsewhere for leadership.

I am particularly indebted to family members whose parents occupied key positions in the Carías era, 1933–49. Aside from their recollections, they provided photographs, correspondence, and memorabilia that helped fill in details about the man and the era. Of particular help were Orlando and Dora Henríques, son and daughter of Benjamin Henríques, director of roads and one of Carías's closest associates for most of his presidency; Francisco Prats and Guillermo Ayes, sons-in-law of Carías; Daisy Carías, a daughter-in-law; Emma Bonilla Laríos, daughter of President Policarpo Bonilla (1894–99); and Miguel Izaguirre, nephew of Carlos Izaguirre, Carías's talented "writer warrior" friend. Last, Roberto Gálvez Barnes, son of Manuel Gálvez, minister of war throughout the Carías era, one-time president, and a member of the governing junta (1956–57), provided a comprehensive and vast overview of his family's role in Honduran politics from the 1930s through the 1960s. His recollections of his father's and his own participation in national politics were extremely helpful. Marcos Carías Zapata, son of Carías's private secretary, Marcos Carías Reyes, and Vicente Williams, son of Carías's vice-president, Abraham Williams, offered insights on their fathers' work in the early stages of Tiburcio Carías's presidency, particularly as the regime consolidated power at the national and local levels.

For an entire year, I met and talked at length in Honduras to people from all walks of life who lived under Carías's rule. Lawyers, businesspeople, taxicab drivers, doctors, and government workers in the capital city and farmers and landowners in remote towns and villages all had stories or personal accounts of their lives that were directly or indirectly affected by Tiburcio Carías. In every sense of the word, these people helped fill in the historical record of the 1930s and 1940s. The Cuevas family—Dr. Adan, Blanca Rosa, and son Juan—was of inestimable help in this regard. Finally, I wish to express my gratitude and thanks to Professor Darío Euraque of Trinity College's History Department, a widely respected scholar of Honduran history, who helped me on more occasions than I can possibly recollect.

Someone once said, "History is never finished." This account hopefully is a start, an effort to recount the life of a major figure in modern Honduran history. All of these people made this effort possible, and to them I shall be forever grateful.

TIBURCIO CARÍAS

Introduction

Twenty years after leaving office as president of Honduras, Tiburcio Carías died peacefully at home in Tegucigalpa, the capital, on December 23, 1969. A few days later, a throng of people lined the streets as party dignitaries solemnly escorted his remains to the presidential palace for public tributes. The procession moved on to the congress, where there were more eulogies for Carías, who had served longer as chief executive than any of his predecessors.

What was striking at these ceremonies was the presence of flags and banners from political groups other than Carías's own National Party. Politicians praised his leadership and some sixty years of public life, during which he was adorned with titles such as "Doctor," "Lawyer," "General," "Restorer of Peace," and "Benefactor of the Nation." Biographical sketches printed in leading newspapers referred to the occasions when he commanded military forces in 1907, 1928, and 1932 and outcomes of elections he supported.[1] Other accounts at the funeral ceremonies mentioned his elevation as constitutional president in free and fair elections. He had accepted election defeats in the 1920s, but after the presidency in 1932, he extended his rule as a strongman, a dictator. Liberal? Conservative? Constitutionalist? Dictator? He was all of these at one time or another. More a pragmatist than an ideologue, Carías combined paternalism with an authoritarian personalistic style. Although from time to time he adopted different political labels, his public life reflected the social and cultural landscape of Honduras in its rural and urban settings. None of his predecessors had succeeded in unifying the country, but he created domestic peace with political and social stability. He did it by force, exiling and incarcerating foes, as well as by persuasion and compromise. At the same time, he allowed old institutions to remain in place, such as local political chieftains and militias.

1. *Revista Extra* (1970), 1; see also *La Época* (Tegucigalpa), 6 July 1933, for his numerous titles and key biographical dates.

How and why did Carías emerge as a *caudillo*, a political leader with enormous power, a strongman governing in a dictatorial way? One scholar has observed, "Caudillos stand in the path of any narrative of Spanish American history, enigmatic and unavoidable."[2] Historians have described several conditions in which caudillos like Carías emerged. Some grew out of close relationships between landlords and political power in the nineteenth century, and from the military organization of rural society. Others gave the propertied classes the spoils of wars and then protected them. Still others became leaders of common people, heroes who engaged a worshipful following.[3]

In many ways the rise of Tiburcio Carías resembles, in varying degrees, each of these conditions producing a caudillo. He came from a landowning family associated with political activity through its kinship ties and alliances with others in the same economic and social class. From their own resources and extended family members, Carías's father, uncles, and brothers created militias to do battle for their particular interests.

Carías's political maturation from the late nineteenth century to the 1930s paralleled the demise of the age of liberalism. He rose to power to fill a vacuum created by the decline of the old order. The era was characterized by frequent outbursts of political instability, civil wars, and chronic economic crises, all unmanageable because Honduran governments lacked the rudiments of a modern bureaucratic state. Carías emerged, like other dictators in Central America in the 1920s and 1930s, when world depression and political unrest paralleled the growth of U.S. economic interests. Carías, like these other caudillos, imposed a domestic peace, centralized a bureaucratic state, and skillfully maintained good relations with Washington.

To those who remember Carías, he was a larger-than-life figure. He strode the stage of Honduran politics for sixty years. He felt his public service during a troubled era was a response to what the nation wanted and needed, namely, to be saved from the disorder and restored to a better era. "I was president for sixteen years," he said, "because the people made me."[4]

Carías was neither a writer nor a diarist. Most of what we know about him comes from the countless handwritten government directives he crafted and

2. John Charles Chasteen, *Heroes on Horseback: A Life and Times of the Last Gaucho Caudillos* (Albuquerque: University of New Mexico Press, 1995), 3.

3. Ibid., 4. Chasteen refers to historians like Julio Halperín Donghi, John Lynch, and E. Bradford Burns.

4. James Dunkerley, *Power in the Isthmus* (London, New York: Verso, 1988), 528.

signed. Interviews with friends and foes alike,[5] and research in official archives and private libraries in Honduras and the United States, also provide insights into his private and public life, revealing traits that contributed to his perceived invincibility.[6] His external demeanor concealed an inner discipline, through which he attended to details with perseverance and patience.

5. Interviews giving the details of Carías's early life and later political career came from many sources, including: Luis Bertrand, grandson of President Francisco Bertrand (1911–12, 1913–15, 1916–19), Tegucigalpa, 2 April 1987; Emma Callejas, whose uncle was Venancio Callejas, a long-time colleague of Carías in the National Party and a critic of the caudillo, interviews, Tegucigalpa, April, May, and June 1987; Miguel Izaguirre, nephew of Carlos Izaguirre, one of Carías's closest confidants through the 1930s and 1940s, numerous interviews, Tegucigalpa, spring 1987; Emma Bonilla de Larios, daughter of President Policarpo Bonilla (1894–99), interview, Tegucigalpa, 26 November 1987; Guillermo Ayes, Carías's son-in-law, interview, Tegucigalpa, 5 November 1987; Raul Barnica, private secretary to Carías 1954–58, interview, Tegucigalpa, 2 November 1987; Francisco Prats Vives, married to Carías's niece María Carías Reyes, interview, Tegucigalpa, 22 July 1987; Presentación Rivera, Carías's chief telegraph operator, 1945–49, numerous interviews, Tegucigalpa, July 1987; Jorge Daniel Carías, son of General Calixto Carías, a nephew of Carías, Tegucigalpa, 3 August 1987; Jorge Fidel Durón, who like his father was a close collaborator of Carías, several interviews, Tegucigalpa, February and August 1987; Daisy Carías, daughter-in-law of Carías, several interviews, Tegucigalpa, April 1987; Vicente Williams Jr., son of Carías's long-time vice-president Vicente Williams, 8 November 1987. A lengthy character description of Carías appeared in *La Época*, "Edición Extraordinaria" (Tegucigalpa), 8 January 1935, 3.

6. For a complete review of the historiography of the Carías regime, see Darío Euraque, "Social, Economic, and Political Aspects of the Carías Dictatorship in Honduras: The Historiography," *Latin American Research Review*, Vol. 29, No. 1 (1994): 238–48. Honduran historians who have written on the Carías era include Mario Argueta, Marvin Barahona, and Alejandro Salomón Sagastume. Argueta's two works, both published in 1989, make extensive use of U.S. and Honduran archives. They are *Tiburcio Carías: anatomía de una época, 1923–1948* (Tegucigalpa: Editorial Guaymuras, 1989) and *Bananas y política: Samuel Zemurray y la Cuyamel Fruit Company* (Tegucigalpa: Editorial Guaymuras, 1989), and Sagastume, *Carías: el caudillo de Zambrano, 1933–1948* (San Pedro Sula: Graficentro Editores, 1988). Barahona's *La Hegemonía de Los Estados Unidos en Honduras (1907–1932)* (San Pedro Sula: Graficentro Editores, 1988) sets the Carías regime in the context of diplomatic history in Central America during this time.

Hagiographic studies on Carías continued in the 1980s with the publication of Rafael Bardales Bueso's *El Fundador de la paz* (unpublished ms., Bardales Library, Tegucigalpa). A Nationalist Party member and intimate collaborator of the dictator, Bardales reveals his bias in the prologue: "it could be said that God put . . . Tiburcio Carías Andino on Honduran soil . . . so that he might uproot and destroy in order to cultivate and create." Carías's Liberal Party detractors who continued to publish in the 1980s and 1990s suffer from the same excesses as his slavish admirers. They portray their subject in the worst light. Emma Bonilla, the daughter of President Policarpo Bonilla, who founded the Liberal Party in 1891, relates the painful difficulties encountered by Carías's opponents

Carías was a large man. He stood over six-foot-two; was barrel-chested, heavy, with a solid build, 250 pounds; and had huge hands and a wide, bristling mustache. His eyes always fixed on his subject, resolute with a consummate presence; his physical features riveted people's attention. Taller than most Hondurans, he filled a room and dominated it. For him, self-discipline, hard work, and tending to details served as a foundation for his lifetime endeavors.

Inherently cautious and circumspect, he made political moves when the moment was propitious. With few close friends, he did not seek a wide coterie of fellow politicians. He kept his distance but at the same time conveyed the demeanor of a simple, plain person, accessible but never intimate, nor too personal. His closest associates were life-long friends. They were people who were as loyal to him as he was to them. Their bonds were shaped in days of civil war, a conflict that stretched from the 1890s through the 1920s and 1930s on to the end of Carías's life. He made acquaintances easily with his natural manner; but they were associations built only on trust, and were connected to his work as party leader, governor, legislator and president of the Republic. Local, departmental, and regional political leaders, ministers of state, and his emissaries abroad held their posts for long periods of time. They remained, however, separate and distinct groups all tied to Carías. Their tenure in office was so long because when Carías became chief executive in 1933, he already had a thirty-year career in politics behind him and had cemented friendships both personal and professional. These were tested allies. They were attracted to his simple tastes and unthreatening manner, but they were smart enough to keep a worshipful distance from him.

Inevitably Carías evokes comparison with other Central American and Caribbean dictators who dominated their countries' politics for decades. Each was a reflection of his nation's social, economic, political, and cultural circum-

---

in the 1940s in her *Continuismo y dictadura* (Comayaguela: Litográfica Comayaguela, 1989). Filander Díaz Chávez, whom Carías jailed and then banished from Honduras in 1944, also published an anti-hagiographic work, *Carías: el último caudillo frutero* (Tegucigalpa: Editorial Guaymuras, 1982).

Euraque (240) cites the following works by Angel Zúñiga Huete, a Liberal Party leader and longtime Carías critic: El *desastre de una dictadura* (Kingston, Jamaica: Times Publishing, 1937); Un *cacicazgo centroamericano* (Mexico City: Imprenta Victoria, 1938); *Idolo desnudo* (Mexico City: Acción Moderna Mercantil, 1939); *Carta Abierta a Tiburcio Carías Andino* (Mexico City: n.p., 1943); *Cartas: una actitud y una senda* (Mexico City: n.p., 1949); and *Conflicto cívico entra la dictadura y el pueblo: mi contribución por la liberación de Honduras* (Tegucigalpa: Imprenta La Razon, 1949).

stances. They all portray common characteristics, especially their personalistic modes of governing, but they were different from one another in many ways. Carías was more a benevolent dictator, and his tenure did not resemble the harsh professional military regimes of Maximiliano Hernández Martínez of El Salvador (1931–44) and Jorge Ubico of Guatemala (1933–44). The Carías era, or caríato, did not impose the draconian and despotic rule of Rafael Leonidas Trujillo of the Dominican Republic (1933–61), nor did the Honduran amass the personal fortunes of Nicaragua's Somozas (1936–79), Fulgencio Batista of Cuba (1934–44; 1952–59), and Marcos Perez Jimenez of Venezuela (1942–58). All of these contemporaries were either assassinated in office or forced from the presidency permanently and exiled from their countries.

The misfortunes of these leaders obviously reflected the conditions of their respective countries, and represented variations in the types of caudillo rule. But whatever the differences and similarities between Carías and them, they all fit into the caudillo mold: coming from the military or relying on its support, governing in a personalist style, staying in office for an extended period of time, and keeping close ties to the United States.[7]

As Carías stood before the National Assembly beginning his presidency in March 1933, another phase of his public life was about to begin. His message on this occasion summed up his passion for the future. "Frequent wars, un-justified factionalism, periodic administrative anarchy, disorder of public services has created a situation in the country lamented by all Hondurans," he said. "Our duty, the obligation of all Hondurans is to end this sad situation."[8] He repeated these words over and over again during his tenure as chief executive. He had already been active politically for some thirty years, and during that time he had weathered political defeats and triumphs. But he also helped build a major party, participate in elections, and lead rebellions. This study explains Carías's governing technique and shows how he created the foundation for a modern Honduran state. It chronicles the dictatorial rule that followed a free and fair election in 1932, gradually concentrated power through one presidential term, and then transformed into a dictatorship. Even once he left office,

7. Russell H. Fitzgibbon, "Continuísmo: The Search for Political Longevity," 210–17, in Hugh Hamill, ed., *Caudillos: Dictators in Spanish America* (Norman and London: University of Oklahoma Press, 1992). See also Howard J. Wiarda and Michael J. Kryzanek, "Trujillo and the Caudillo Tradition," ibid., 246–49.

8. *Mensaje del Señor Presidente de la Republica, Primera Parte, 1933–36* (Tegucigalpa: Talleros Tipo-Litografica Riston).

Carías continued to exert considerable influence in politics for two decades, as party leader and a viable candidate for public office again.

Carías's entire political life was spent ending regional differences and rivalries of local politicians—building the foundations of a modern state. He did this by drawing on the resources and support of the country's chief geographical features: the city, rural village, and extended family of traditional Honduran society.

I

Honduran Political Culture

City, Village, Rural Family

The Landscape of
City, Village, and Rural Family

Honduras is a hilly country with approximately 80 percent of its territory scattered in elevations of over a thousand feet. In the western region, the mountains reach ten thousand feet. They do not follow a particular geological range formation but create a landscape of valleys and small villages. Isolated communities have characterized the country's territory, leaving populations in clusters that depend on subsistence agriculture. Internal trade and commerce did not develop easily, as these small enclaves were unable to reach one another easily. The political culture was basically regional.[1]

Unlike in neighboring countries, the Honduran landowning class did not emerge as a powerful economic and political force in the late nineteenth century. A thin and infertile soil generally left it with the remnants of subsistence agriculture or raising cattle. The cash export crop of bananas was controlled by U.S. companies in the first decade of the twentieth century. The profits from farming and ranching did not flow into the hands of an oligarchy which created a centrally administered state from the wealth of its exports, as it did in El Salvador, Guatemala, and Costa Rica. Those in the Honduran "oligarchy," the country's rich, were "poor" in comparison with their Central American neighbors. An abundance of land for subsistence farming left room for the peasantry to till the soil, without an agro-export elite pushing them off their fields.[2]

From the beginning of modern Honduran history, with the advent of the Spanish conquest in the sixteenth century, this portion of Central America had remained an isolated region in the great vice-royal kingdoms of Latin America.

1. William Stokes, *Honduras: An Area Study in Government* (Madison: University of Wisconsin Press, 1950), 226–27. See also Darío Euraque, *Reinterpreting the Banana Republic: Region and State in Honduras, 1870–1972* (Chapel Hill: University of North Carolina Press, 1996), 43–57. .

2. Darío Euraque, "La reforma liberal en Honduras y la hipotesis de la oligarquía ausente, 1870–1930," *Revista de Historia* (San Jose, Costa Rica), No. 23 (1991): 7–56.

Lacking the vast mineral and human resources of México and Perú, and with no good ports or harbors or easily crossed landscapes connecting oceans like in Nicaragua and Panamá, Honduras remained an administrative subdivision of the Captaincy General of Guatemala. It was also cut off from the main arteries of Imperial Spain's great metropolitan centers. All of these factors—geography, the local landscape, its place in the wider structure of colonial-imperial rule—reinforced localism in its politics.

Soon after the break-up of the United Provinces of Central America (1824–38), Honduras embarked on a history of economic and political instability. With no national institutions or established political parties, regional factions with local leaders tried to dominate the political landscape. No general agreement had established a constitution under which all Hondurans would be governed. Making peace and stability more difficult to attain were threats of invasion from neighboring states, whose political leaders found favor with different factions in Honduran politics. Political and economic alliances of liberal and conservative groups established during the Central American Confederation (1824–38) continued to cut across national boundaries as states struggled toward their separate independent paths.

The middle decades of the nineteenth century were times of great upheaval in all of Central America. The failure of liberalism and its efforts to create a union of states left a wake of constant turmoil in most countries. Personalism in politics offered little hope for building national and cohesive organizations. Yet as a response to the long period of chaos following the fall of the United Provinces of Central America, rule under liberal efforts in the 1880s and 1890s began to build the economies of several states, write constitutions, and give some direction and order to the national polity in Central America. In Honduras, the scarcity of good land, preponderant localism, and isolation from world markets prevented national integration efforts during the nineteenth century. Political leaders in neighboring countries like El Salvador and Guatemala began efforts to establish modern states, yet a unified-cohesive ruling class did not emerge in Honduras to promote, or even benefit from, an expanding export economy in the late nineteenth and early twentieth centuries.

Referred to as modernizers or liberals, the generation of the 1870s in Honduras made serious efforts to develop the country by directing the state authority to encourage the growth of industry, agriculture, and commerce. They came from elements of the old aristocracy and an emerging bourgeoisie.[3] Like their counterparts in other Central American states, most wanted to introduce some of the basic tenets of economic development prevalent in Western Europe, the United States, and México under President Porfirio Díaz (1876–1911). These included promoting foreign trade, exports, and investment, as well as encouraging immigration. They were enthusiastic adherents of positive materialism, a social and economic philosophy that called for the increased wealth of a state with bureaucratic efficiency.[4] Liberal regimes emerged in Central America in the 1870s, one in Honduras led by Mario Aurelio Soto (1876–83), for example, and others in Guatemala under Justo Rufino Barrios, José Santos Zelaya in Nicaragua, and Tomás Guardia in Costa Rica.[5] Honduran liberals drafted two constitutions, one in 1880, the other in 1894. They wrote civil and commercial codes, established obligatory public education, decreed the separation of church and state (secularizing Catholic Church property), and made public lands available for private ownership. They also created national postal and telegraph systems, as well as a Casa de la Moneda, an institution to give some order to financial transactions by the national government. Efforts were begun to create departments like the Ministries of Government, Justice, Foreign Relations, War, and Development. The rudiments of an organized Honduran Liberal Party took shape in the 1890s. Its basic tenets came from the doctrines of the French Revolution and the Constitution of the United States, with acceptable theoretical precepts but little practical application to Honduran politics. Generally it supported a separation of church and state, a Central American Union, economic progress based on sound fiscal policies, strict adherence to a written constitution, and, if need be, a resort to revolution should elections be set aside. A basic overall objective was to stimulate domestic and foreign investment by formulating codes regulating commerce and promoting mining investment.

Honduran economic development progressed without a well-established

3. Stokes, *Honduras*, 211. See also Francisco Guevara-Escudero, "Nineteenth-Century Honduras: A Regional Approach to the Economic History of Central America, 1839–1914" (Ph.D. diss., New York University, 1983).

4. Ralph Lee Woodward, "The Rise and Decline of Liberalism in Central America: Historical Perspectives on the Current Crisis," *Journal of Interamerican Studies and World Affairs*, Vol. 26, No. 3 (1984): 291–312.

5. Ibid.

entrepreneurial class in control of a national governmental apparatus. The effort to promote an infrastructure for development and to gain wealth focused on the sale of vast tracts of land in the form of concessions to foreign entrepreneurs for the construction of railroads, mines, and banana interests. Although an agrarian law in 1898 stipulated that the country retain title to national lands assigned to villages and municipalities, the sale of property within eight kilometers of the sea coast proceeded on a grand scale anyway. North coast ports and cities became centers fostering trade with the Atlantic-Caribbean and the United States. Their economies became almost exclusively tied to the banana trade, and these northern urban centers grew in population, especially in the 1920s as a result of large-scale internal migration for work. Eventually, these coastal cities became Honduras's most urbanized areas.[6]

By the end of the nineteenth century, bananas constituted a substantial percentage of all exports. Commerce in this commodity had begun in the 1860s and 1870s, but expansion in shipping made possible its extraordinary growth by 1892. Major economic enclaves of banana production in the republic's north coast departments of Cortés, Atlántida, and Colón emerged. By the 1920s three companies, the United Fruit Company, the Standard Fruit Company, and the Cuyamel Fruit Company, dominated the production and marketing of this industry.

The Vaccaro family of New Orleans controlled much of the northeastern coast with its Standard Fruit Company (now Dole). This enterprise grew with land concessions in return for building railroads and obtaining exemption from taxes. Specifically, grants of lands were made as a right of way to cut timber, build houses, and construct other structures for operations. Companies were also allowed to use a certain amount of territory for each kilometer of railroad track built. In most concessions, the banana enterprises could use land immediately upon signing a contract, even though title did not come into effect until the railroad line was completed.[7]

In 1902, a tract of property surrounding the Cuyamel River near Omoa on the north coast was sold to a German, William Streich. This property of some two thousand hectares was in turn purchased by Samuel Zemurray of New Orleans, who in 1910 formed the Cuyamel Fruit Company. The United Fruit Com-

6. Euraque, "La reforma liberal," 15.

7. Charles Kepner and Jay Soothill, *The Banana Empire: A Case Study of Economic Imperialism* (New York: Vanguard, 1935). See also their subsequent Spanish edition, *El Imperio Bananero: las compañías bananeras contra la soberanía de las naciones del caribe* (Mexico City: Ediciones del Caribe, 1949).

pany (known as El Pulpo, "the Octopus") became the largest banana producer in Honduras. It expanded significantly in 1929 when Zemurray sold his company to United Fruit for cash and 300,000 shares of stock worth $32 million. He became its largest stockholder. The Tela and Trujillo Railroads also were part of the enterprise, making his company a dominant economic force on the north coast.[8]

Standard and United controlled the entire infrastructure along Honduras's Caribbean territory. Their holdings included railroads, docks, communications systems, sugar mills, commissaries, electric power systems, soap, and brewing factories. They published newspapers and owned Banco Atlántida, one of two banks in Honduras.

The vast and diversified activities of the fruit companies employed thousands of Hondurans as laborers, accountants, and lawyers for their operations. Banana enterprises also introduced considerable investment for the development of other northern cities such as Tela, El Progreso, and San Pedro Sula. The rapid expansion of the banana industry and its corresponding influence and control over all economic enterprises in the north contributed to a steep decline of Honduran independent banana growers. In effect, a segment of the country's economy was indeed growing but without the administration, ownership, and direction of a Honduran entrepreneurial elite.

Against this background of a dominant banana export industry, a large segment of the country's landed oligarchy measured their status in relation to these north coast enterprises rather than seeing themselves as an independent socioeconomic class. This connection was characterized by the powerful influence these companies exerted in Honduran politics, primarily through financial interests. Political leaders felt the power and influence of these foreign entrepreneurs. Competing political groups were often financially backed by them. Enterprises like Standard and United supported different candidates for political office in order to enhance their respective economic and political interests.

While the north coast economy expanded and prospered on banana exports, Tegucigalpa, the political capital to the south, languished with empty treasuries and constantly changing governments. Two conditions dominated the country's political landscape, fratricidal warfare among caudillos and

8. Thomas Schoonover and Lester Langley, *The Banana Men: American Mercenaries and Entrepreneurs in Central America, 1880–1930* (Lexington: University Press of Kentucky, 1995); Argueta, *Bananos y política*.

the inability of governments to maintain peace and order. The two conditions were inextricably linked. Well-known journalists and writers like Froylán Turcios (1877–1943), Carlos Izaguirre (1895–1956), and Paulino Valladares (1881–1926) lamented the country's failure to modernize and create a strong central government. They attributed these inadequacies primarily to the lack of political leadership. Moreover, they blamed self-serving politicians who headed militias that conducted wars, grabbing power for their own gain and interest.

Militias were recruited locally and paid for by a region's economically prosperous commercial and landed class. They were the appendages of the armed will of caudillos. These figures were responsible only to local interests. "Matters of state" extended to the boundaries of a village or a region. Consequently, political parties with national goals and objectives did not appear until the end of the nineteenth century. Elections and presidential terms were mostly resolved by machetismo ("the use of force, a machete, to influence elections").[9] Because Honduras lacked a well-established oligarchy supported by an economy with revenue from cash crop exports, public affairs was reduced almost entirely to the ambitions of local figures.[10]

During this era of "economic development," particularly on the north coast, Liberal Party presidents such as President Celeo Arias (1872–74) and Marco Aurelio Soto (1876–83), although strong advocates for modernizing the nation's administrative institutions through constitutions (1880 and 1884), were not identified entirely with a party label. They governed under personalized rule with loyal followers committed to them, and they promoted centralization of administrative procedures, constructing a communications system, encouraging foreign investment, and attempting to build a banking structure. Political organizations were named after them as they had been for their predecessors. Their names, not party labels, symbolized political interests. They wanted to control the state through legal procedures if possible, but they did not hesitate to take up arms if thwarted. By the first decade of the twentieth century, a broad and loose coalition of liberal parties in Central American states once strengthened by the Guatemalan Justo Rufino Barrios in 1876 had disintegrated.[11] Honduran politics from the 1890s to the second decade of the

9. James A. Morris, Honduras Caudillos and Military Rulers (Boulder: Westview Press, 1984), 4.

10. Ibid., 9.

11. Euraque, Reinterpreting the Banana Republic, 44.

twentieth century continued to be marked by civil wars between caudillos, the factional leaders who also sought to control government through a spoils system. Armed political conflicts, rather than regularly scheduled elections as the constitution prescribed, continued on into the twentieth century.

Before turning to a detailed account of national politics, it is necessary to take a closer look at one family's role in regional politics. It was in the local area that Tiburcio Carías and so many of his contemporaries made lifelong friends and enemies in Honduran politics.

This brief review describes the setting from which Tiburcio Carías rose to power as a regional leader, then as president for sixteen years (1933–49) and continuing thereafter to exert a significant influence on national politics until his death in 1969. Carías was born in Tegucigalpa on March 15, 1876. His father, Calixto, was a businessman in the city but also lived in Zambrano, a small village some thirty-five kilometers northwest of the capital city. As in most countries in Central America, the Carías family lineage, along with its land ownership, determined its social status. The upper class to which it belonged was divided geographically into three areas: a cosmopolitan sector in the capital, a group in the northern city of San Pedro Sula, and landowners in the rural districts. Generally, families who held property in the interior identified with politics there and with their economic resources raised militias for local security and to wage war against competing interests elsewhere. Carías was raised in Zambrano, located in Central Honduras, a village with fewer than twelve hundred inhabitants, mostly *campesinos* with plots of land cultivated for food production. Towns like Zambrano were surrounded by mountains with few good roads. A strong feeling of localism existed along with a deep suspicion of neighbors. Zambrano was unique in one respect: a road from Tegucigalpa passed through it and went on to points north, so people traveled through it to points north and south. Although distant from larger cities like San Pedro Sula and Tegucigalpa, it was accessible to these two main urban centers.

The Carías family held about 150 hectares of acreage, given mostly to crop cultivation for local consumption and cattle. Like the rest of the Honduran rural oligarchy, they lived simply, in a plain rural setting. The Carías home was a one-story, whitewashed building that had passed through several generations of the family. It was located just a few feet from the unpaved road connecting Tegucigalpa north to Comayagua and on to San Pedro Sula, then to the Caribbean-coast banana port cities. Like other village residences of the more prosperous inhabitants, the home, built with bamboo frames filled with mixed stones and mud dried to make walls, was also a *bodega* ("restaurant").[12] Passengers traveling north and south stopped for meals, rest, good food, and gossip. A logical place to stop, it was about halfway from San Pedro Sula to Tegucigalpa and right next to the "highway."[13]

The Carías family ancestors could be traced back to eighteenth-century artisans and members of the lower clergy.[14] Because Calixto was away during much of the year, his wife Sara Francisca de Paula Andino raised and educated young Tiburcio Carías and his five brothers and sisters.[15] Calixto, propertied but not rich, with a leather shop in Tegucigalpa, was a local politician, a member of the Liberal Party who occupied much of his time forming political alliances and organizing militias in the last two decades of the nineteenth century. He raised his children in both the city and the rural village, giving them education and friends in two worlds—the Spanish metropolitan center of the capital city and the campesino environment of a small town.

Probably around 1894 (the date is not certain), Tiburcio remained in Tegucigalpa for formal schooling. He attended a high school named El Espiritual Siglo, which had been founded to provide boys with a "practical education" following the basic tenets of liberalism in the late nineteenth century. There he studied math, languages, history, and natural sciences.[16]

After finishing his secondary schooling, young Carías entered the National University, then called Universidad Central (Central University), to study law. He joined the Faculty (school) of Jurisprudence and Political Science. Known as serious, conscientious, and hard working, he earned grades well above average. Records of his academic performance show consistent attendance in classes, and that he took the full range of legal studies. These included natural and Roman law, civil codes, and criminal procedure, along with administrative, commercial, and international law—a demanding schedule. He received his undergraduate degree in 1898.[17]

---

12. Called *bahareque*, a bamboo frame filled with stones and mud.

13. Díaz Chávez, *Carías*, 75, 77, 78.

14. Juan B. Valladares, "Algunos datos sobre la ascendencia del General Tiburcio Carías Andino," *Anales del Archivo Nacional*, No. 8 (August 1970): 66–67.

15. Marcos Carías Zapata, interview, 17 November 1987. Zapata is the son of Marco Carías Reyes, Carías's private secretary.

16. *Revista* (Tegucigalpa), 15 May 1969, 9.

17. Expedientes de Licenciatura, 1898–1900 (Universidad Central), thesis no. 322204, Biblioteca de Universidad Nacional de Honduras (UNAH), 8–11.

In 1900, Carías wrote a master's thesis entitled, "Has the Appearance of Machines Improved the Conditions of the Needy?"[18] in preparation for a teaching career.[19] He described how the machine was rapidly replacing the unskilled laborer and outlined the dangers it posed for the working person. Carías speculated that workers would lose jobs, creating widespread unemployment. He observed that rather than discount the use of innovative machine technology, people should take steps to apply its uses wisely and thus simultaneously protect the interests of labor. He pointed out that while machines were replacing a work force, over time they created new jobs. Finishing his academic career, Carías became a teacher. He worked in a secondary school in Tegucigalpa, offering courses in math, algebra, and geometry.

The friends he made in Tegucigalpa during his secondary and national university years were the sons of the professional elite. Yet while new contacts were important in the capital, the roots of his early youth remained strong. As he traveled back and forth to his father's farm, he became more active in local politics, spending most of his time in Zambrano planning military campaigns or plotting strategies for elections.

Before he reached twenty, young Tiburcio entered the politics of civil war in what was once described as "a country without law or God."[20] The major candidates for national office in the first decade of the twentieth century were Policarpo Bonilla (1894–99) and Manuel Bonilla (not related) (1903–7, 1911–13), Miguel Dávila, Francisco Bertrand, and Domingo Vásquez. No strong ideological framework existed in the Liberal Party. Rather, political fortunes rose and fell on the personal loyalty of people. Choices for a leader were made based on who could provide posts at the national level and distribute favors locally.

Early in 1893 (the exact date is not certain), young Carías fled with his father to Nicaragua after supporting an unsuccessful military campaign against President Domingo Vásquez (1893–94). Probably again in the early part of 1901–2, he left Honduras for El Salvador with his father, who was exiled in a political squabble. There he taught in a high school, Colegio El Carmen, in Sonsonate.[21]

18. Ibid.

19. Rafael Bardales Bueso, interview, Tegucigalpa, 13 November 1987. Bardales was a close friend and confidant of Carías for many years and a leader in the National Party going back to its early years.

20. El Cronista (Tegucigalpa), 20 October 1932, 3.

21. Bardales, "El fundador de la paz."

Despite his two exiles, and as a follower of the Liberal Party chieftain Poli-carpo Bonilla, Calixto Carías continued to organize and lead militias defending his patron. The first Carías family battle with a militia supporting Policarpo Bonilla was fought either in 1893 or 1894 at a place called Tatumbla, twenty kilometers east of Tegucigalpa in the Department of Morazán.[22] Later in 1904, father and son again fled to El Salvador when Manuel Bonilla defeated Poli-carpo and became president (1903–7).

In 1907, Calixto and his son Tiburcio again escaped to Nicaragua to gain the backing of Liberal Party president José Santos Zelaya (1893–1909) and acquire arms to mount a campaign supporting his fellow Liberal Policarpo Bonilla in a war against the conservative Manuel Bonilla. Zelaya, with his own designs for assisting an ally in Honduras, granted several lucrative concessions to foreign-ers on the Nicaraguan-Honduran border. A friendly government in Teguci-galpa would help immeasurably in this project.[23]

Washington, concerned by the continued threat of civil unrest in Hon-duras, called a conference of Central American nations to seek measures for re-ducing armed conflict between political factions and states. Specifically, the United States chargé d'affaires in Tegucigalpa arranged a peace settlement that provided for the installation of a Liberal, Miguel Dávila, as president (1907–11).[24] With an ally installed as chief executive, Tiburcio Carías was named to several administrative posts, building ties to local and regional leaders. During the Dávila regime he served throughout the country, either as a military com-mander or as a political chief with administrative duties. He moved up through the ranks in militias from lieutenant to colonel then general through "self-promotion." This meant a leader would form a militia or a guerrilla band, and if a successful campaign ensued, officers like Carías would have their ranks confirmed by a new government.[25]

22. Romualdo Elpidio Mejía, 4 de Julio 1944 (Tegucigalpa: Talleres Tipográficos Aristan, 1945), 22; see also Cultura (Tegucigalpa), 31 December 1948, 7, 10–11.

23. Gerardo Martínez Funes, Viajando por el istmo a traves de Honduras: recopilaciones de impresiones y de ideas de una visita a vuelo de pájaro (Tegucigalpa: n.p., 1941). Funes and members of his family were close friends of Calixto Carías and his sons. This account relates in some detail the travels in mili-tias by Calixto and his son Tiburcio into Nicaragua, southern Honduras, and even El Salvador.

24. Manifiesto, Presidente Dávila, Biblioteca y Archivos Nacionales, Tegucigalpa, 6–9; see also La Bandera Liberal (Tegucigalpa), 2 May 1907, 3–4.

25. Steve Ropp, "The Honduran Army in the Socio-Political Evolution of the Honduran State," in James A. Morris, ed., Honduras: Caudillo Politics and Military Rulers (Boulder: Westview Press,

Two Honduran chief executives, Liberals Celeo Arias (1872–74) and Marco Aurelio Soto (1876–83), were most likely the first political leaders to create the semblance of an organized Liberal Party, a disciplined group with both an ideological base and a national organization.[26] Even Policarpo Bonilla built rudiments of a disciplined party too with committees established at all levels, systemizing and organizing public administration at all levels of government. He made himself a dominant force in the party organization as presidents before him, and continued the politics of personalism. His successors too, Juan Angel Arias (February to March, 1903), Manuel Bonilla, Miguel Dávila, and Rafael López Gutiérrez (1920–24), continued the tradition of Honduran politics by leading movements more under their names than party labels. All through this early part of the twentieth century the Carías brothers served in Liberal Party administrations. For example, President Miguel Dávila had once been a professor of Tiburcio Carías at the National University,[27] and their friendship remained close for several years. Marcos was political governor of the Department of Tegucigalpa in 1907 and later minister of *fomento* ("development") and agriculture. Tiburcio was named *fiscal general de hacienda* for a few months in 1907, and then political chief in the Department of Copán in western Honduras. He later held these two positions jointly in Cortés.[28]

Miguel Dávila, like late-nineteenth-century liberals, placed great emphasis on integrating regions of the country long since left to the interests of local politicians. His goal was to govern effectively throughout Honduras from Tegucigalpa, especially areas of the country that had fallen into political chaos and fiscal disarray. For example, he lamented the central government's failure to administer properly areas on the north coast which had vast underdeveloped resources. Three of these, Copán, Cortés, and Atlántida, had only recently been made departments.[29] Newspapers editorialized on the need for competent ad-

---

1984), 505. See also William Krehm, *Democracies and Tyrannies in the Caribbean* (Westport, CT: Lawrence, Hill, 1984), 29.

26. Stokes, *Honduras*, 211. See also Guevara-Escudero, "Nineteenth-Century Honduras."

27. Vicente Cáceres Lara, interview, Tegucigalpa, 30 September 1987. Cáceres Lara was a political associate of Tiburcio Carías in the National Party and a prominent historian.

28. Together in Copán and Cortés, Carías served from 1907 to 1911. *La Bandera Liberal*, 15 July 1907, 1. See also *La Gaceta* (Tegucigalpa), 5 October 1907, 43; 19 August 1907, 1. He apparently was *comandante de armas* and *jefe político* in Copán for only a few months.

29. Copán in 1869, Cortés in 1893, and Atlántida in 1902.

ministrators to bring these regions under efficient administrative control and
to end the power of local political bosses who governed without legal constraints.[30]

The Miguel Dávila government set aside approximately one hundred thousand lempiras for the construction of roads, schools, and houses and for the
establishment of new commercial enterprises in these northern regions.[31] The
expanding banana companies' trade with the United States was growing, and
the central government was not effectively administering revenue derived from
these activities.[32]

Dávila believed Cortés and Atlántida were the greatest potential resources
for the country's economic development. As seaports near the burgeoning
commercial northern city of San Pedro Sula, they held the possibility of securing greater revenue for the central government.[33] First appointed to the western department of Copán, Carías issued the area's first *gaceta municipal*. This
was a monthly report on his major administrative activities in the area, reflecting his propensity for detail and efficiency. Among the items covered were
reports on income from Copán, work done by the council members in the Department as well as reports on its deliberations, the number and lengths of
roads constructed, and the number of schools built. The publication of the
gaceta in August 1907 was an early and vivid indication of Carías's interest in
order, administration, and efficiency. His performance reflected the operations
of an agent of the central government, not the local caudillo.[34]

Soon after, Carías was reassigned to the north coast city of Puerto Cortés, a
bustling, prosperous port exporting products to neighboring countries like

30. La Gaceta, 30 May 1907, 1.

31. Ibid., 2; 30 June 1907, 1.

32. Darío A. Euraque, "Los recursos económicos del estado Hondureño, 1830–1870," in Arturo
Taracona and Jean Piel, eds., *Identidades Nacionales y Poderoso en Centroamérica* (San José, Costa Rica:
Editorial de la Universidad de Costa Rica, 1995), 138–42.

33. Paulino Valladares, a leading journalist and a key supporter of Tiburcio Carías, wrote numerous articles on this subject in 1908. He referred to Carías's competent and efficient administration in Cortés from 1908 to 1911. See Valladares's editorial in *La Prensa* (Tegucigalpa), 16 October
1908, 2; and later, *Sufragio Libre* (Tegucigalpa), 8 December 1923, 4.

34. The Gaceta municipal report was published in *La Bandera Liberal*, 26 August 1907, 4. The Gaceta was suspended in 1911 when Carías left his posts in northern Honduras. It was resumed,
though, in all departments when he was president in 1935. See Antonio Coello, ed., *Anuario Estadístico Comercial de los Departamentos de Tegucigalpa, Cortés, y Atlantida* (Tegucigalpa: Tallares Tipográfica
Nacionales, 1935).

Guatemala and Nicaragua. Carías again assumed the dual titles of *jefe político* ("political chief") and *comandante de armas* ("military commander") of Cortés as he had done in Copán. He administered and dispensed funds appropriated by the central government for road construction, linking several towns to the port city. Money was spent building schools, bridges, and dams; purchasing land and materials for planned municipal buildings; and encouraging new enterprises by exempting them from paying taxes and import duties on new equipment.[35]

Throughout his tenure in Copán and Cortés, Carías expressed deep suspicions of an organized local armed force linked to a national professional army. Consequently, from these early days on the north coast he focused attention on the structure of departmental, local militias, building units without administrative support from Tegucigalpa. Instead, Carías recommended in 1911 that the Dávila government send cadets from the Escuela Militar in Tegucigalpa to train local forces when he defended the north coast from Manuel Bonilla's invading forces who were attempting to install Bonilla as president. Rather than training solely in military tactics, Carías emphasized basic education in reading and writing. He also established a departmental school solely for corporals and sergeants.[36]

Carías's political fortunes took a sharp turn in 1911 when he abruptly left his administrative post in Cortés. Manuel Bonilla, a longtime family political rival from New Orleans, successfully invaded Honduras and with logistic support of

35. Several interviewees pointed out that Carías was cautious about building an army, choosing later a plan to build an "air force" instead. Interviews with Roberto Gálvez Barnes (member of governing junta, October 1956–November 1957, ambassador to the United States, and son of Carías's minister of war, navy, and air force, 1933–1949), Tegucigalpa, 2 September 1987; Manuel Gálvez (president, 1949–1954), Tegucigalpa, 30 October 1987; Jorge Daniel Carías, 3 August 1987; Rafael Bardales, 5 March 1987, 24 June 1987, 15 July 1987, 13 November 1987; Colonel Carlos Castillo Caceres (archivist, ministry of defense), Tegucigalpa, 1 September 1987; Tomás Martínez (commander, Mounted Police, national police force under Carías, 1933–1949), Tegucigalpa, 9 April 1987, 11 November 1987; Rodolfo Velásquez, La Esperanza, Intibucá, 27 October 1987; Gonzálo (Chalo) Luque, San Pedro Sula, 10 September 1987; Juan José Flores (whose father was an early carísta), San Pedro Sula, 13 September 1987; Francisco Sánchez, El Progreso, 12 September 1987; Baltazar Vigil Claros, La Esperanza, 26 October 1987; Oscar Guerrero (whose father, Francisco, became a close friend of Carías as comandante de armas in the Department of Atlántida), Tegucigalpa, 23 October 1987.

36. Gonzálo Chalo Luque, *Memorias de un Sanpedrano* (San Pedro Sula: Talleres Litigráficos de Empresora Hondureña, 1979), 1:12, 132. See also Tiburcio Carías, "Informe del Gobernador," in *Mensaje del President Miguel Dávila* (Tegucigalpa: n.p., 1909), 296–97.

Sam Zemurray, head of the Cuyamel Fruit Company, declared himself president. The former chief executive reached Belize (British Honduras), then took the Islas de Bahía off Honduras's north coast, moved to the mainland, and set up a provisional government at La Ceiba. Carías unsuccessfully attempted to defend the north coast departments against Bonilla. To stop the war from escalating and protect American lives and property, the United States dispatched the warship *Tacoma* to Cortés, to mediate the conflict. Washington eventually persuaded President Dávila to step down, making Francisco Bertrand provisional president until elections. In what was considered a fair political contest, Manuel Bonilla became chief executive, governing the country from 1912 to 1913.

During Bonilla's tenure as chief executive, Carías sought the quiet of Zambrano as a retreat from public affairs, planning his next move. Despite his political setback with Dávila's ouster, he continued planning a political career at a time when many of the late-nineteenth-century political leaders were dead or dying off. Carías was already considered a successful military commander in the south and a competent administrator in western and northern departments. While serving the central government in these posts, he made friends in the country's regional communities.[37] In fact, he built the foundations for his own political organization in the Departments of Copán and Cortés during the Dávila administration (1907–11), which later became important during his presidency from 1933 to 1949.

No leader in the first decade of the twentieth century could form a strong national party and create a platform for governing. Liberals were still a collection of factions who followed a politician. Similarly, party unity lasted as long as a person could command the respect of his followers. "Policarpistas" and "Manuelistas" better fit the title of organized groups in these early years of Tiburcio Carías's political life. Neither Policarpo Bonilla nor Manuel Bonilla could maintain "party" discipline for very long. Honduras's political leaders also sought military, financial, and political support from neighboring countries like Nicaragua, El Salvador, and Guatemala, as well as from local banana companies. Exercising political power and completing a presidential term eluded most presidents.

37. *Sufragio Libre*, 8 December 1923, 4.

Elections with Ballots and Bullets

Throughout Honduran history presidential succession has been largely contingent on the outcome of civil wars. These conflicts determined the course of politics itself, specifically the installations and resignations of chief executives. The Liberal Party remained deeply divided well into the twentieth century, continuing to be an organization based on personalism, led by party chieftains who had been nineteenth-century presidents, such as Marco Aurelio Soto (1876–83), Luis Bográn (1883–91), Ponciano Leiva (1891–94), Policarpo Bonilla (1894–99), Terencio Sierra (1899–1902), and Manuel Bonilla (1903–7, 1911–13). Yet despite these men's important philosophical beliefs, internal conflicts continued until 1919. Conflicts affected even Manuel Bonilla's two terms as president, a period of continuity that should have brought peace to the party. When Bonilla died in office in 1913, he was succeeded by his vice-president, Francisco Bertrand. Bertrand created a central committee to promote exclusively his own candidacy in the next scheduled election in 1915. A year later, organized groups loyal to Bertrand were established in most of the country's departments. They called themselves Liberal Constitutionalists.[1] When President Bertrand tried to install his brother-in-law, Nazario Soriano, as president, General Rafael López Gutiérrez, military commander and governor of Tegucigalpa, objected. This development and Washington's effort to avoid a civil war by threatening to intervene sealed Soriano's fate, and Bertrand promptly fled to Costa Rica. Similar to the 1912 U.S. intervention, this incident made a lasting impression on the young Tiburcio Carías, who had learned first hand that unless civil wars were ended, external intervention from Washington would occur.[2]

Despite the fact that civil wars persisted just before elections in 1894, 1911, and 1919, the emergence of General López Gutiérrez as president in 1920

1. Stokes, *Honduras*, 222.
2. Euraque, *Reinterpreting the Banana Republic*, 45–46.

(1920–24) marked a turning point in the relationship among what one histo-rian has called "militarist politics, Honduran society and the state."[3] The 1919 election took place in a setting much different from any previous one. There were several reasons for this. First, U.S. investments grew significantly be-tween 1908 and 1919. Land concessions to banana enterprises in particular ac-celerated at the same time government revenues declined precipitously. Most of this income (about 50 percent) was lost to these enterprises through grants in the same time period. Moreover, the number of workers in banana planta-tions reached approximately ten thousand. Other sources of revenue, espe-cially from municipal institutions, declined considerably. U.S. banana compa-nies actually subsidized a significant portion of the central government's expenditures.[4] Facing this fiscal crisis, President López Gutiérrez asked a U.S. financial expert to review all government finances.[5] Along with these develop-ments, profound changes in the Honduran political landscape took place. The Liberal Party fell into disarray again amid constant civil wars, largely precipi-tated by Liberal president López Gutiérrez's announcement that he intended to stay in office. This decision, along with the accelerating fiscal crisis, forced po-litical groups to reshape and redefine their organizations.

The Liberal Party (created in 1891) saw a chance to redefine its goals from those of its nineteenth-century forerunners. New leaders, such as Ángel Zúñiga Huete, a thirty-five-year-old lawyer, added more radical features to the party platform, calling for an end to mining monopolies, limitations on state grants of land to individuals and companies both foreign and national, and "the so-cialization of land and labor."[6] The Liberal Party adopted the Mexican Revolu-tion (1910) and a model for nationalism, creating state monopolies managing the country's economy. People like Zúñiga Huete supported popular anti-Yankee movements in Central America, such as that in Nicaragua led by Augusto César Sandino, who opposed the U.S. military intervention there (1927–33).[7]

The Democratic National Party (1919) emerged to oppose President López Gutiérrez's plans for extending his term in 1924; between 1920 and 1923, it re-organized into the National Party. Members came principally from President

3. Ibid., 48.
4. Ibid.
5. Ibid.
6. Ibid., 51.
7. Ibid., 51–52.

Francisco Bertrand's old Liberal Constitutional Party (1916). The new organization was conservative on social and economic issues, interested primarily in reforming government finances and encouraging foreign investment. It reflected many aspirations of a generation of Hondurans who had grown tired of civil wars that had disrupted the economy and made effective administration of government difficult. By 1923–24, Carías wanted to adopt the word "national" as a party name—reflecting a more broadly based movement as his nineteenth-century hero, Liberal president Trinidad Cabañas (1852; 1853–55), had during Honduran civil wars from 1826 to 1829. In that period Cabañas had backed fellow Honduran Francisco Morazán, president of the United Provinces of Central America (1823–38), who during two separate terms (1830–34, 1835–38) tried to compel states to stay with the Middle American Union. Having been embroiled unsuccessfully in wars in Guatemala and El Salvador, Cabañas saw the futility of armed conflict used for political gain. As president from 1853 to 1855, he turned to constitutional government and national unity at home. After bringing a modicum of political peace, he embarked on economic development, especially promoting public education as a way to encourage economic growth and political stability. He signed a contract with the North American Ephraim George Squier in 1854 for the construction of an interoceanic railway across Honduras to promote commerce and trade. Although not entirely successful, Cabañas's efforts to establish peace by drawing up a blueprint for economic progress later appealed to Hondurans like Carías in the second decade of the twentieth century.

Carías and others, not all active politically but influential in the country's public affairs, once again stressed a national agenda for economic progress, building on the strong infrastructure begun by Cabañas. Reinstituting nationalism and unity to end the politics of combat became the key theme of the National Democratic Party. Carías later placed a bust of Cabañas in his presidential office and frequently referred to the nineteenth-century president's efforts to create peace in the country.[8] When Alberto Membreño, one of the party's founders, died in 1921, Carías assumed leadership of the organization. He considered himself heir apparent, as he had been the deceased candidate's running mate in the 1920 presidential race. His rise in the National Democratic

8. See El Cronista, 6 May 1925, 2; La Época, 19 November 1937, 1; Raúl Arturo Pagoaga, Honduras y sus gobernantes (Tegucigalpa: Imprenta Soto, 1979), 34.

Party was assisted in part through efforts by journalists who had written about his administrative skills in Copán and Cortés, talents they said were needed in the political arena.[9]

Among leading organizers of the National Democratic Party, later the National Party, were journalists and members of congress. Chief among them was Paulino Valladares, who served in the national legislature in 1908, and private secretary to the Liberal Party president Miguel Dávila (1907–11). He also founded La Prensa in Tegucigalpa and later served as editor of El Cronista in the same city. Using the press as a propaganda weapon, he wrote extensively on the need for ending the persistent political chaos that plagued the country.[10] Having served in liberal administrations, admiring, then lamenting their failure to create efficient government machinery, he called for a new political party. He took note of Tiburcio Carías's work as jefe político and comandante de armas in Cortés and, particularly, his leadership skills.[11]

Valladares wrote an editorial in 1915, "Tiburcio Carías," praising the candidate's excellent educational background as a teacher, disciplined and efficient in his work. In the same article he deplored the chaotic administrative conditions of Honduras since independence and the civil wars that made matters worse. Although Carías was young, time and maturity, he said, would one day make him a leader.[12] In other editorials, Valladares called for competent people and institutions to govern above politics, like the U.S. Civil Service did, administering fiscal and financial matters.[13] All segments of society, like capital and labor, he said, should be directed and protected by the state.[14] Government needed organization, a political framework to guarantee order. He believed stability was the main goal, and if it was secured, freedom and progress would emerge. He used the term falange, adopted from the Spaniard José Antonio Primo de Rivera, as a model which placed government above politics as the best way to achieve national unity.[15]

9. Abel Villacorta Cisneros, Reseña história del Partido Nacional de Honduras (Tegucigalpa: Publicaciones del Comité Central del Partido Nacional de Honduras, 1966), 10–11.

10. Lucas Paredes, Biografía del Dr. y General Tiburcio Carías Andino (Tegucigalpa: Tipolitografía Ariston, 1938), 287.

11. Sufragio Libre, 8 December 1923, 4.

12. El Cronista, 22 November 1915, No. 933, reproduced in Revista 15 de Mayo (Tegucigalpa) 1970, 15.

13. El Cronista, 12 January 1926, 2.

14. El Cronista, 13 January 1926, 2.

15. Ibid.

Another journalist, Carlos Izaguirre, a flamboyant figure with eclectic tastes, was to become one of Carías's closest confidants. He always carried a weapon, the Bible, and a novel.[16] He founded several newspapers, El Esfuerzo (1917), La Voz del Sur (1918), and Alba Nueva (1919), all in the Department of Choluteca, as well as El Marino and El Debate in Puerto Cortés (1921), and La Voz de Trujillo (1932) in Colón. He authored novels and other books on political issues. Truly a versatile person, he flew planes, wrote essays, and recited poetry, and he provided the otherwise taciturn and reserved Carías with distraction from the serious matters of state. He spoke English and had studied in the United States and worked for Cuyamel Fruit Company (1919–21). Known as Elefante Pichón ("the little elephant"), he once served as secretary to his brother-in-law, President Vicente Tosta (1924–25), and held a post in the Honduran legation in Washington (1925–28). Izaguirre rarely appeared at social functions, preferring to exert his influence behind the scenes. During Carías's presidency, he would undertake several overseas missions for the chief executive.[17] As inspector general of consulates abroad he received a salary of $1,000 a month.[18] Like Valladares, he too deplored the chronic civil wars in Honduras and rallied public support for Carías through articles in Tegucigalpa's El Cronista. He advocated the creation of a political party that would give the country peace and order. He also called for a new constitution giving vast powers to the chief executive. Izaguirre admired the fascist regime of Benito Mussolini, not for its ideology but for the order and stability it imposed.[19] He wanted the Honduran congress reorganized, abolishing the representation system by party, with a single chamber of deputies from industry, farming, professional, and religious organizations.[20]

16. Jorge Fidel Durón (close collaborator of Carías, 1930s–1949), interviews, Tegucigalpa, January 1987; 8 February 1987; August 1987; 18 October 1987; Eliseo Pérez Cadalso (secretary to Carías's adviser and confidant Carlos Izaguirre), Tegucigalpa, 1 December 1987; interviews with Bardales and Bertrand.

17. Luis Mejía Moreno, El calvario de un pueblo o un doble error constitucional (Tegucigalpa: Tallares Tipográficas Nacionales, 1937), 198.

18. Office of Military Intelligence, U.S. Embassy, Honduras, Report, 25 May 1945, in National Archives of the United States and Confidential Post Records, Central America, Honduras, 1930–1945, ed. Paul Kesaris (Frederick, MD: University Publications of the Americas, microfilm, 1985) [hereafter, Confidential U.S. Diplomatic Post Records].

19. Carlos Izaguirre, Readaptaciones y cambios (Tegucigalpa: Imprenta Calderón, 1936), 53, 64–65.

20. Ibid., 60–62, 53.

Izaguirre admired Carías for his purposefulness and his total commitment to politics as an administrator and practical politician.[21] Like the Honduran writers Froylán Turcios (1877–1943) and Rafael Heliodoro Valle (1891–1959), Izaguirre wrote in a combative vein, deploring the corruption, civil wars, and anarchy that plagued the country in the 1920s. He preferred democratic, representative government in the Western, liberal mode.[22]

Other journalists urging the creation of a strong central state included Julián López Piñeda (1882–1959), who wrote for El Demócrata (Tegucigalpa), and Fernando Zepeda Durón (1894–?), director of La Época, later the official periodical during the Carías dictatorship. In his Democracía y Redentonismo (1942), López Piñeda observed that "it will not be possible to achieve internal peace in Honduras if a capable dictatorship is not established, capable of dominating the blind forces of ambition and ignorance." He likened the extreme form of dictatorship to totalitarian rule in the Soviet Union, Nazi Germany, and Fascist Italy and proposed instead a benevolent dictatorship that ended anarchy but did not bludgeon people with one ideology, nor persecute and enslave them. His models for a political leader were nineteenth-century Latin American presidents Antonio Paéz of Venezuela (1790–1893), Ramón Castilla of Perú (1797–1867), Rafael Nuñez of Colombia (1825–94), and Julio Roca of Argentina (1873–1942). These rulers were harsh, even at times brutal, but, López Piñeda said, they imposed peace and built nation-states, something he hoped Carías would do with the National Party.

All these journalists viewed México's National Revolutionary Party (PNR, after 1929 the Institutional Revolutionary Party [PRI]) as a model for a Honduran political movement. La Época, the National Party newspaper, frequently discussed the failure of liberalism and the need to create a government with a dominant organization like the PNR, which Mario Vargas Llosa, the Peruvian novelist, later called the "perfect dictatorship."[23]

---

21. Interviews with members of the Izaguirre family: Miguel (nephew) and Matilda Izaguirre Tosta de Fiallos (daughter-in-law), Tegucigalpa, 3 September 1987. See also Raúl Arturo Pagaoga, Carlos Izaguirre y su múltiple actividad mental (Tegucigalpa: Imprenta Soto, 1947), 16.

22. Pagaoga, Carlos Izaguirre, 24. See also Revista Ariel (Tegucigalpa), Froylán Turcios, Arturo Martínez Galíndez (directors), 15 June 1925, No. 7, 1.

23. The party was first called the PNR, National Revolutionary Party (1929), then the PRM, Mexican Revolutionary Institutional Party (1938), finally the PRI, Institutional Revolutionary Party (1946).

Creating corporate entities, representing the nation's economic and social groups, and defending the country from foreign economic interests, PNR leaders along with México's president, Plutarco Elías Calles (1924–28), were often quoted in articles by Carías's journalistic partisans, who advocated a similar role and structure for the National Party in Honduras.

The ever-cautious Carías took no public stand on the wide-ranging and sometimes controversial views of these publicists in the 1920s or 1930s. Instead, he built a party in which "national" meant governing above narrow political interests, calling revolution indefensible in circumventing the electoral process. Yet he shrewdly cultivated these writers, using them to promote peace and order, the new themes of the party.

Combative figures with strong opinions and volcanic personalities, Paulino Valladares, Fernando Zepeda Durón, and Carlos Izaguirre were not political threats to Carías. He had no interest in their tastes for poetry, romantic novels, and travel abroad. But they were useful as journalists who could disseminate propaganda about order and peace.[24] Newspapers they edited and owned in the 1920s were few in number, but they reached a tiny, literate population that could shape public opinion, especially in cities like Tegucigalpa, San Pedro Sula, and the small towns along the Atlantic coast.

Actually, these publicists formed only a segment of Carías's world. They were from the city, articulate, literate—Carías's friends growing up in Tegucigalpa. His other world, not theirs, was the regional departments and municipalities where he had served in military and political posts since 1907. These writers and journalists never held permanent positions in government, nor were they local, regional political figures. Many of them, like Paulino Valladares and Carlos Izaguirre, initially helped organize the National Party then took on specific assignments for Carías, returning to their old pursuits as journalists. Yet Carías's pragmatism attracted their attention. He was useful to them, especially Izaguirre and Fernando Zepeda of La Época, in that he provided access to power. He personified the kind of political figure they wanted, a proven administrator, not flamboyant but careful, deliberate, someone who understood and appreciated good management. He was also a political figure with allies in the countryside where many of the Honduran civil wars were waged, a political realist, and a pragmatist who could plot political campaigns

24. *Sufragio Libre*, 17 February 1923, 4; 21 July 1923, 1; 1 December 1923, 2.

too. Carías was perceived as someone who built friendships with rural political leaders, landowners, and tenant farmers, craftsmen whose economic resources like land were affected by civil unrest. These journalists were not offended by his lack of intellectual interest or theories of how to run government; rather, they were confident that based on his practical experience he could end the politics of machetismo and lead a party under the banner of national unity.

From the wide assortment of proposals for renovating the republic and building a unified state, Carías rejected the extreme views—Carlos Izaguirre's call to create a Mussolini-like fascist state or Zúñiga Huete's vague social reforms. He was also skeptical of the politics of a representative democracy proposed by Froylán Turcios. Instead, he combined many ideas of the theorists with practical politicians he had known for years. Caudillismo or personalism, the politics of the leader, would endure, but under a centralized bureaucracy with a dominant National Party. Democratic institutions with genuine separation of powers, an independent judiciary, free press, and fair elections would only be symbols in a Carías paternalistic, benevolent dictatorship. With the National Party already taking shape, he embarked on a quest for the presidency in 1924. Listening to his "theoreticians" and cultivating the friendships of rural politicians, he planned for the election campaign from his rural home in Zambrano, his main headquarters for these civic endeavors.

Honduras in the 1920s and 1930s was still a country of villages whose people had virtually no impact on national politics. The total population was approximately 800,000, less than 10 percent living in cities with over 9,000 people, and less than 5 percent living in towns exceeding 10,000 people. Women could not vote (until 1955). The lives of most citizens were linked to a local politician. Personal rivalries of these regional leaders were in turn tied to the ambitions of one figure. The urban dwellers in Tegucigalpa and San Pedro Sula, cities with fewer than 50,000 people, were small in number but extraordinarily influential and powerful.[25] As yet no one ever had ever successfully mobilized departmental leaders into a hierarchical structure of a political party. Carías gradually assumed leadership of the new party, where members heaped praise on him and extolled his virtues. The following is an example of a poem praising him in the mid 1920s:

25. Ministerio de Gobernación, 1935–1936 (Tegucigalpa: Imprenta Nacional, 1937), 36.

TRIUMPHANT MARCH
(dedicated to our candidate, General Carías)

I

All the people hail you fervently
Pronouncing your name with pride,
Since they know that you are the man
That shows us the olive branch.
We cannot be conquered by the despicable ones
Who want to keep us in yokes.
Because we no longer want hangmen
That make us suffer their pretentiousness!

2

Today we want a man that, young,
Without trappings of horrible parties
Steers us toward progress, already united,
Without hateful and disloyal division;
We do not want ancient tyrants
That power has made mighty,
With the death of so many valiant ones
Whose ambition was taken to the grave.

3

To Doctor Tiburcio Carías
And of the triumph that hits the palms,
Because he reigns proudly in the souls
Of this proud and virile town.
They cannot conquer us, those
Tyrants who erase the forgetting,
Missionaries who always have wanted
To keep us in civil war!
                    Santa Barbara, January 17, 1923[26]

When Carías assumed leadership of the Democratic National Party, which he renamed the National Party in 1922, he established its headquarters in Tegucigalpa, calling it El Club Trinidad Cabañas after his hero the nineteenth-century Liberal president.[27] Paulino Valladares created the party's administrative

26. *Sufragio Libre*, 24 February 1923, 3.
27. *Sufragio Libre*, 10 February 1923, 1.

machinery in the capital and, with his network of journalists and their newspapers in San Pedro Sula, Puerto Cortés, and Tela, established clubs in those cities. From these regional urban centers, departmental, municipal, and town headquarters were founded with club names of past presidents, all Liberals: Celeo Arias, Marco Aurelio Soto, Manuel Bonilla, and Policarpo Bonilla.[28] National Party organizations also included occupational interests of members such as El Club La Voz de La Mujer ("The Voice of the Woman Club"), El Club del Entusiásmo Feminino ("The Club of Feminine Enthusiasm"), and El Club del Campesino ("Rural Farmers Club").[29]

Valladares included his own name, Carías's, and those of other prominent party organizers in the titles of new headquarters. The leadership of the National Party was placed under the direction of local politicians whom Carías had known as comandante de armas and jefe político in several departments during the first two decades of the twentieth century.[30]

Carías spent a good part of his time in Zambrano from 1920 to 1924 during the planning and organizational stage of party building. From there he appeared at functions campaigning for the 1924 presidential contest, but rivals competed for stewardship of the party as well. Miguel Paz Barahona, a highly respected medical doctor and owner of pharmacies along the north coast, and Venancio Callejas, a lawyer from Tegucigalpa, also wanted the party's nomination at the top of the ticket.[31] Even Paulino Valladares was prominently mentioned as a possible candidate. Never enjoying the political limelight, he supported Carías as the best choice of the party. His reason was simple: Carías had always been closely associated with both the rural, regional sections of central Honduras and Tegucigalpa. From the "Village Capital" of Zambrano, as he called it, he backed Carías, who was supervising and building ties to departmental and municipal party chieftains.[32]

In April 1923, Carías was selected by the National Party's Central Commit-

28. *Sufragio Libre*, 2 December 1922, 1; 27 January 1923, 1; 10 February 1923, 1; 24 February 1923, 2–3; 16 June 1923, 2; 6 October 1923, 1.

29. *Sufragio Libre*, 9 June 1923, 1; 13 October 1923, 2.

30. In addition to "El Club Trinidad Cabanas," "El Club General Manuel Bonilla," "El Club Paulino Valladares" (in Tegucigalpa), other party organizations had names of local caudillos such as "Inocente Trimino" (El Paraíso), "Carlos Sanabria" (Colón), "Jose León Castro" (Lempira), and "José Antonio Ortega" (Choluteca).

31. *Sufragio Libre*, 2 December 1922, 1; 27 January 1923, 1; 14 April 1923, 1.

32. Simeon Hernández, minister of war, navy, and aviation, in his *Memoria* (1911), 405, and in President Miguel Dávila's *Mensaje* (same year) paid special tribute to Carías for his military defense

tee directed by Valladares as the organization's candidate for president, with Miguel Paz Barahona, a cousin of two former presidents, as his vice-presidential running mate.[33] Barahona, chosen because he came from the coffee-growing western area of Santa Barbara, had grown up and prospered along the north coast. This choice gave a regional balance to the ticket.

The incumbent chief executive, Rafael López Gutiérrez, a Liberal elected president in February 1920 (1920–24), faced a series of major crises at the start of his administration. The Liberal Party, still plagued with personalism, split again in 1923, when Juan Ángel Arias and Bonilla each launched a campaign for the presidency. Both had been active party figures since the late nineteenth century.[34]

Added to this, there were allegations of interference in the elections by U.S.-owned fruit companies. Banana enterprises along the north coast were purchasing land in exchange for railroad construction, vastly extending their economic power. By the 1920s they owned about 80 percent of the banana plantations there. The Honduran government had amassed a foreign debt largely owed to these U.S. companies. The presidential candidates accused one another of having ties to these enterprises and allegedly receiving cash contributions for their campaigns. Carías allegedly received a sum of money from United Fruit during the 1924 election to purchase arms in the United States and allowed his military forces to use its boats to move military equipment and personnel.[35]

A constitutional crisis loomed during the 1924 electoral campaign. Presidential candidates often were unable to attain an absolute majority of votes in general elections. By law, the congress was required to select a president if the popular vote failed to do so. Against this background of national debt, unemployment, and political stalemate, the Liberal Party, the largest bloc in congress, was plagued by factionalism, and President López Gutiérrez and his cohorts could not decide on his successor. Carías at this time was often referred to as an "old liberal," merely one "army general" among many with a personal following, not the National Party standard bearer.[36]

The presidential campaign was a bitterly contested election, and Carías was

---

of the north coast, especially Puerto Cortés in 1911 against the invading Bonilla forces. See also Bardeles interview, 5 March 1987.

33. *Sufragio Libre*, 3 February 1923, 1; 14 April 1923, 1.

34. Pagaoga, *Honduras y sus gobernantes*, 45.

35. *Sufragio Libre*, 17 February 1923, 1; 21 July 1923, 1; *El Cronista*, 15 August 1923, 2.

36. Gustavo S. Castañeda, *El congreso de 1924* (Comyaguela: Empresa "La Sol," 1925), 6.

frequently attacked in the press as a renegade, a Liberal who had deserted the party. The National Party mouthpiece, El Sufragio Libre (Tegucigalpa), pointed out that the standard bearer had served in Liberal governments but did so honorably and loyally. The paper saved its invective for the old Liberal war horse, Policarpo Bonilla, a presidential contender too. The paper described him as irresponsible, dogmatic in his views, and untrustworthy. Worse still, it accused him of being the incumbent chief executive's choice as a successor. El Sufragio Libre, expressed outrage when El Cronista was shut down and its editor, Carías's staunch ally Paulino Valladares, fled to Nicaragua.[37]

Carías did not travel around the country campaigning, which was not easy to do as there were fewer than 500 kilometers of roads. He was not a good public speaker, like Miguel Paz Barahona. The vice-presidential candidate did a vast amount of barnstorming where he had the strongest following, namely in Copán, the western part of the country, and all along the north coast. Carías allowed political allies to campaign for him alone in their own departments, a strategy he followed throughout his entire political career.[38]

Elections were held in the fall of 1923, but no candidate received a plurality of votes. Carías obtained the largest number of ballots, 49,591, but failed by 3,181 to receive the required number for an absolute majority.[39] By law, the congress was required to select a president. In December, President López Gutiérrez declared a state of siege, suspended the constitution, and announced he would continue in office to keep the peace.

The National Party, convinced that there was no chance to win by an election, closed all possibilities for compromise and prepared for a military campaign to defeat the president. Its reason for taking up arms was that a legitimate election had been held and its standard bearer had been denied a victory he had won by a majority vote. In the newly elected single-chamber congress, Juan Ángel Arias's Liberal faction had eighteen deputies, Policarpo Bonilla nine, and Carías's National Party, fifteen.[40]

37. Sufragio Libre, 24 February 1923, 1; 7 July 1923, 1; 1 December 1923, 2.

38. Sufragio Libre, 21 July 1923, 1.

39. The National Party issued the following vote count: Carías, 49,591; Bonilla, 34,855; Arias, 20,718 (Sufragio Libre, 10 November 1923, 1). The government later amended these figures after a vote certification: Carías, 49,953; Bonilla, 35,474; Arias, 20,839, for a total of 106,266 votes.

40. Congress confirmed the following figures on 23 January 1924: Carías, 49,541; Bonilla, 35,160; Arias, 20,426. Carías, by this count, was 2,375 votes short of an absolute majority. Sufragio Libre, 1 December 1923, 1. Paredes, Biografía Carías, 85, 89–90.

Considerable controversy surrounds the political picture at this point. Did Liberals in congress deliberately obstruct the selection process? Since their party was deeply divided between "Policarpistas" and "Aristas," the Liberals together could not have reached a consensus and selected a president. Debates in congress on the issues seemed to go nowhere and when it did vote to select from among three candidates, Carías received the expected fifteen, Bonilla, nine, and Arias, eighteen. Carías and Juan Ángel Arias agreed to renounce claims to the presidency and back the former's running mate, Miguel Paz Barahona, for president. In return for this concession, the National Party standard bearer could appoint two people to the supreme court, Arias, three. Other posts in the government would be evenly divided. This political maneuvering failed when Policarpo Bonilla persuaded Arias to break the agreement.[41]

Carías saw no choice but to take up arms and prevent López Gutiérrez from extending his term beyond 1924. He had the most to lose if the president did so. Proclaiming his electoral victory, Carías seized on the disgruntled feelings of Liberal departmental leaders who resented President López Gutiérrez's highhanded tactics, and offered them support soon after the chief executive extended his term of office.[42]

When hostilities, called the War of Revindication, began in February, it became evident that President López Gutiérrez could not maintain the allegiance of his party in several departments. Although Liberals challenged his authority to declare a state of siege, they were not prepared to give Carías unqualified support either.[43] Some backed him, however, once his forces occupied Tegucigalpa in late April and early May.[44] Carías had organized his army in the east, near the Nicaraguan frontier, and marched toward Tegucigalpa. He had Carlos Izaguirre fly a rented airplane over Tegucigalpa and bomb several military barracks. Meanwhile, Gregorio Ferrera, the Liberal populist who hated López Gutiérrez, headed toward Comayagua from the western departments of Copán and Intibucá. He was joined by another Liberal Party rebel, Vicente Tosta, proceeding from the south, marching north to San Pedro Sula.[45]

41. Paredes, Biografía Carías, 113. See also Daniel Ross, "The Honduran Revolution of 1924 and the American Interventions" (master's thesis, University of Florida 1969).

42. Telegrams, May 1924, Vol. 12, n.d., Biblioteca de Telegramas, Biblioteca y Archivos Nacionales, Tegucigalpa.

43. Ibid.

44. Ibid.

45. Longino Becerra, Evolución histórica de Honduras (Tegucigalpa: Editorial Baktun, 1983), 139–

The López Gutiérrez government was surrounded and paralyzed. At this point, U.S. Secretary of State Charles Evans Hughes sent Sumner Welles as a special representative and marines to protect the North Americans' property on the north coast and end the civil war. The Washington Peace Treaty of 1923, negotiated under the aegis of the United States, had recognized the right of Central American states to withhold recognition from any regime that had seized power by a coup. Representatives from the contending forces sent delegates to the Honduran southern port of Amapala for a conference on the U.S. ship *Milwaukee*. They signed an accord on May 3, which called for the creation of a provisional government headed by General Vicente Tosta until elections were held. According to the agreement, figures in the Liberal and National Parties who had participated in the civil war were excluded from running in the presidential election. This of course meant Carías.[46]

The National Party standard bearer in the 1924 contest willingly accepted the Amapala accords. He had two reasons for not contesting the treaty's provisions. First, he was anxious to show Washington his willingness to cooperate in bringing a peaceful end to the civil war and to gain their support for a future contest. "We lost and we accepted it," he said later.[47] He persuaded the United States of his sincerity on this point successfully.[48] Second, his vice-presidential running mate, Miguel Paz Barahona, was subsequently elected to a four-year term as chief executive in February 1925. As titular head of his party, Carías was content to have his partisans appointed to several ministerial posts, including

---

41. Several people offered uncorroborated evidence that Carías dispatched Carlos Izaguirre to Choluteca to pick up a plane and fly it to Tegucigalpa. They include Miguel Izaguirre, interview, 6 April 1987. Captain Lucas, the first Honduran recruited by Carías to become a pilot, said the military barracks in Tegucigalpa were struck; interview, Cerro de Hule, 21 February 1987. Charlie Matthews, a TACA pilot in early 1930, confirmed the story as well; interview, 31 May 1987. U.S. marines landed at the north coast port cities for a few hours to protect U.S. property and citizens in La Ceiba on 27 February 1924; at Telas on 3, 4, and 8 March 1924; and again at La Ceiba on 20 April 1925. See Captain Harry A. Ellsworth, *One Hundred Eighty Landings of United States Marines, 1800–1934* (Washington, DC: Historical Section, Headquarters, U.S. Marine Corps, 1934), 96–98, 128–33.

46. Text, Pact of Amapala, 19 April 1924, Bardales Library, Tegucigalpa, 8–12, and in the Rafael Teresero Papers, Benjamín Henriques Family Library, Tegucigalpa, marked "Milwaukee Conference," 19 April 1924.

47. *El Cronista*, 21 November 1928, 2.

48. Dispatch, U.S. legation to State Department, Honduras, 31 October 1932, reel 15, 296, in Confidential U.S. Diplomatic Post Records. The dispatch reads in part, "Carías acted in good faith. Without his aid [the] election could not have been a success."

the Supreme Court, steps that would further strengthen his political position.[49]

At this point, Carías was fully aware of Washington's role in Central American politics and its determination to enforce stability there. He saw how the internal instability of Honduras was linked to regional rivalries, sometimes fought in his own country, particularly between Guatemala's Manuel Estrada Cabrera (1898–1920) and Nicaragua's José Santos Zelaya (1893–1909). He saw the U.S. reaction to civil war with its use of force to create political stability. Both Washington conferences (1907 and 1923) with Central American participants had pledged not to recognize regimes that came to power by coups and revolutionary activity. Therefore, two basic tenets of Carías's foreign policy later as president would be gaining full and unqualified support of the United States and maintaining peace with his Central American neighbors.[50]

Carías found collaborating with Paz Barahona much to his liking. The administration addressed issues of special interest to him (less so to Paz Barahona), such as reducing the country's internal and foreign debt, balancing the budget, and restructuring the Supreme Tribunal of Accounts, whose specific duty was to oversee government costs, expenses, and income. In fact, Carías was primarily responsible for legislation that enumerated the duties and responsibilities of the accounts office, attempting to give more executive authority on budget matters.

Overall, the Paz Barahona administration showed considerable fairness, appointing some Liberals to office. In fact, the chief executive was open, congenial, and nonconfrontational when dealing with his political opponents. His promise not to serve another term beyond 1928 further reduced political tensions, convincing Liberals that their chances for capturing the presidency through the ballot box were better than through taking up arms.[51]

Carías continued to devote considerable time and effort organizing the National Party in all departments from his farm in Zambrano. This time he built a political organization in each area of the country with loyal veterans, those who had served with him in the War of Revindication in 1924. From there he managed the 1926 congressional campaigns and increased his party's majority in the legislature. All this politicking in 1926 was an effort to make another run for

---

49. Members of the Supreme Court were selected by Congress. *Decreto de Congreso*, 1929–1930, Decreto No. 10, 8–9.

50. *Manifesto de Miguel Dávila*, 1908, Imprenta Nacional, 9, 13; *La Prensa* (Tegucigalpa), 28 August 1908, 2; 31 August 1908, 2; 1 September 1908, 2.

51. *La Gaceta*, 12 October 1928, 1546.

president in 1928.[52] Other candidates included General Vicente Tosta, once a head of the Independent Republican party, Liberals Vicente Mejía Colindres, administrator of revenue on the Islas de la Bahía off the north coast, and José María Ochoa Velásquez, a political unknown. Two weeks before the October 1928 election, all Liberal Party contenders agreed to back Mejía Colindres, making the contest more difficult for Carías.

Having won his party's nomination, Carías faced a contentious and heated campaign. Editors of a leading newspaper hoping to derail his candidacy proposed that representatives of all parties, Nationals, Liberals, and Tosta's Independent Republican Party, meet to select one candidate with no contest.[53] The paper argued that civil war was so endemic it would break out again during the election. Carías saw this as a ploy to deny him the presidency. He and his partisans felt Tosta would support a Liberal because Carías had bypassed him in 1925 and backed Miguel Paz Barahona as the party's choice for president.[54]

As in 1924, U.S.-owned banana companies became a major issue in the campaign. Seizing on a controversial boundary dispute between Guatemala and Honduras, the Liberal Party accused Carías of being in the pay of United Fruit Company, which had acquired a land concession from the Paz Barahona government, while Standard Fruit had negotiated a similar arrangement with Guatemala. United Fruit was accused of wanting to see that the next Honduran president did not charge it for the land it had leased.[55]

El Cronista said Carías never examined closely, or publicly denounced, the land claim made to United nor questioned the financing arrangements made by government concessions to the fruit company's Trujillo Radio and Telegraph Company.[56] Carías vigorously denied the charges in an open letter published both in Tegucigalpa and Puerto Cortés.[57] He organized committees in the National Party to distribute his printed answer to the charges, and copies were dispatched to all departmental capitals and municipalities within a week.[58]

52. Paredes, Biografía Carías, 212.

53. El Cronista, 6 July 1928, 2; 4 August 1928, 2.

54. Stokes, Honduras, 251.

55. El Cronista, 7 August 1928, 2; 14 August 1928, 2.

56. Ibid. El Cronista said "Carías continues silent . . . silent like a rock. . . . May God forgive him" (23 August 1928, 2). See also 9 July 1928, 2; 13 July 1928, 2.

57. Carías denied any association with United Fruit Company. El Demócrata (Tegucigalpa), 12 May 1928, 2.

58. Letter to National Party's members, 8 May 1928, Bardales Library and Papers.

Elections were held on October 28. Mejía Colindres defeated Carías, 62,319 to 47,945. The Liberal candidate's victory was decisive and President Paz Barahona was credited with remaining neutral and managing a fair election.[59] Carías conceded defeat and made a pact with the new president to cooperate on critical economic issues. Two years later, in 1930, he was elected to congress and, with his party in the majority, became its presiding officer.[60] There is a story that describes how Carías got elected to preside over congress. Apparently, elected Liberals and National Party deputies were equally divided in the legislature with twenty-one members each, with one Independent, Lorenzo Vásquez from the Department of Intibucá. When voting to elect a president of the congress began, Vásquez supported Carías. Yet a Liberal representative was missing, thereby giving Carías the election. It seems the unaccounted-for Liberal deputy, José María Palacios, who also was from Intibucá and married to President Colindres's niece, was enticed into too much alcohol, put on a plane owned by United Fruit's Tela Railroad, and whisked out of Tegucigalpa. He was returned to the capital city after the vote.

Critical financial and budget issues began to surface as government deficits were increasingly covered by emergency loans. Revenues were cut by declining banana exports. Despite the economic and fiscal crisis, Carías, using the power of his office, was able to approve diplomatic appointments, name people to the Supreme Court and Tribunal of Accounts, and, of course, appoint party loyalists to key committees in congress.[61]

Meanwhile, Carías consolidated control of the party apparatus at all levels of government from the very smallest *aldea* to the national legislature. From 1924 on he built National Party committees in San Pedro Sula; in the north coast cities of Puerto Cortés, La Ceiba, and Trujillo; and in Copán and Intibucá in western Honduras. These entities were headed by well-known political figures all loyal to Carías: Carlos Sanabria, Efrain Pireda Zacapa in the Department of Colón, Vicente Ayala in Copán, Aureliano Bustillo in the Department of Tegucigalpa, Hipólito Pavón in Olancho.[62] A new generation of leaders also was

59. El *Cronista*, 7 November 1928, 2; 21 November 1928, 2. El *Cronista* on 7 November gave preliminary figures of 57,000 for Colindres, 44,000 for Carías.

60. Carías accepted defeat and signed a pact with Mejía Colindres. El *Cronista*, 21 November 1928, 2; 13 December 1928, 3.

61. República de Honduras, *Decreto del Congreso*, 1929–1930, No. 48, 76, Biblioteca y Archivos Nacionales.

62. These names were listed later in an article covering the 1928 campaign; La *Época*, 7 February 1936, 1.

emerging even in the Liberal Party following the deaths of Policarpo Bonilla and Vicente Tosta. The popular and charismatic rural leader Gregorio Ferrera from Intibucá was killed by an unknown assailant in 1931, so a political vacuum had emerged allowing Carías to strengthen his organization in that region in an alliance with Rodolfo Velázquez, once a Ferrera partisan who entered congress and remained there for forty years.[63] Carías drew mainly on the loyalty of political allies from the 1924 and 1928 elections to lead his efforts in the departments for a 1932 race. For example, he put pressure on municipal officials to join National Party organizations before his next try for the presidency in 1932.[64] His Liberal Party opponent in 1932, Ángel Zúñiga Huete, a brilliant lawyer and effective public speaker, chose a diplomatic post in Nicaragua in 1928, leaving the party in the hands of President Mejía Colindres, who had little influence over rank-and-file members. Worse, Mejía Colindres secretly approved and signed contracts with United and Standard Fruit enabling them to use national waters without paying taxes or fees. This step further antagonized Liberals, divided the party, and even provoked military uprisings as the 1932 election approached.[65]

The political crisis within the government, large-scale unemployment, and a mounting national debt contributed to Mejía Colindres's loss of party support.[66] Uprisings began, both in support of and opposed to Ángel Zúñiga Huete, who was accused of arranging for his nomination only with the approval of his party's Supreme Council, not the national convention.[67] Mejía Colindres's partisans both in and out of government wondered if they could

63. Velázquez interview, 27 September 1987. See also Rafael Bardales Bueso's *Biografía del Profesor: Rodolfo Z. Velázquez* (Tegucigalpa: Impresa Cettena, 1985).

64. This understanding of Carías's strategy is based on several interviews with Gonzalo "Chalo" Luque, San Pedro Sula, 1987. He also discussed the significance of the 1924 generals in his *Memorias de un soldado Hondureño*, vol. 1 (San Pedro Sula: Impresora Hondureña, 1980). Liana Zúñiga Caceres, whose father was director of the Central Committee Liberal Party in the 1930s and 1940s, made frequent reference to Carías's total commitment to the National Party organization at all levels of government; interview, Roatan, 14 August 1987. See also *Sufragio Libre*, 27 January 1923, 1, for a detailed account of his organization of the National Party and its committees in all parts of the country.

65. Stokes, *Honduras*, 252–53.

66. Euraque, *Reinterpreting the Banana Republic*, 57–58.

67. *El Cronista*, 18 August 1932, 3. See also reports from jefe político, Department of Atlántida, Biblioteca de Telegráficos, Biblioteca y Archivos Nacionales, 15 January 1932, Vol. 21, Tel. no. 19; 15 August 1932 (no vol. no.), Tel. No. 23, both to Ministerio de Gobernación.

maintain order in light of the president's growing unpopularity, even as regional Liberal leaders like Justo Umaña from Intibucá, Filiberto Díaz Zelaya in Copán, and Gregorio Ferrera (before he died) dropped their support for the president.[68] The government was simply too weak to maintain control and order in the country, as seen when the Department of Olancho in the east (frequently called "the Independent Republic of Olancho") negotiated a commercial treaty with another department, Morazán. "Olancho," said a newspaper, "needs strong administration."[69]

Carías soon realized that threats to Mejía Colindres's government and the potential for his overthrow affected his own chances for election as chief executive in 1932. Mejía Colindres was prevailed upon to establish *Juntas Patrioticas* in each department with representation from both Liberal and National Parties to ensure fairness in the election and oversee its process. This development offered a glimpse of hope for a fair election. Meanwhile, the president, not sure of his party's own political backing and desperate to hold on to power through the election, turned to Carías for logistical support in ending armed resistance to his government in what he called the "War of Traitors" (dissident Liberals).[70]

Seizing an excellent opportunity, Carías quickly organized his forces to support Mejía Colindres and free elections and to ensure that a peaceful transfer of power took place.[71] President Mejía Colindres was aware of his untenable position, with uprisings all over the country and forces approaching the capital from several directions. His opponents were even mobilized on the Nicaraguan and El Salvadoran borders, obtaining arms in those countries. Amapala, in the south, was actually in the hands of Liberal rebel forces headed by General Santos Chinchilla. General José María Reina, a Carías ally, successfully took Amapala from Chinchilla, but he complicated matters by declaring himself provisional president of the republic.[72]

Just prior to the election in October 1932, several Liberal Party comandantes

68. El Cronista, 28 May 1932, 3; 7 June 1932, 8.

69. El Cronista, 22 September 1932, 1.

70. Tegucigalpa, 17 July 1932, 1–2; 20 November 1932, 2.

71. Telegram, U.S. legation, Tegucigalpa, No. 453; 10 June 1932, No. 505, Confidential U.S. Diplomatic Post Records, reel 4, 940.

72. Teresero Family Papers (Tegucigalpa), family of Benjamín Henriques, Comandante de Armas, La Ceiba, telegram, President Mejía Colindres to Benjamín Henriques, 1 December 1932. Also, Dispatch, U.S. legation, Tegucigalpa, to Department of State, 15 December 1932, reel 5, 561, in Confidential U.S. Diplomatic Post Records.

de armas, under intense pressure from National Party leaders, resigned their posts, replaced by Carías supporters, all with the approval of President Mejía Colindres. These changes occurred in Comayagua, Yoro, Intibucá, Tela, Colón, and Ocotopeque. Several new appointments were critically important, such as the Sanabria brothers—Manuel, Carlos, and Salvador—who took over Ocotopeque, Colón, and El Paraiso, respectively. Francisco Martínez Funes, a longtime Carías ally, became comandante de armas in San Pedro Sula.

Special "expeditionary forces," all led by officers loyal to Carías, were organized in Tegucigalpa to spread out across the country to maintain peace. Several of these forces had previously rebelled against President Mejía Colindres: one unit commanded by General Camilo Reina, who later headed Carías's national police, controlled all the southern departments. Colonel Tomás Martínez, on Reina's staff, later known as cakita ("the shit"), became commander of the republic's mounted police force.[73]

Other special expeditions led by Carías partisans were Generals Lino Zúñiga, central zone (department of Morazán); Manuel Trejo, Santa Barbara de Copán; and Generals Juan Chávez and Gregorio Zelaya, both sent to the "Independent Republic of Olancho" to put down armed resistance there. Commissions for these officers requested by Carías were approved by President Mejía Colindres.[74]

The balance of military and political power gradually moved in Carías's direction in the summer and early fall of 1932. Carías skillfully adopted measures to deploy arms and reconnoiter the countryside with airplanes to spot dissident rebel forces. Lowell Yerex, a World War I fighter pilot from New Zealand and later founder of TACA (Central American Air Transport), joined Carías on a contract basis in his fledgling "air force." With a five-seater Stinson, a single-engine monoplane dubbed "Espíritu de Honduras," Yerex picked up Enfield and Remington rifles in neighboring El Salvador, and, using the southern city of Amapala as a fuel base, hit rebel targets there, en route north to Tegucigalpa,

73. Acuerdos, October 1932, 15 November 1932, No. EM 294; Acuerdos, October 1932 to January 1933, Secretaría de Estado, dispatch, Marina y Aviación, Biblioteca y Archivos Nacionales. See also Acuerdos, 4 November 1932, No. EM 163; El Cronista, 18 November 1932, 2; 24 November 1932, 1; 25 November 1932, 1; 30 November 1932, 1; 1 December 1932, 1.

74. Acuerdos, No. EM 295, 13 November 1932; No. 311, 19 November 1932; Nos. 31–320, 23 November 1932; No. 337, 24 November 1932; No. 350, 26 November 1932; No. 349, 26 November 1932; No. 356, 29 November 1932; No. 417, 8 December 1932; No. 419, 9 December 1932; No. 447, 12 December 1932. Dispatch, Ministerio de La Marina y Aviación, Biblioteca y Archivos Nacionales.

and in the capital itself. Yerex was particularly helpful in the campaign because he had collected good maps of Honduras since his arrival in the mid-1920s. Such information was very useful to Carías's ground troops. Carlos Izaguirre also flew a plane across the north coast back and forth from Tela and La Ceiba with supplies for Carías partisans.[75]

Mejía Colindres meanwhile denied that Carías was in command of government military forces and called for Liberal rebels to lay down their arms.[76] While overseeing tactical operations, Carías proceeded to establish political ties with Liberal Party regional caudillos if the opportunity arose. For example, Gregorio Ferrera, the popular figure from western Honduras, began his campaign to oust Mejía Colindres for granting numerous land leases to the United Fruit Company. Many called him "the Honduran Mexican Emiliano Zapata." When Ferrera was shot in the spring of 1931, his followers blamed Mejía Colindres and shifted their allegiance to Carías, who allegedly instructed his local followers to oppose land grants to banana companies in order to gain support for Ferrara's allies.[77] The change in political alliances in the Ferrera case reflected another way the National Party candidate had built his power base. In 1930, Carías, aware of Ferrera's popularity, decided not to field candidates in congressional races against him in Intibucá. Although remaining a Liberal, Ferrera was ever grateful to the National Party leader for his decision.[78] Followers of the dead leader, furious with Mejía Colindres and grateful to Carías for not contesting the 1930 election, willingly backed the National Party ticket.[79]

Carías also drew on the continued popularity of former President Miguel Paz Barahona. In several campaign speeches, he promised his administration would be a continuation of the former chief executive government's policies

75. Photos showing planes purchased, Archives, Escuela Militar de Aplicaciones, 24 December 1933; David Yerex, *Yerex of TACA: A Kiwi Conquistador* (Carterton, New Zealand: Ampersand Publishing, 1985), 62–63; Telegrama #23, Alcalde, Department of Atlántida to Ministerio de Gobernación, 17 October 1932, Biblioteca de Telegramas; *La Época*, 23 October 1933, 2; interview with Captain Luis Fiallos, First Commander Honduran Air Force, Tegucigalpa, 21 February 1987. Matthews interview, 5 May 1987.

76. *El Pueblo* (Tegucigalpa), 19 November 1932, 7.

77. Luque, *Memorias de un soldado Hondureño*, 1:10; Velásquez interview, October 1987.

78. Telegrams, U.S. legation to Department of State, 25 April 1931; U.S. consul, Puerto Cortés, to U.S. legation, Tegucigalpa, 26, 27 April 1931, Confidential U.S. Diplomatic Post Records, reel 2, 868, 875, 897; Dispatch, U.S. legation to Department of State, 6 September 1930, 2, reel 1, 587, 800-H, reel 7, 567, 800-H, reel 4.

79. See note 78 for sources.

on fiscal reform and toleration for the opposition, even calling Paz Barahona the "Founder of Honduran Democracy."[80] The ex-president was escorted around the republic by National Party chieftains giving addresses supporting the Carías candidacy as he had done in 1924. Close friends and party stalwarts like Abraham Williams, Carías's vice-presidential running mate, flew in airplanes making whistle-stop speeches all over Honduras. When the Liberal Party standard bearer Ángel Zúñiga Huete, also using a plane, gave his typically dramatic and fiery speeches, he was immediately followed by a Carías backer offering a rebuttal.[81] Even Ángel Zúñiga Huete recognized Carías's superb organizational abilities, not requiring him to travel around the country promoting his candidacy during the 1932 campaign.[82]

The United States hoped for a Carías victory, and Washington's legation in Tegucigalpa viewed the rebel campaign of the anti-Yankee Augusto César Sandino in nearby Nicaragua as an ally of the Liberal Ángel Zúñiga Huete, whose party attacked North American fruit companies. Yankee diplomats reported from Honduras that the latter's election would accelerate anti-American "radical sentiments in the region."[83]

The War of Traitors raging in the late summer and fall months of 1932 was one more example of Honduran political violence. So Carías, as he had done in 1924 and 1928, campaigned on the slogan of peace and agreed to abide by the election results. This strategy appealed to a large segment of the population, especially those of his own generation who had tired of civil war, and the United States. By 1932, the Honduran population was approximately 900,000. The National Party had been recruiting and organizing a cross-section of people since 1924, especially landowners large and small and shopkeepers in large cities like Tegucigalpa, San Pedro Sula, Puerto Cortés, and Tela;[84] even arti-

80. El Cronista, 20 August 1932, 1.

81. Ángel Zúñiga Huete received $30,000 from Guatemalan Liberal chief executive Jorge Ubico. Kenneth J. Grieb, Guatemalan Caudillo: The Regime of Jorge Ubico (Athens: Ohio University Press, 1979), 112. El Cronista, 11 June 1932, 3; 9 August 1932, 1; El Pueblo, 13 August 1932, 7.

82. Zúñiga Huete, Un cacicazgo centroamericano, 8.

83. Dispatch, U.S. legation, Tegucigalpa, to Department of State, 16 August 1930, Confidential U.S. Diplomatic Post Records, reel 1, 582. Two years later, the legation reported that there was a distinct possibility that Zúñiga Huete and Sandino were friendly, specifically that the latter was giving military assistance to the liberal standard bearer. Dispatch, U.S. legation (Tegucigalpa) to State Department, Honduras, 22 October 1932, reel 5, 224.

84. La Época, "Edición Extraordinaria," 8 January 1935, 8–9. This was a series of interviews with people who knew Carías in the 1920s.

sans, government bureaucrats, and campesinos were enrolled.[85] Carías, with the help of his old allies, recruited a substantially wide-ranging cross-section of voters. The overriding theme attracting these people to the ranks of the party was Carías's call for peace and order to enable government to function. Few people could find fault with a campaign calling for both an end to armed political warfare and economic recovery.

Carías was elected president on October 28 with a 20,000-vote majority, electing deputies to congress in fourteen out of seventeen departments. Approximately 151,000 votes were cast, the largest turnout in Honduran history. U.S. legation staffers were thankful that a Honduran government was in Carías's hands, not, as one dispatch to Washington said, "the other crowd [Liberals] of craven and incompetent swashbucklers [sic] who were anti-Yankee and anti-fruit company."[86]

Ángel Zúñiga Huete conceded defeat without protest, and Carías made the transition process look amicable and smooth.[87] When he later met Mejía Colindres for photographs, shaking hands, he said, correctly, that a peaceful transfer of executive power without precedent had been accomplished. Carías likened his victory to Franklin Roosevelt's sweep in the United States election of the same year.[88] He spoke prematurely, as several Liberal Party militants refused to accept their party's electoral defeat. For example, La Esperanza, the capital of the department of Intibucá in the west, declared the National Party candidate's election null and void and created a "de facto government" that was short lived.[89] In response to this uprising and others, Carías made plans to build an air force to ensure his installation as chief executive in February 1933. He dispatched two of Lowell Yerex's TACA pilots to the United States with $25,000; they bought two planes and flew back to Tegucigalpa. Carías continued his strategy of deploying aircraft around the country when there were threats of revolts.[90]

85. *Libro de Oro del Partido Nacional de Honduras, 1933–1940,* n.d., Biblioteca y Archivos Nacionales, Part V, 4.

86. Dispatch, U.S. legation, Tegucigalpa, to Department of State, 6 January 1933, Confidential U.S. Diplomatic Post Records, reel 7, 109; see also 27 January 1933, reel 7, 132.

87. *El Cronista,* 31 October, 1932, 1.

88. *El Cronista,* 16 November 1932, 1.

89. Ibid.

90. Telegram, U.S. legation, Tegucigalpa, to Department of State, 24 April 1933, Confidential U.S. Diplomatic Post Records, reel 7, 216; 27 April 1933, reel 7, 217; 19 May 1933, reel 7, 228.

Outgoing president Mejía Colindres and Carías exchanged remarks before the swearing-in ceremonies on February 1, 1933. Mejía Colindres deplored the disorder and uprisings that had plagued his administration. Subdued and exhausted, he called on the president-elect to begin a reconstruction of the country, politically and economically. Facing Carías at the inaugural ceremonies, Mejía Colindres concluded, "I hope you may be able to deliver the presidency in the legal manner in which I do, [now] standing erect, scorning the injustices that may rain upon you, head up, looking ahead without fear of anything or anybody . . . in a few moments you will exercise the office of president, that is to say, you will begin combat."[91]

Carías took his oath of office and briefly, in his usual low-keyed manner, recalled the tumultuous political history of his country. He mentioned civil wars, poor administration, and economic disaster, and he pledged national reconstruction, fiscal reform, political stability, and order. Ironically, all these national short-comings had contributed to his political rise.

The 1933 inauguration was both an end and a beginning in Carías's career. Fifty-six years old, he had already established a political party, giving it structure and organization. Futile attempts by earlier politicians like Policarpo and Manuel Bonilla, both Liberals like him, failed to build a party. Unlike Carías, these political chieftains had little or no contact with local politicians. They simply formed a party without the organization to sustain and support it. Equally important too was that these figures were not able to give their organizations an identification with a regional leader, someone who could provide the structure and force of a party locally. But Carías broke this cycle of factional disputes because in 1933 he represented a generation of people weary of disorder, chaos, and poor administration and desirous of stability and order. He built a following from both the urban sector and the village, especially Zambrano, where he had cultivated interests as rancher, landowner, and farmer. His "capital" would also be in Zambrano, on the main dirt road connecting Tegucigalpa to San Pedro Sula, joining north and south, east and west.

Carías would work to centralize his administration and, at the same time, continue strengthening his party at the local level. He was a product of his past—the politics of regional political personalism and the old liberalism, the party of "progress," in the late nineteenth century—but he had the instincts to

91. El Cronista, 31 October 1932, 1; Address, Dr. Mejía Colindres; First message, President Tiburcio Carías, 1 February 1933, translation in Dispatch no. 720, U.S. legation to Department of State, Confidential U.S. Diplomatic Post Records, reel 7, 175–76,.

link power in the periphery (the village) to Tegucigalpa. His election to the presidency in 1932 offered a promise of what he would do, but it would take certain talents, skills, and powers of persuasion, even the use of brute force, to bring about order and peace. His blueprint for governing in 1933 did not provide for the transformation of society. His goal was to create fiscal responsibility and build an infrastructure promoting more and better trade and commerce. People were urged to join his party to form occupational and professional groups collectively expressing their interests and views, not to foster individual representative democracy. Washington was delighted with Carías's election, as stability, its chief goal, now seemed possible. Said a Yankee diplomat, "This legation should be able to get anything it asks for from the new administration, congress and the supreme court, except money."[92]

92. Dispatch, U.S. legation, Tegucigalpa, to Department of State, 15 December 1932, Confidential U.S. Diplomatic Post Records, reel 5, 561.

II

The Politics of
Benevolent Paternalism

3

Vox Populi—Vox Deus

The Voice of the People Is the Voice of God

Although caudillismo always leads to despotism and often to terror, it is still not possible to condemn outright its role in the national evolution of Spanish American countries. Caudillismo is a general social phenomenon, the result of social structures and ideologies that prevailed in all the Spanish American countries at one time, although each caudillo is a personality distinct from all the others. Thus it would be useless to sketch the portrait of the typical caudillo and paint it black or white. Latin America, which has had so many of them, has had all types. Different in their ideologies—progressive or reactionary—wise men or illiterates, some caudillos were agents of progress for their countries, others ruined them: still others, the great number perhaps, did their countries a great deal of harm but at the same time a little bit of good.

—JACQUES LAMBERT
Latin America: Social Structures and Political Institutions (1969)

Tiburcio Carías was a personalist leader, who by persuasion, intimidation, and force promoted allegiances to his regime characterized by excessive praise and adulation. He fostered a cult of the leader, proclaiming order and stability, the sacred themes of his regime. His elaborate titles and the public works named after him attested to his self-proclaimed uniqueness as head of both government and nation. Yet beneath this picture of an omnipotent leader lay the calculated and deliberate strategies for governing through others, many more competent in certain areas than he.

A visitor to Honduras in the era of Carías would find imposing portraits of him on the walls of all government offices. One got a sense of his bigness from these pictures, which seemed almost too large for their frames: his heavy-set face, full mustache, and a presidential sash draped across his broad chest. In town he dressed in a three-piece suit with a watch chain; he was always neat in appearance, meticulously groomed. Below the presidential portrait displayed everywhere was the statement, "Honduras acclaims General Carías the voice of the people is the voice of God."[1] A passage on a plaque still displayed in the Palace of the Central District of Tegucigalpa reads:

FACING THE PORTRAIT OF GENERAL CARÍAS
by Alejandro Alfaro Arraga

We are revealed before him, his name inspires
this moral strength that carries the symbol
and the glory has encircled his head like a halo.
At his triumphant pass all bow
and the land proudly goes forth
confidently toward the zenith of its grandeur.

We are revealed before him, carry the motto
HONDURAS above all;
in the ghostly hour in which the world lives
like a good legionary burning in his breast
calls of Liberty, with a profound
blow to the conquests of the Right.

We are revealed before him. He and the land,
The land and he, the two one same ideal;
[Behind] this ideal we are forging the present
and ONE is our soul and our mind,
united in a fraternal embrace.

We are revealed before him, as if we were
contemplating in effigy the Superman;
and placed on his temple a Cincinato
revering the sounds of his name
and leaning, looking at his portrait.[2]

From any part of Tegucigalpa one can still see the huge Monument to Peace on Mount Picacho in the center of the city. It has sixteen columns surrounding it inscribed "March 15, 1876," Carías's birthday. It was thought better to commemorate his birth with the motto of his regime, "Peace and Order," than to adorn the structure with his bust, which many of his advisers thought could be

1. La Cultura: Organo del Institúto Normal de Varones (Tegucigalpa), 30 November 1940, 73.
2. These words appear on a plaque located in the main entrance hall of the Palace of the Central District of Tegucigalpa.

easily cut down.[3] During his regime, and for some time thereafter, the Honduran flag was displayed at the imposing round structure on his birthday to commemorate "a day of peace and to give thanks to God" along with Dios, Patria y Paz ("God, Country, and Peace").[4]

Stories abound as to the origins of the circular monument with its sixteen columns. The most commonly accepted account is that Carlos Izaguirre raised 80,000 lempiras for a statue of Christ as a symbol of peace. Consequently, one was commissioned in Italy. En route to Honduras, possibly sometime in late 1936, the ship carrying the statue sank in the Atlantic. Carías therefore decided a monument ought to be built near the sports stadium dedicated to the Olympic Games of 1936. Sixteen pillars were constructed around the structure, and he called it the Monument to Peace. The pillars represented the length of the caudillo's rule, 1932–48. The monument remains today but without the caudillo's birth date, which was removed not long after his term ended.[5]

Schoolchildren in the Carías era began each day with the "Hymn to Peace." On special occasions they marched from their schools to the Presidential Palace paying homage to the "Benefactor to Peace." Crossing any bridge leaving Tegucigalpa, one would read that Carías had built it; and it was usually named after him. Most of the towns or villages one entered displayed a plaque in the central park that said "Tiburcio Carías—the Builder and Renovator of the Community."[6]

Praise to the dictator was lavish. Members of congress and ministers frequently began and ended their speeches with reference to the president who they said by some "intercession by God brought blessings"—because of the peace and order established under his regime. General Benjamín Henriques, director of roads and one of Carías's most loyal associates, was oftentimes effusive. At the end of a long drought he said, "Thanks to the peace and order that exists in Honduras with Carías, we have been given an abundance of rain, he [Carías] is the maximum leader of the destiny of Honduras, symbol of man, founder and sustainer of Honduran peace, and benefactor of the country."[7]

Slogans covered the country, on all public buildings, squares, and newspa-

3. Boletín del Congreso Nacional Legislativo (Tegucigalpa), Imprenta Nacional, 16 July 1946, 15.

4. Sufragio Libre, 24 September 1943, 2.

5. Francisco Prats Vives, interview, Tegucigalpa, 22 July 1987. Prat, an architect, designed the monument. He was married to Carías's niece, María Carías Reyes.

6. Sufragio Libre, 14 February 1936, 13.

7. Henriques family papers, Tegucigalpa, newspaper clippings, n.d.

per and magazine mastheads. Roads, too, were named after him or dedicated to the peace and order he was giving the nation. A segment of the Pan-American Highway that ran through southern Honduras was called Camino del Sueño ("Road of Dreams"—in reference to the pleasant, hopeful future).[8] Schools, hospitals, and libraries were also named after the president, who usually dedicated them. During elections, the slogan of a National Party candidate would extol the virtues of the caudillo, not those of the office-seeker. For example, one would see a picture of the local candidate but read, "Vote for a man who is strong, like a tree who is clear as the sun, and lonely as the moon, vote for the most beautiful man of Honduras—Carías and the National Party."[9] Praising a candidate was done only in the context of exalting the chief executive.

The country's two "ships," actually motorboats, one on the Atlantic north coast and the other anchored in Amapala, on the Pacific Ocean, were the Elena and the Zambrano, named after Caríias's wife and his much-loved country residence.[10] Many ports were also named after his wife and constant companion.[11]

Those who wisely contributed funds for the construction of a park, bridge, or building dedicated to Carías had their names inscribed on a plaque located nearby.[12] Yet public works projects were also dedicated to Carías's close friends, advisers, and ministers, as well as to his hero President Trinidad Cabañas (1852–1855). Even National Party committees in many cities and towns were named after recognized influential figures in the hierarchy of the regime.[13]

This propensity to share the limelight while praising the principle of order and peace characterized the style and manner of the Carías administration. His strategy was to blend direct, personal rule with his political experience as a regional leader. While his image clearly dominated all parts of the nation, his power and prestige were enhanced too through the popularity of those who governed for him at the local level. His governing style and administrative skills touched everyone.

8. El Cronista, 24 August 1936, 7, as quoted from The Lamp, published by Standard Oil of New Jersey, n.d.

9. La Época, 7 February 1936, 1; 6 August 1936, 1, 4; 8 December 1938, 1; 12 September 1938, 1; Boletín Legislativo, 15.

10. Memorias de guerra, marina, y aviación, 1933–1934, Biblioteca y Archivos Nacionales, 10. A new ship was purchased and named General Carías in 1938; see Memorias de guerra, marina, y aviación, 1937–1938, 12, Anexos, Memorias de guerra, marina, y Aaiación, 1942–1943, 17.

11. La Época, 20 March 1940, 1.

12. La Época, 3 June 1940, 2; 3 December 1942, 2.

13. La Época, 7 January 1938, 1; 14 August 1936, 1; 14 October 1939, 1.

Honduras was largely an illiterate and politically indifferent society, where homey, country manners were common. Only a small segment of the population needed to be influenced through the press or radio. Although Carías appeared frequently at ribbon-cutting ceremonies around the capital, he never toured the rest of the country, as travel by land was almost impossible. He never flew in an airplane, yet he kept open channels of communication at all levels of government. Carías was not a political leader like Juan Perón of Argentina or Fidel Castro of Cuba, who enjoyed public speaking from a balcony to multitudes below. He never delivered long, emotional addresses but offered instead a few simple, short introductory comments at a dedication ceremony, then turned the proceedings over to a minister, or a local political ally, someone more directly involved with the project.[14]

His main rival for years was the colorful Ángel Zúñiga Huete, an excellent speaker and a prolific writer, who traveled throughout the country by plane in his campaigns of 1932 and 1948.[15] Yet unlike Carías he never built a political organization with the discipline of the National Party. Ángel Zúñiga Huete was not a product of the politics of las montañas, not a general de las montañas. His political ties were almost entirely from urban Honduras. Therefore, his political constituency was but half of the country's political divide; the other half, towns and villages, was controlled by Carías.

Called el hombrón ("the strongman") and la buchona ("the caudillo from Zambrano"), Carías always conducted himself in a solemn fashion, as a ceremonial leader, symbol of order and peace. Never criticizing his Central American neighbors, the United States, or banana companies,[16] Carías also rejected the anti-imperialism espoused by the Nicaraguan rebel Augusto César Sandino in the 1930s, thereby gaining Washington's favor. He wanted to end interference by states in the internal affairs of other countries in Central America, which he remembered from his earlier political career. His was a regime that

14. Izaguirre Tosta de Fiallos interview, 3 September 1987; Durón interviews, spring 1987; Perez Cadalso interview, 1 December 1987.

15. Some works by Ángel Zúñiga Huete include El desastre de una dictadura (Kingston, Jamaica: Times, 1937); Un cacicazgo centroamericano (Mexico City: Imprenta Victoria, 1938); Idolo desnudo (Mexico City: Acción Moderna Mercantil, 1939); Carta abierta a Tiburcio Carías Andino (Mexico City: n.p., 1943); Carías: una actitud y una senda (Mexico City: n.p., 1949); and Conflicto cívico entre la dictadura y el pueblo: mi contribución por la liberación de Honduras (Tegucigalpa: Imprenta La Razón, 1949). These are mentioned in Euraque, "Social, Economic, and Political Aspects of the Carías Dictatorship," 240.

16. Gálvez Barnes interviews, 2 September, 30 October 1987. Gálvez Barnes served on the governing junta in 1956 and as ambassador to the United States in 1957.

wanted to gain respect from neighbors and largesse from North America to achieve stature and prestige at home, as well as revenue from trade abroad. Carías believed a low-key, orderly, closely managed administration was necessary to accomplish these objectives.

As a "general" in the army, Carías typified the regional caudillo. He passed through the ranks from captain to general in the 1920s, reflecting his rising stature as a political force. Over the years he was assigned to domestic posts as an administrator, never abroad to diplomatic positions, nor did he ever travel outside the country after becoming president. In the first decade of the twentieth century, when actively engaged in civil wars, he visited Nicaragua and El Salvador but only to gather arms and spend brief stints in exile. He always dispatched his sons and loyalists to consulates on missions for specific purposes.[17]

Everywhere, on the mastheads of government publications and in his annual address to congress, Carías's governing principle was first stated: "Peace engenders order, order security, security facilitates work and work creates progress."[18] These words reflected his own daily habits as well as his goals as the country's chief magistrate. Since politics was his life, he labored at it full time, with farming in Zambrano as his only diversion. Carías had a photographic memory for names and remembered special matters in a person's life, always recalling them when he met someone.[19]

Not surprisingly, Carías was an extraordinarily self-disciplined person with an enormous capacity for work; he paid especially close attention to details. Methodical and persistent, he began his day at five in the morning, reading and sending telegrams from his office to jefes políticos and comandantes de armas in all seventeen departments. He expected immediate responses from them with a full account of all the issues and questions he had raised.[20] He worked until noon, and every day at the same hour after lunch, following the same route, a chauffeur drove him and his wife Elena in a black, four-door 1930 Packard, armed, to Villa Elena, an aldea just outside Tegucigalpa in Guasculile. Returning to the capital at six, he resumed work, mostly receiving petitioners,

17. La Época, 18 September 1935, 1.

18. Revista de Policía: Organo de la Institución (Tegucigalpa), August–October 1941.

19. Interview with Henry Gilbert, Carías's dentist and close friend, Tegucigalpa, 12 April 1987.

20. Interviews in Tegucigalpa with José María Lagos (known as "Lagitos" or "Chemita"), Carías's bodyguard, 1937–39, 22 October 1987, and Francisca Paca Antunez Rivas, Carías's private secretary, 1949–62, 10 October 1987.

people from all walks of life appearing for personal requests. With an "open door," he scheduled appointments on Tuesdays and Thursdays and rarely, if ever, changed this routine.

Carías never used a telephone, only the telegraph, when dealing with political associates in the far-flung regions of the country. He expanded the telegraph system to towns in every administrative department by 1935. In the city, a messenger would be dispatched with his car to bring someone to his office over the main entrance in the rotunda of the presidential palace for a meeting. He never met his cabinet as a group, but only with ministers individually in his private office. His desire for secrecy reflected a need to oversee every detail in government offices and to maintain control over employees. Attending to matters of state at all levels, from major issues to the most minute, his signature was affixed on contracts with U.S. companies like Squibb, Westinghouse, and Standard Oil of New Jersey, even as he approved expenditures for typewriters and paper. He assessed fines for failing to perform duties properly in a government post and reviewed petitions of all kinds—requests for scholarships, permission to increase a government office telephone allowance—or sent messages to employees ordering them to reduce the number of phone calls and messages.[21]

The telegraph system became the means by which Carías maintained daily control of the country.[22] Its headquarters in the capital was housed in a separate building, but Carías created his own telegraph office in the presidential residence with his personal telegraph operator, Presentación Rivera, who lived in a room next to the chief executive's office. From the second-floor presidential office in Tegucigalpa to towns and cities in the republic, a daily flow of telegrams passed uninterrupted back and forth for sixteen years. Like other dictators in Latin America, Porfirio Díaz in México, Jorge Ubico of Guatemala, and Vicente Gómez in Venezuela, Carías made effective use of this technology to help consolidate his regime and govern the country personally. Previous Hon-

21. *Acuerdos*, Ministerio de Gobernación, 1, 2, 3, 4, 7, 24, 25 April 1941, Biblioteca y Archivos Nacionales. See also *Notas Varias*, año 1933, Ministerio de Fomento, *Acuerdos*, Ministerio de Fomento, 20 October 1934, Biblioteca y Archivos Nacionales.

22. The Telegram Library in the Biblioteca y Archivos Nacionales contains few if any messages from a president or his ministers prior to 1932. In the waning months of upheaval in the Mejía Colindres government, one sees the number of telegram directives increase noticeably, and they are sent by Tiburcio Carías to comandante de armas and jefe políticos, mostly his own followers around the country defending the incumbent regime against its detractors.

duran chief executives used the telegraph system sparingly but never made it the key instrument for governing.

Presentación Rivera's tasks were simple but critically important, and of course they required complete loyalty. His job was to send directives each day to political chiefs and military commanders and to await their responses at the Central Telegraph Office for transmission to his boss for review. By six o'clock, he had sent dispatches throughout the country with assignments or simply a request to learn what was happening in a particular locale.[23] If no significant matter needed attention, a reply was necessary anyway. Therefore, "*sin novedad*" ("nothing new") often clattered in on the telegraph from a political chief. The president always insisted on a response.[24]

The constant traffic between the chief leader and his loyalists made the careful selection of telegraph operators throughout the country possible without Carías having to conduct periodic visits to rural areas.[25] Candidates' family backgrounds, political activities, and demonstration of loyalty were investigated with details of these reports sent to the president. Without exception, the final selection was given to a National Party loyalist, never someone associated with a local political chief or military commander.[26] No one receiving the paid appointment could work in more than one location, and those employed along the north coast or the once British-held Bay Islands of Honduras had to know English as well as Spanish.[27] After a lengthy search, Antonio Raquel, a long-time Carías follower, was chosen as director of telegraphic communications in 1933. He had held this position from 1904 to 1907, and again from 1911 to 1919 in Cortés when Carías was comandante de armas in 1907. A premium was therefore placed on attachment, devotion to the caudillo in Tegucigalpa, as opposed to technical skills, which Raquel lacked.[28]

23. Rivera interview, 4 July 1987.

24. Rivera interview, 16 July 1987.

25. Rivera interview, 2 September 1987.

26. "Copias de Notas," April 1933, Doc. No. 705, Vol. 1701, Ministerio de Fomento, Biblioteca y Archivos Nacionales; see also "Copias de Notas," July–September, Vol. 1770; Rivera interview, 2 September 1987.

27. Rivera interview, 2 September 1987; "Copias de Notas," July–August 1934, Doc. 281; 24 December 1934, Doc. 276; 17 December 1934, Doc. 614; 22 November 1934; República de Honduras, "Notas Ministeriales," 1935, Ministry of War, Navy and Aviation, 2 January 1935, 21 October 1935 (no doc. no.); *Tegucigalpa*, 26 November 1933, 9.

28. Perfecto Bobadilla, "Monografía del Departamento de Cortés," *Revista del Archivo*, Vol. 18, September 1940, 227.

Carías's close scrutiny in selecting and supervising the telegraph system grew out of his experience in the fall of 1932 and in the winter and spring of 1933 trying to place loyalists in key local posts to end the military conflict called the War of Traitors. Although not always successful in obtaining his objective, he had learned some important lessons. No longer would military commanders in departments report to the minister of defense; rather, they would communicate directly to the president. The same applied to political chiefs, who would now report to Carías rather than to the appropriate minister.[29] Local leaders, civil and military, were connected first to the president's office and then, if necessary, referred to his cabinet officers, such as Juan Manuel Gálvez, the defense minister, or Abraham Williams, minister of government.

All departments and municipal districts were to have a telegraph operator, a Carías loyalist, linked to the center of administration in Tegucigalpa, the Central Telegraph Office, and the presidential residence. No one other than these local Carías operatives was ever permitted to use the system. Political leaders, if considered disloyal, were punished by being excluded from using the telegraph. For example, when Mariano Bertrand Anduray, a Nationalist Party deputy from Choluteca, challenged Carías's appointment as director of the party while serving as chief executive, he was prohibited from communicating with his collaborators through the national telegraph system because his activities "tended to evoke partisan passions with intent to provoke disorder," according to the directive.[30]

Sometimes government officials used the Tropical Radio Telegraph Company, a subsidiary of the United Fruit Company.[31] Carías even allowed TACA (Central American Air Transport), run by his confidant Lowell Yerex, to install telegraph radio stations in Tegucigalpa, San Pedro Sula, La Ceiba, Santa Rosa, and Tela. But these TACA-owned units would be under the Central Telegraph Office in the vice-president's Ministry of Fomento.[32] For the first time a radio-telegraph system was linked to the Central Telegraph Headquarters in Tegucigalpa from the Mosquita, Honduras's northeast coast.[33] Carías even had con-

29. "Correspondencia Telegráfica, 1933, de Choluteca," Biblioteca de Telegramas, Biblioteca y Archivos Nacionales, Telegramas, February–April 1933.

30. "Copias de Notas," *Acuerdos de 1933*, 22, 23 February 1933; *Acuerdos*, Ministerio de Gobernación, 1 April 1941.

31. Ibid., Doc. 323, 22 September 1934, 168.

32. Ibid., Vol. 331, Doc. 1610, 3 April 1940.

33. "Notas Ministeriales," 1938, Biblioteca y Archivos Nacionales, Ministry of War, Navy and Aviation, 19 February 1938.

gress pass a bill marking April 30, 1933, as "Telegraph Operators' Day," in commemoration of the anniversary of Samuel F. B. Morse's invention of the wireless.

Carías assumed the presidency in an atmosphere of crisis during the 1930s. His predecessor, Mejía Colindres, admitted that political upheaval, civil war, and rebellion had stopped his government from functioning effectively.[34] Moreover, the armed resistance to his regime had disrupted the economy, making worse the already desperate fiscal conditions. The general loss of life, property, and agricultural goods was incalculable. A cross-section of the population, particularly campesinos, landowners, and artisans in small towns and villages whose property and livelihood had been destroyed, had reached the limit of their tolerance and longed for some order in a state that appeared to be disintegrating. A simple declaration that peace and stability would be the basis for a new administration was enough to rivet people's attention and draw them to Carías.[35]

Carías's initial statements as chief executive propounded the very issues the public wanted: restore order and bring organization and efficient administration to all levels of the government.[36] To do this, he established a framework through which he would govern the country by creating a loyal personal staff, members of his family. At the ministerial level he appointed individuals skilled in certain fields such as finance, budget, banking, education, and foreign relations. In the departments of the country, jefes políticos and comandantes de armas, usually local political rivals, were placed in charge of their respective areas. Carías personally directed the operations of each of these three segments of his administrative system using different strategies to ensure loyalty, competence, and dedication to him personally.

He kept several competent ministers who had served in the Mejía Colindres government and placed National Party loyalists in top posts as well, including ministers for development, governing with jurisdiction over justice; war, navy,

34. Memoria, Ministerio de Hacienda, 1930–1931, Biblioteca y Archivos Nacionales, 3, 11–12, 15.

35. Luque interviews, 10 September 1987, 14 September 1987. Chalo Luque describes death and destruction in Honduras during the era 1924–32, with an estimated dead of 5,000 in 1924. Luque, Memorias de un soldado Hondureño, 1:120–24.

36. Abraham Williams, Carías's vice-president, describes his immediate tasks as given him by the new president in February 1933, in Manuel Santoveña and Alejandro Novas Gardela's book Hombres y cosas (Tegucigalpa: Tallares de la Democracía, 1933), 18–20; see also Memorias, Minister de Gobernación, Biblioteca y Archivos Nacionales, 1933, 15–16, 19–20, 36–37, 39.

and aviation; finance; public education; and foreign relations. His goals were to end civil strife, to get the country's finances in order by reducing international and domestic debt, to expand the number of diplomatic representatives abroad,[37] and to punish those guilty of idleness, theft, damage to property, and criminal offenses.[38]

There was a degree of continuity in the government transition of 1933, as Carías had assumed the tasks of defending the Mejía Colindres administration from its detractors in the summer of 1932, using the telegraph system and then deploying loyal militias, from the Ministry of War.[39] Telegrams to all parts of the country poured out of the presidential palace from the day he took office, swiftly placing loyal National Party figures and military allies in their posts. Each was required to report steps they were taking to end revolutionary violence.[40] Departmental figures who would become household names—Carlos Sanabria, Julián Mejía, Martínez Funes, and Benjamín Henriques, loyal to Carías since 1924—now filed volumes of telegrams to the caudillo from their respective posts across the country.[41]

The transition of administrations was not entirely smooth, for Carías ran into great difficulty ending resistance soon after taking office. To expedite matters he established a National Police Force with mounted units to begin pacifying the central region of the country from Tegucigalpa south to Amapala, and north to San Pedro Sula, contracting out assignments to people with aircraft in search of pay and adventure. He built this "air force," as he called it, using small single-propeller aircraft, whose pilots transported arms and supplies to his loyalists in other departments.[42]

When Carías took office in 1933, the constitution of 1924 was in force, which limited the chief executive's power, giving extensive authority to congress on financial matters.[43] The liberal constitution of 1894, amended somewhat in 1924, contained provisions for individual rights with obligatory voting.

37. "Interview with President Carías," in Santoveña and Novas Gardela, Hombres y cosas, 10, 13, 15. See also Mensajes Presidenciales, 1933–1935, Biblioteca y Archivos Nacionales, 6, 15, 16, 31.

38. Correspondencia Telegráfica, 1933, Biblioteca de Telegramas, Biblioteca y Archivos Nacionales, Telegramas January, February 1933, to several ministers, jefes politicos, and comandante de armas.

39. Ibid., May, June 1933.

40. Ibid., March, April 1933. See also El Cronista, 2 December 1932, 1.

41. El Cronista, April, May 1933.

42. Martínez interviews, 9 April 1987, 11 November 1987.

43. Durón interviews, 8 February 1987; 10 August 1987. See also Stokes, Honduras, 80.

Free, lay, compulsory education was provided and the role of the Catholic Church was vastly reduced. The unicameral congress was given the responsibility to ensure the implementation of executive actions in areas such as agriculture, industry, and commerce. It was also empowered to approve or disapprove the president's expenditures and limit his power of the state of siege.

The president was elected to a four-year term, allowing for reelection once.[44] Congress could call into question, review, and even censure ministers for their actions. It also had the responsibility for ascertaining whether a presidential and vice-presidential candidate had obtained an absolute majority in the election. In several contests since 1894, the legislature failed to make this determination out of partisan interests, so resolution of presidential races was almost always left to military conflicts. The powers later granted to Carías constitutionally were considerable, yet the main political issues that ushered in his election were order, peace, and the pressing need for economic recovery. Carías and his cohorts felt swift action and a decisive executive hand were needed.

His followers who played key roles in his election, Carlos Izaguirre and journalist Fernando Zepeda Durón, also wanted a strong executive with expanded authority. But before any changes could take place, Carías was prepared to use the patronage spoils system, keeping the National Party under his direct control. The administration of government in 1933 required immediate attention. The prospect of losing control to departmental political leaders was always a possibility; it had happened to other chief executives before him. Beyond the appointment of cabinet officials, Carías had no power to name heads of departments or municipal districts. These were all officially determined by elections. Personalism could greatly enhance the power of a president if he chose because at the local level, the leader of the party exercised real power. Although pressure groups existed, they were not well organized at the national level, so a party loyalist or a military commander could remove a governor of a department if he chose.[45]

The political conditions at the local level do not explain how Carías managed to administer the republic for so long—and so effectively—as a dictator. The country had no national army or police force that could singly or jointly impose authority over the republic. Militias, at the local level, had historically advanced the interests of a single leader. This was an advantage and a disadvan-

44. Stokes, Honduras, 80.
45. Ibid.

tage to the new president. No institutionalized national armed force could manipulate or even cast him out. Yet these local, regional military forces, under the command of a local political figure, could ignore his authority. Carías therefore embarked on a strategy to control regional authority and build a strong personal party with ties to him at the national level. As a caudillo, he built his regime on an inner core of loyal people who provided the needed administrative expertise to see that his directives reached cabinet officers and political subalterns in the far-flung departments of the country. With no standing professional military to challenge or disrupt this inner core of loyalists, Carías could be reasonably assured that his orders were carried out unimpeded.

Two people who fit into this category, José María "Chema" Albir and Marcos Carías Reyes, the president's nephew, served as personal secretaries from 1933 to 1948. Both were writers and journalists, people who in their considerable published works wrote on the need for the creation of a country devoid of civil war and political upheaval. Albir, known as "Pico de Oro" ("golden tongue") was an excellent speaker who delivered radio addresses weekly, expounding passionately and forcefully on the president's accomplishments.[46] An effective, polished orator, Albir was never confrontational; his career in Honduras had been spent as an executive assistant, an administrator, once for President Miguel Paz Barahona, though he also served in congress in 1926. Considered brilliant and something of a dandy (called a "philosopher of action"), he was happily consumed by his tasks, as long as efficiency and authority were properly executed.[47] The range of his interests never extended beyond Tegucigalpa and was never political. His father, a Honduran, married Adelaida López Vallecillos of Ocotal, Nicaragua, so when a border dispute with Managua erupted in 1938, he resigned his post, not wanting to embarrass Carías, and left the country to become the Honduran consul general in San Francisco, California.[48]

Marcos Carías, the president's other close confidant and secretary, became a full-time journalist in the early 1920s, writing for *Sufragio Libre, El Obrero, El Demócrata, El Cronista* (all in Tegucigalpa), and *La Vanguardia*, a publication devoted exclusively to the Carías campaign in 1932. Like Albir, but more pro-

---

46. *La Época*, "Edición Extraordinaria," January 1937, 2.

47. Margot Lainfiesta, *Cámara lenta* (Tegucigalpa: Talleres Tipográficos Nacionales, [1935]), 28–29; *El Diario Comercial* (San Pedro Sula), 2 May 1933, 1.

48. Minister, Foreign Relations, to Juan Albir, 26 August 1938, Doc. no. 69a, Correspondencia Despachada, Ministry of Foreign Relations, Republic of Honduras, Archivos Palacio Nacional.

lifically, Marcos wrote extensively in the genre of the better-known Honduran writer, Froylán Turcios's *Ariel.* He emphasized the need to build a strong nation-state and avoid civil wars. When special, confidential assignments arose, Marcos Carías went on missions abroad for the president.[49] He could be trusted, was competent and personally loyal, and his ties to journalists were also important when the chief executive needed to explain or promote his policies.[50]

Another nephew, Calixto, became Carías's main link to the development of an air force, purchasing planes, arms, and equipment abroad. Called "general," he never received any military training yet became commander of the Amapala military district (southern Honduras) and directed the National Artillery School there.[51] He was considered less reliable than others in Carías's inner circle because he drank too much and was given to displays of pompous showmanship.

Carlos Izaguirre was unique among Carías's advisers. Like Marcos Carías Reyes, Paulino Valladares, and Froylán Turcios, he wrote novels, essays, and articles for newspapers and never was a permanent fixture in a Carías cabinet. Rather, his assignments varied from serving in congress to flying planes delivering arms to Carías's partisans, and from time to time he went abroad as inspector of consulates to allow him to carry out sensitive tasks for the president. He was always at Carías's side offering advice or simply amusing and entertaining the taciturn president with good stories and gossip.

Surprisingly, Izaguirre, with all his eclectic talents and exuberance, was taken seriously. He spoke several languages, traveled extensively at home and abroad, and knew a wide range of people. Although he and Carías had different personalities, each one appreciated the intelligence and competence of the other.[52] Izaguirre was intensely committed to building a centralized state, a government that could bring order and effective administration to the country,

49. *Tegucigalpa,* 6 August 1933, 27.

50. El Día (Tegucigalpa), 16 February 1949, 1;Zapata interviews, December 1987.

51. *Acuerdos de Guerra, Marina y Aviación,* 1941–1942, Acuerdo No. 66, 15 August 1941; No. 316, 5 January 1942, Palacio de los Ministerios; Julian Caceres, Honduran Minister, Washington DC, to Minister of Foreign Affairs, Salvador Aguirre, 15 October 1940; *Correspondencia Diplomática Recibida de la Legación de Honduras,* 1940–1941, Archivo, Foreign Minister, Comisión de Soberania y Fronteras, Comayagua, Tegucigalpa, Registro de Pasaportes, October 1935–December 1938, 1940–1943, Archivos, Palacio Nacional; Confidential U.S. Diplomatic Post Records; Dispatch, U.S. legation , Tegucigalpa, to State Department, 30 June 1938, reel 17, 406, Honduras.

52. Cadalso interview, 1 December 1987.

and Carías was his model. He had observed him closely as an administrator and political organizer for years.

Carías gave ministerial posts to a number of friends who were not necessarily personally close but professionally competent in law, accounting, business, foreign trade, and diplomacy. Most of them, including Vice-President Abraham Williams, served the full sixteen years in the Caríato (the Carías regime). The president as dictator rarely if ever had to shift individuals from post to post or oust them from office in order to stay in power. He relied on his political instincts and sound judgment to make appointments to his satisfaction in the early stages of his administration. Carías had known these people for years, mostly in Tegucigalpa as schoolmates and social friends. Many of them, like Vice-President Abraham Williams, Minister of Development Salvador Aguirre, Julio Lozano who headed finance, and Antonio Bermúdez who directed foreign affairs, spoke foreign languages, particularly English, which they learned in the United States and in their work as lawyers or accountants for banana companies. Their ties to the U.S. corporations further linked Carías to those vast enterprises with their wealth and power. These friends, after studying at the National University, had entered their professions at home and abroad while Carías went to his family's rural estate in Zambrano, and to political-administrative posts throughout the country during the turbulent years of the 1920s and 1930s. Political upheaval and the collapse of the economy in the 1930s rekindled their friendships.

Never personally or politically close to Carías, these cabinet officers had no ties with local, regional interests. None even were political leaders, *coroneles del cerro* ("generals of the mountain"), nor did they represent a particularly powerful, cohesive national oligarchy. Although they had extensive experience in national posts, they were never politically threatening to chief executives. Loyalty, service, and many longstanding links to private industry (mostly in the United States) gave the regime its desperately needed stability.[53] They were placed in positions where Carías made known his main priorities at the start of the new administration—financial recovery, creating sound fiscal policies, and ending lawlessness. Carías formed a cabinet of individuals who lacked charisma and had no interest in building a popular base of support to challenge him.[54] All of

53. Paul Lewis, *Paraguay under Stroessner* (Chapel Hill: University of North Carolina Press, 1980), 115, offers an interesting and similar account of Alfredo Stroessner's cabinet.

54. Even Vice-President Abraham Williams served faithfully until the end of the Carías era. Later he led an insurgent movement in the National Party to capture his party's nomination in the mid-1950s.

them together established cordial relations with other Central American re-gimes, the fruit companies, and Washington.[55]

Carías filled six ministerial posts before his inauguration in 1933. Many of the officers had past experience in similar positions and could be relied upon to assume these tasks once again. In order of importance, according to the way Carías set his priorities, were, first, ministers of government; then war, navy, and aviation; finance; fomento ("development"); foreign relations; and public education.[56] His vice-president, Abraham Williams, oversaw the National Po-lice Force and Ministries of Internal Security, Justice, and Gobernación ("govern-ment"). The Ministry of War, Navy, and Aviation was filled by a lawyer, Juan Manuel Gálvez (1887–1972), who had represented several of the U.S. banana companies in the 1920s. Never a "political-general" or a participant in revolu-tionary campaigns, Gálvez was a mild-mannered, trusted aide, someone who never built a political base with regional leaders but rather spent his profes-sional life as an attorney for Samuel Zemurray, "the banana man," head of Cuyamel Fruit Company (later United Fruit). He had served as a councilman and lawyer for the municipality of San Pedro Sula in 1921, 1922, 1924, and 1931 and from 1924 to 1928 was private secretary to President Miguel Paz Barahona. Gálvez held shares with Zemurray associates in Companía Hondureña de In-versiones and in United Fruit's Companía Editora, both in South America.[57] Because of Gálvez's financial association with banana entrepreneurs, Carías valued his contacts with these U.S. enterprises. The companies exercised an extraordinary financial influence over the country and would make loans to the Carías government arranged by Gálvez, whom United Fruit Company officials called "the best lawyer in Honduras."[58]

Salvador Aguirre, known as the "dean of the cabinet" at age seventy-eight, held several posts starting with the Ministry of Development, which included agriculture and labor. Julio Lozano, a one-time accountant with banana com-

55. Mensajes Presidenciales, 1933–1945, Biblioteca y Archivos Nacionales, 1 February 1933, 16–18; "Mensajes de 1935," 31.

56. Tegucigalpa, 12 February 1933, 1.

57. Darío Euraque, "Industrialists and Merchants in Northern Honduras: The Making of a Na-tional Bourgeoisie in Peripheral Capitalism, 1870–1972" (Ph.D. diss., University of Wisconsin, 1990), footnotes pp. 174–75. See also Fausto Lara Cerrato, ed., Aspectos culturales de Honduras (Teguc-igalpa: n.p., 1951), 138.

58. Dispatch, U.S. legation, Tegucigalpa, to the Department of State, 17 February 1933, Con-fidential U.S. Diplomatic Post Records; Gálvez Barnes interview, 30 October 1987.

panies, served as minister of finance, as he had during Miguel Paz Barahona's administration. Foreign relations, initially the area of least interest to Carías, but one that required a steady hand, was given to the dependable, competent lawyer and supreme court judge Antonio Bermúdez, also an attorney for a U.S.-owned fruit enterprise.

Consideration for selection to the Carías cabinet was based on geographical representation, too. Abraham Williams was from Choluteca in the south; Gálvez, San Pedro Sula in the north; Antonio Bermúdez, the east (Olancho); and Rodríguez from Copán in the west.[59] But none of these figures had spent their lives as political leaders in these areas. Some, like Gálvez, had relations with financial or land interests in these regions but played no direct role in local politics. The exception, Vice-President Abraham Williams, the grandson of an Englishman from Wales, was a mining proprietor who later prospered and became a wealthy farmer and cattle owner in Choluteca. The family became powerful political leaders in Valle and El Paraíso (southern Honduras). They claimed liberalism as their "political preference," but rarely was the family happy with meddling politicians, Liberals or Nationals, from other areas.

The vice-president's father, Emilio Williams, was a close associate of Carías when both backed Policarpo Bonilla for president, then Alberto Membreño in 1919.[60] Abraham graduated from high school in Boston, Massachusetts, and later earned an engineering degree from Union College in Schenectady, New York. He did graduate work at the Massachusetts Institute of Technology, went to work for the New York Central Railroad, then returned to Honduras. He continued his professional career as commander of ports in Amapala and La Ceiba.[61] Serving briefly as undersecretary of war in the Miguel Paz Barahona government and later in congress (1930), his primary interest was building aqueducts and bridges, not politics. When Abraham's brother, Emilio, was assassinated by a Liberal Party member, he joined Carías and the National Party.[62]

Williams assumed command of a Carías militia that took the eastern section of Tegucigalpa in the War of Traitors in 1932. Carías had never built po-

59. "Cabinet Appointments," Dispatch, U.S. legation, Tegucigalpa, to Department of State, 17 February 1933, National Archives, Record Group 59, 8:15/00, 8:15/002.

60. El Cronista, 15 March 1932, 8; Williams interview, 18 November 1987.

61. Tegucigalpa, 15 February 1942, 5–6.

62. Williams interview, 18 November 1987. See also Military Intelligence Section, Office of U.S. Military Attaché, United States legation, Tegucigalpa, 25 May 1945, Confidential U.S. Diplomatic Post Records, reel 41, 166–167.

litical ties in the south or the east (Olancho). Williams's selection as vice-president was judged on political-regional considerations. Yet his recognized skills as an engineer meant a great deal to the president. Williams was dependable, reliable, and efficient, qualities Carías admired.[63] The National Police Force, under Williams's jurisdiction, was assigned to a longtime Carías ally, Camilo Reina. Williams actually devoted much of his time building roads and bridges, not managing a police force. The ever-loyal Reina minded the police.

Salvador Aguirre, who held the posts of development, agriculture, and labor and served for a time as foreign minister (1939–1943), was a longtime Carías acquaintance. Although never particularly close, the two were comandante de armas and jefe políticos in the Miguel Dávila government (1902–11).[64] Aguirre was also a journalist and editor of El Demócrata (Tegucigalpa) in the early 1920s, then a member of the supreme court (1929–33).[65] At seventy-eight, Aguirre had reached the twilight years of his public career. Yet, still agile and alert, he took on tasks as needed by the president, changing posts not for political reasons but because the assignment needed his expertise and experience, domestic or foreign.

Julio Lozano, an accountant and minister of finance, served a good part of his professional career with Zemurray's Cuyamel Fruit Company in Puerto Cortés, fully supporting the enterprise's role as the country's chief exporter. Lozano felt its financial influence, controlling the export trade, offered worthwhile benefits to the country. For several years he held posts as customs administrator in Tela, La Ceiba, and Puerto Castilla. Never having held elective office, he was not interested in politics, preferring administration instead.[66]

A U.S. diplomat reporting home on the profile of a Carías cabinet appointee said, "His reputation is excellent, he has a pleasant, but colorless personality. He is not the type to appeal to the masses . . . he has no popular following . . . he is very close to Carías."[67] These few words could apply to all the

63. Williams interview, 18 November 1987; Lainfiesta, Cámara lenta, 34–35.

64. La Bandera, 21 August 1907, 4; Apuntes biográficos hondureños, 16.

65. Philip Raine, Honduran section, Regional Division, Coordinator of Inter-American Affairs, to U.S. legation, Tegucigalpa, 8 April 1943, in Confidential U.S. Diplomatic Post Records, reel 39, pp. 29–41; Lainfiesta, Cámara Lenta, 45–49; La Época, 2 September 1933, 3; 19 September 1933, 1.

66. Euraque, "Industrialists and Merchants," 167 n.55. Julio Lozano later served as vice-president under Manuel Gálvez (1949–54) and as president (1955–56). He held three different posts under Carías: minister of finance and public credit, foreign minister, and minister to the United States.

67. Dispatch, U.S. legation, Tegucigalpa, to Department of State, Intelligence Report, "Political Leaders," received 12 September 1932, Confidential U.S. Diplomatic Post Records.

cabinet officers. They remained loyal to the chief for sixteen years and there were no major turnovers; none was ever imprisoned, executed, or exiled. From time to time changes were made, but ministerial posts were altered to meet a particular need, provide a certain skill a person could perform well. For example, if an international financial issue became important, Julio Lozano might be changed from his position as minister of finance to foreign affairs. Basically it was a group of people with certain skills related to administration. Lawyers, accountants, diplomats, and educators, they formed a technocracy, committed to bringing efficiency and order to the country. Carías imposed a peace; they in turn prescribed the policies and administered them. A common thread united them, promoting domestic calm and bringing order to a fiscal crisis in the 1930s that pushed the government deeper in debt.

Unlike that of his cabinet ministers, much of Carías's political and professional experience rested with regional leaders. Now, as president, maybe for the first time in Honduran history, a chief executive could meld the interests of local leaders with a cabinet of technocrats and extend the power of the state through the National Party. With his newly formed government in place, Carías's task turned to administering and managing these political leaders in the villages and towns who for generations felt no compulsion to obey a central government.

4

Watching the Lords of the House

Tiburcio Carías's first main challenge as president in 1933 was to consolidate his authority. Although he was already a major political figure by 1932 and had several rural chieftains as longtime allies, these chieftains still considered themselves "sovereign" in their respective departments. How to extend his power became a major preoccupation, and because his political experience was in the countryside, he knew these chieftains' strengths and weaknesses, which enabled him to manipulate and ultimately dominate them.

Carías could wield power and impose his authority easily in Tegucigalpa. However, the far-flung regions, the rural towns and hamlets, were not easily reached, either administratively or logistically. The authority of the local politician was in many areas absolute. "I am not a Carísta," Carlos Sanabria, the boss of Atlántida and Colón once said; "I am La Ceiba; I am the Lord in my house."[1] The mountains that divided the chieftains' territories and protected them from outside incursions limited their ambitions, too. There was no national standing army; only militias, personal armies they commanded, made them independent from central power. These were civilian generals who appointed themselves or were chosen by those who followed them for personal gain. They administered their jurisdictions through personalism and paternalism, extending favors in exchange for loyalty. Yet while they dominated their departments, none could easily extend power beyond their jurisdiction. While they could not control others, no one could dominate them either.[2]

Carías, like his contemporaries a *general de cerro* ("general of the mountains"), rose to power within the political culture of these regional figures. From 1907 on, he raised and trained militias for his own political purposes, as

1. *La Época*, 8 October 1936, 3.

2. Edward McGinnis, U.S. Vice Consul, La Ceiba, 1933–36, personal communication to author, 15 December 1986, describes the almost limitless power of political chiefs and militia commanders like Carlos Sanabria in northern Honduras.

his father had done. Through this, he formed friendships with people, more often than not to stay the power of presidents, limiting their terms or unseating them. He fought with and led local armies when elections failed.

There were basically three ways in which Carías governed his "lords of the house" once he assumed the presidency in 1933: through personal loyalty, identifying with local heroes and popular figures regardless of party affiliation; by recognizing and accepting the economic interests of regional leaders and allowing them to prosper, with lucrative perks, contracts, and shares in profits of local enterprises both public and private; and by allowing regional departmental chiefs to have limited authority on security matters, in effect making them sovereign up to a point but with constraints he imposed.

The many civil wars Carías fought in the first three decades of the twentieth century reflected the inability of any president to govern effectively. Like his predecessors, he could not easily abolish the power of the local chieftains. Neither he nor they had an army to do it, or the resources to build one. Yet the lifelong friendships the president made with regional politicians from the 1890s to 1932 enabled him to use budget power and economic rewards to limit their influence. He blended his interests as chief executive with theirs locally.

Carías was not interested in commanding troops and occupying all parts of the country after he became president. He could not do it anyway, as there were few resources to create a national military institution. Carías was interested in confining military forces and their operations to small towns, training officers and troops locally. This strategy involved fostering the economic interests of the local chieftains and promoting competition between military commanders and political chiefs. Carías continued to allow them to control their departments under their tutelage, but in time he would centralize his management of them. He waited to create military districts and professional schools for officers until he had the resources to do so.

Carías knew that it was the successful military campaigns of the Sanabria brothers in the north and Francisco Martínez Funes in the south that had ensured his installation as president.[3] He was aware too that to stay in office, their personal, economic, and security interests had to be maintained. Carías extended his personal power through patronage, with jobs managing customs

---

3. At one point in the late 1930s, Carías sent Francisco Martínez Funes to the United States to receive a new means of medical treatment. The president paid for his travel and all expenses for the operation. *Acuerdo de la Oficial Mayor, Archivos de los Ministerios* (1939–1940), Acuerdo No. 44, 20 July 1939.

houses, awarding rum and *aguardiente* (liquor) franchises, and government contracts to build roads and bridges. Loyalists came from a wide economic and social spectrum—shopkeepers, artisans, owners of small industry, schoolteachers, small farmers, petite bourgeoisie of towns and villages, ranchers, and merchants. Yet their support did not mean that Carías would undertake major transformations of their standards of living or give them a new freedom to criticize government policies.

Personal loyalty remained the foundation of caudillo politics in the Carías regime. For example, Gonzálo "Chalo" Luque (1905–92) was a longtime carísta in San Pedro Sula. He supported himself by selling fish and fruit. He recalled in his *Memorias* learning of Tiburcio Carías Andino as a good governor and military commander of Cortés,[4] and he remembered newspapers in the north praising Carías's work and even suggesting that he would be a good candidate for president.[5] Chalo Luque recalled that after Carías created a School for Corporals and Sergeants in San Pedro Sula, he became a soldier, a salaried recruit in a local militia.

Chalo Luque looked to leaders who gave him financial security, leadership, and discipline, remembering Carías at one point closed billiard halls and bars to stop idle play and drunkenness.[6] Entering what he called "combat . . . Honduran politics" during the 1920s and 1930s, Luque recalls:

> General Justo Umaña Alvarado [a caudillo in western Honduras] asked me what I thought of the liberal president Mejía Colindres government (1928–1932), *hijo de puta* ["son of a whore"], I told him it was a disaster, the government cannot do anything. It can't repair telegraph lines, school teachers don't get paid. Umaña then told me that those who helped President Colindres come to power were treated as if they were his enemies. Why don't we throw him out? But I replied, now I have a home, wife and child. I forever renounced revolution as a sport in 1930. Now I prefer a bad government to a good revolution. What did I gain in revolutions? No one would help me get an education, now I have work. We Hondurans are either "Blues or Reds," Nationalists or Liberals. Umaña told me that General Gregorio Ferrera opposing Colindres could offer me a better job than the one I had now. Ferrera hated those men in the government. I sympathized with him but I was still thinking of my wife and my family. I admired Justo Umaña too.

4. Luque, *Memorias de un Sanpedrano*, 2. His *Memorias de un soldado Hondureño*, Vol. 1, makes similar biographical references.

5. Luque, *Memorias de un Sanpedrano*, 108.

6. Ibid., 108, 132.

He could enter a barracks day or night firing his .45 at the building, swing his machete then enter into combat. But I was still thinking of my home and family. I felt apart from all these things. I didn't worry because my work was with a private company. But a man was a Red or Blue. I was a Red. [Gregorio] Ferrera was a Red so Umaña and I started our journey on the road over Santa Rosa [in the western department of Copán]. I was captured by Ferrista revolutionaries. But I discovered that my captors were friends. I told them that I was finished with revolutions, fighting for Reds or Blues. Umaña said if you don't join us the Reds will capture you and then you will have to fight for a bad government. But I thought of my wife and child. Umaña said he had about 80,000 pesos given him as a contribution—to pay for us. I continued with these soldiers led by Umaña as his prisoner. The next day a train passed us with its crew. Several of them knew me. When they reached San Pedro Sula they were called before the comandante de armas to explain what the revolutionaries were doing, and the men they had seen. They gave the authorities my name. So the government thought I was a revolutionary. Now I was its enemy. Soon General Gregorio Ferrera entered the town [Cofradía in the department of Copán] with 900 revolutionaries. Others like Umaña from the area joined him. In all, there was an army of 1,200 men, all volunteers. . . .

When General Ferrera arrived, Justo Umaña saluted him. He introduced me to him and said, "Look, General, see who is with us." Ferrera extended his hand and said, "It makes me happy to have you with us, my friend, Luque." I had joined the revolution but I did not have a pistol yet. So General Ferrera pulled out a .45 caliber and gave it to me. From that moment I had joined his revolutionary army. If now the government captured me one of three things would happen. They would shoot me, put me in prison, or I would grab a rifle and defend the government.

We then left for San Pedro Sula. I thought of my wife and family as we approached the city. How could my wife know that after renouncing revolution I could do a thing like this? I went to a friend's house in the city. He said to me Chalo, I don't think you have any enthusiasm for this revolution. I said he was right I did not have any enthusiasm for this, not like those wars of 1919 and 1924. I fought hard then because there were no responsibilities. My friend offered to help me escape from the Ferrera army. But I said no, now I am on bad terms with the government. I know what would happen to me if I deserted this revolution. It's like this. I am in a main role now and have "to bear the rough knocks." So we began the attack on Santa Rosa de Copán on April 31, 1931. We shouted, "Long live the revolution, long live Ferrera, death to the government, death to [President] Mejía Colindres—sons of bitches."[7]

7. Luque interviews, spring 1987. These reflections are also chronicled in Luque's two works cited in note 4.

Why did men like Gonzálo Chalo Luque fight in revolutions and support Carías? They joined civil wars sometimes to take vengeance because the Blues (Nationalists) or the Reds (Liberals) in a government had assassinated a father or son; others fought because they were forced to leave Honduras and could not return by any other means but war for employment and adventure.[8] People like Chalo Luque fought to obtain a job (*chamba*) when a victory was won and, if possible, to get rich. At one time he joined Carías only to obtain money to study in Tegucigalpa if the revolt against President Mejía Colindres was successful.[9]

Chalo Luque's personal story describes the motives and reasons of those who supported the rise of Tiburcio Carías in the 1920s and 1930s. Frequently these loyalists participated in efforts to prevent the extension of presidential terms, such as that of Liberal president Domingo Vásquez (1893–94). Neither ideology nor Liberal Party discipline evoked loyalty to Vásquez. This was a campaign to oust an autocratic president. Again in 1903, 1919, and 1924, Carías and others rejected the efforts of Liberal presidents Manuel Bonilla, Francisco Bertrand, and Rafael López Gutiérrez to extend their terms. Alliances between politicians were made to protect local interests that chief executives were thwarting.[10]

In 1928, candidate Carías faced division within his own organization when General Vicente Tosta crossed party lines and joined Liberals trying to keep him from winning the presidency. Sometimes Carías forged alliances by agreeing to stay out of local politics, leaving the political lands in the hands of fellow caudillos. On occasion he even took sides with Liberals who fought against his *coreligionarios* for local domination if they backed him personally. For example, in the mid-1920s, he supported members of the Williams family, prosperous ranchers in the Liberal Party of Choluteca (southern Honduras), and they in turn were closely associated with many other merchants and entrepreneurs, thereby enlarging Carías's interests there.[11]

8. Luque, *Memorias de un soldado Hondureño*, 2:26.

9. Ibid., 2:126.

10. Several letters in the Rafael Teresero Family Papers in the possession of the Benjamín Henriques family (Tegucigalpa) offer examples when in 1924 Carías collaborated closely with local chieftains who objected to President López Gutiérrez's meddling in their departmental affairs. In 1924, Carías wrote to his ally Benjamín Henriques on how to help his friends. Carías to Benjamín Henriques 7, 9 April 1924, Benjamín Henriques Papers.

11. Williams interview, 8 December 1987. By 1924, deputies to congress from the department, some once Liberals, were now Carías followers.

In 1932 when President Mejía Colindres could no longer manage the country's failing economy or keep local leaders happy, dissident Liberals banded together to oust him and declared the Nationalist carísta election null and void.[12] Wishing to defeat his opposition, with few troops, no arms, and no money, Mejía Colindres turned to Carías for help. For pragmatic reasons the Nationalist presidential candidate had everything to gain by obtaining funds, however meager, and supplies from the government, but at the same time he relied on longtime local leaders, and Liberals, to guarantee his succession to the presidency, a strategy Mejía Colindres was unable to put into action.

Another weakness of Mejía Colindres was that he was from the western department of Intibucá and tied solely to the economic interests of the landed elite. But power in the 1920s had shifted to political leaders who raised militias and met the financial needs of new groups such as campesinos and artisans who simply wanted work. Mejía Colindres, governing from the capital city, failed to pay close attention to these shifts in local politics. Political figures like Gregorio Ferrera and Vicente Tosta (provisional president April 1924–February 1925) emerged in Intibucá fully capable of ignoring the chief executive's authority in Tegucigalpa.[13] When fissures like these broke out between the Liberal Party president and his local partisans, Carías deftly stepped in to take advantage of the situation.

Carías often turned away from the Nationalists to gain local support. Sometimes the party's goals and Liberal interests contradicted one another, but that made no difference if they had a common foe. Another example of how Mejía Colindres lost power also took place in Intibucá. For years the Liberal Gregorio Ferrera fought bitterly against his party's leadership in Tegucigalpa. He was a populist, loved by the campesinos and often he took up arms in the southern and western parts of the country when government land policies encroached on small farmers. Sensing Ferrera's popularity, Carías frequently made provisions for the transportation and medical treatment of Ferrera's wounded to hospitals, a gesture the general did not forget.[14]

12. Carías's elections were declared void by Liberals and a de facto government in the Department of Intibucá; República de Honduras, Memorias de guerra, marina y aviación, 1932–1933 (Tegucigalpa: Miguel Paz Reyes Library, n.d.), 4.

13. Gonzálo Chalo Luque, Las Revoluciones en Honduras (San Pedro Sula: Tallares Tipo-Litográficos de Central Impresora, 1982), 2:69–81.

14. Tiburcio Carías to Benjamín Henriques, Comandante de Armas, Tonkintin Airport, 9 April 1924, Benjamín Henriques Papers.

Ferrera's assassination in summer 1931 left a void in Intibucá's Liberal Party. As expected, different factions fought to gain power, but none could field a successful candidate for mayor of La Esperanza, the department capital, in 1932. The congressional seat was easily won by a Nationalist and a Carías partisan, Rodolfo Zacarías Velásquez (1896–?), who served in the legislature until 1970.

Velásquez gained immeasurable influence locally by supporting Ferrera's war on Mejía Colindres. Later, he became a backer of the fallen leader's followers and enhanced his authority by adding dissident Liberals to his ranks. When Carías became president, he provided Velásquez with funds and government contracts to be distributed in Intibucá. In effect, Carías played two sets of political maneuvers in defending Mejía Colindres in Tegucigalpa and allying with Ferrera Liberal dissidents. Velásquez opposed the former because the president, in his words, "couldn't pay teachers, like me, our salaries." "So," said Velásquez, "I became a revolutionary with those men in the War of Revindication."[15] Through Rodolfo Velásquez, a schoolteacher and head of primary and secondary schools, Carías strengthened the National Party by adding Liberal Ferreristas to its ranks and utilizing Velásquez's network of schoolteachers in the neighboring departments of Lempira, Copán, and Ocotepeque to build a power base.[16] After Carías took office, funds poured into Intibucá, selectively handed out by the ever faithful Velásquez. The money was spent on agricultural development, cattle ranching, diversification of crop production, roads, and water projects. Velásquez's power soared, and he boasted of the newfound power, saying, "I ran these [development] programs for Carías and managed his political campaigns. I had become a general, too. The militia soldiers here elected me colonel, then a general."[17]

Even as he sought to increase his own influence, Carías defended Mejía Colindres from rebels seeking to nullify the 1932 election and made alliances all across Honduras for this purpose. Nationalists like the Sanabrias—Carlos in the Department of Colón; Gregorio, director of police in La Ceiba; and Manuel, a cousin, military commander in the Department of El Paraíso in the southeast—were persuaded to support Mejía Colindres. If they remained loyal to Carías, they received arms and supplies by air from Tegucigalpa.[18]

15. Velásquez interview, 27 September 1987.

16. Bardales, Biografía Velásquez, 44–48.

17. Velásquez interview, 27 September 1987. See Bardales, Biografía Velásquez, 66.

18. E. L. McGinnis, Silver Spring, MD, former U.S. consul in La Ceiba in the 1930s, letter to author, 15 December 1986.

The decision to deploy aircraft to loyal friends in 1932 tipped the balance of power in Carías's favor. Benjamín Henriques, briefly military commander of La Ceiba in the north, reported the movement of anti-Carías partisans in his part of the country.[19] He then received a cache of arms and reconnaissance intelligence from pilots dispatched from Tegucigalpa.[20]

Local politicians became useful to Carías in other ways. Carlos Sanabria, once a Ferrera loyalist and military commander of Colón, was reputed to be the most autocratic of all local chieftains[21] and wielded absolute power across the northern part of the country.[22] A story goes that when his rule became particularly repressive, Carías was asked to remove him but said no with the comment, "how I wish I had 17 Carlos Sanabrias for each of the departments of Honduras."[23] A competent administrator who got things done, Sanabria was the architect of efforts to develop that region's economy and trade with the United States, supporting small merchants, particularly importers and exporters. He was the sole conduit through which funds and patronage came back and forth from the capital to the departments of Atlántida and Colón throughout the Carías presidency.

Most Carías loyalists in the interior of Honduras were veterans of wars in 1919, 1924, 1928, and 1932. Many were legends in their respective departments and excellent military strategists. The most prominent of them were Justo Rufino Solís, in Atlántida;[24] Gonzalo "Chepe" López, in San Pedro Sula; Julián Mejía, in Ocotopeque; Francisco Martínez Funes, in Choluteca;[25] Alvaro Suazo (father of President Robert Suazo, 1982–86), in La Paz;[26] Juan Fletes and

19. Ibid.; Carías to Henriques, 7 April 1924. Bombs were dropped on Mount El Piccacho as a diversionary tactic drawing military attention, according to Carías, away from ground action he planned outside Tegucigalpa.

20. Carías to Benjamín Henriques, 9 April 1924, Benjamín Henriques Papers. Carías's letter states that both Carías and Henriques were cooperating with the Liberal militia leader Gregorio Ferrera to oust Liberal president Rafael López Gutiérrez (1920–24).

21. Santoveña and Novas Gardela, Hombres y cosas, 16.

22. Carías to Henriques, 9 April 1924.

23. La Época, 29 September 1936, 4. See also 10 October 1936, 4.

24. José Ruiz and Rogelio Triminio, eds., Apuntes biográficos: Hondureños e información para el turista (Tegucigalpa: Imprenta Hernández, 1943), 36.

25. La Época, 7 February 1936, 1. See also República de Honduras, Acuerdos de la Fiscalia Mayor, 20 July 1939. Carías took care of the many needs and bills of Martínez Funes.

26. La Época, 8 January 1935, 12. According to this account, Carías urged Suazo, a Liberal, to join him and the Alberto Membreño National Democratic Party Committee in 1923 to go to the Nica-

Hipólito Pavón, who someone said on Carías's orders "cleaned up the free and Independent State of Olancho in 1938";[27] José León Castro in Lempira; and Vicente Ayala in Copán. These local party leaders also helped Carías keep President Mejía Colindres in office long enough to fill his term and make possible a Carías succession.

President Carías gave added incentives to his regional supporters by having easy access to funds provided periodically by the United Fruit Company. He did this in the first month of his term by decreeing a state of siege, which allowed him to avoid accounting for expenditures from the banana enterprise. In so doing, he was able to consolidate power significantly at the departmental level, appointing his associates to positions of military commander and political chief and paying them in part from this unattributed fund. With arms and newly salaried recruits, the Sanabrias, Justo Rufino Solís, Francisco Martínez Funes, Julián Mejía, and others were instructed to "clean out the departments of opponents and establish order."[28] Aside from the ad hoc funding by the banana companies, these newly designated "commanders" were attracted by lucrative salaries from the standing "special budget" the United Fruit Company frequently replenished. These payments were distributed by the minister of war and the vice-president.[29] "Agreements" were drawn up fixing the sum to be paid for a position, and Carías personally signed the contracts.[30] Justo Rufino Solís and Carlos Sanabria were put on the government payroll for the department of Colón and the port city of La Ceiba, respectively. Similar payments

---

raguan border and organize a militia to oust the autocratic Liberal president Rafael López Gutiérrez, who declared a state of siege that nullified the 1924 elections. Suazo did and backed Carías from then on.

27. La Época, 2 July 1938, 4.

28. Mensaje, 1935, 30–31; 44–45. Dispatch, U.S. consul, La Ceiba, to U.S. legation, Tegucigalpa, "Political Report," 2 March 1933, Confidential U.S. Diplomatic Post Records, reel 7, 183; Dispatch, U.S. minister Julian Lay, U.S. legation, Tegucigalpa, to Department of State, Confidential U.S. Diplomatic Post Records, reel 7, 514.

29. It is possible that the availability of funds (about $75,000) at this time (1931–33) came from the United Fruit Company. See Dispatch, U.S. minister Julian Lay to Department of State, 10 June 1933, Confidential U.S. Diplomatic Post Records. See also "Special Budget," Ministry of War, Estado Mayor, Acuerdos de Mantenimiento del Orden Público, Archivos de los Ministerios (1932–1933), Acuerdos 1165–90 for payments—salaries to commanders in Comayagua, 31 May 1933; Yoro, 30 May 1933; Olancho, 30 May 1933; Tegucigalpa, 31 May 1933; Intibucá, 30 May 1933; Gracias y Copán, 31 May 1933.

30. "Special Budget," Appointments and Salaries; Acuerdos, 568–73, 4 February 1933.

were made for military commanders in El Paraíso, Choluteca, Lempira, Copán, La Paz, and Ocotepeque.[31] On average, these commanders were paid between 8,000 and 10,000 lempira a month.[32]

Political chiefs, National Party loyalists, were also named to departmental, district, and municipal posts. More often than not they were rivals of the military chiefs in their departments. Carías made these appointments obviously to "divide and conquer" the local power structure. For example, Efrain Piñeda Zacapa, a longtime Carías National Party follower in the Department of Colón, was named jefe político for the department. He was a bitter critic of the comandante de armas there, Carlos Sanabria, who was equally loyal to the president.[33] Another example could be found in the Department of Cortés, where political adversaries Governor Ramón Discua and M. José López Muñoz, the military chieftain, competed for Carías's attention and beneficence.[34] Sometimes the chief executive played on the rivalries of the military commanders. General Isabel Espinosa was named acting comandante de armas in Colón while serving as the head of a Special Expeditionary Force sent to a department by Carías for a special task. He was dispatched north to keep an eye on Mariano Reyes and Carlos Sanabria, each of whom had served as military chiefs there at one time.[35] Both civilian and army commanders were watched by telegraph operators, who provided the communication link between the president and these local bases. They were named to their posts by the party, but in fact Carías personally approved their appointments and paid their salaries.[36]

Carías developed a pay system that secured the allegiance of all his parti-

---

31. Salaries for Military Commanders, Choluteca, El Paraíso, *Acuerdo* (Estado Mayor) No. 750, 27 February 1933; for General Incocente Triminio, *Acuerdos* (EM) No. 780, 2 May 1933, and No. 833, 11 March 1933; *Acuerdo* (EM) No. 837 for Carlos Sanabria, 11 May 1933. Salaried positions went to General Filiberto Díaz y Zellaya in Cortés, 300–400 lempiras a month, General Lem Castro, Ocotepeque, *Acuerdos* (EM) No.723, 22 February 1933; No. 724, 22 February 1933; No. 725, 22 February 1933, all for the same salary, 300–400 lempiras monthly.

32. *Acuerdo* No. 155, 13 December 1933. Political chiefs were also named to departmental, district, and municipal posts generally without a salary. They were in many cases longtime rivals of the military commanders in their regimes.

33. Secretary of the Junta Central, interview, Trujillo, Department of Colón, 16 August 1987.

34. U.S. consul Puerto Cortés to U.S. legation, Tegucigalpa, 2 March 1933, Confidential U.S. Diplomatic Post Records, reel 7, 183. See also U.S. consul, 26 November 1943, ibid., reel 7, 2, 5.

35. *Acuerdo* (EM), 1 August 1941; *Acuerdos* (EM), 1939–40; 1941–42 Archivo, Ministry of War, Ministry of Defense.

36. *Acuerdo* No. 1750, 15 February 1933, Ministerio de Fomento.

sans. Money was allotted to longtime associates "for past services" (presumably during the War of Traitors, 1931–33) and current duties.[37] Sometimes these payments were allocated for *fuerzas extraordinarias* ("special forces"). From time to time, when an emergency arose, an ever loyal but never implicitly trusted political veteran—the Sanabrias, Martínez Funes, Justo Rufino Solís, or Juan Fletes—was made commander of one of these units.[38] The commander was never given this assignment in his own department[39] but was sent to other regions on contract for a stated period of time with troops paid directly by Carías.[40]

A commander of a "special forces" unit was given a temporary assignment as chief military official in a department; then the unit was disbanded and the contract terminated.[41] Payments for these tasks often came from a more closely guarded fund than the general budget allocations of the war minister, known as the *presupuesto especial de Guerra* ("special budget for war"). From March to July 1936, 15,000 of a total of 28,290 lempira went to Carlos Sanabria

37. *Acuerdos* Nos. 108 and 110, 6, 9 November 1933, Ministerio de Guerra, Marina y Aviación, Acuerdos de Mantenimiento del Orden Público, 1933–1934.

38. *Acuerdos* (EM) No. 51, 7 August 1937, and No. 232, 18 January 1940, Archivos Ministerio de Guerra, Marina y Aviacíon, Sección Estado Mayor, January–August 1937, Archivo, Palacio de los Ministerios. "Fuerzas extraordinarias" were sometimes called "expeditionary forces" or "special forces."

39. Ibid., Shifting commanders in the departments of Valle, Tegucigalpa, El Paraíso, *Acuerdo* (EM) 1.004, May 1933. See also Luque, *Memorias de un Sanpedrano*, 117. He noted that General Francisco Martínez Funes was given as assignment in San Pedro Sula but was a prominent caudillo in the Department of Choluteca.

40. *Acuerdos* (EM), Nos. 140–41, 10 August 1933. Soldiers, salaried with funds from the Supreme Tribunal of Accounts, were assigned to Trujillo, Department of Colón, to Colonel Francisco Soto to guard the Honduran-Guatemalan frontier; *Acuerdo* (EM) No. 105, 10 August 1933, to Filiberto Díaz Zelaya, Commander of Special Forces in Departments of Cortés, Yoro and Copán, to General José León Castro, Commander of Special Forces, to Departments of Gracias, Ocotepeque, Santa Rosa de Copán, *Acuerdo* No. 375, EM 5 September 1933; Troops to General Mariano Sanabria, Commander of Special Forces, Department of Tegucigalpa, Valle, El Paraíso, *Acuerdo* (EM) No. 367, 4 September 1933.

41. *Acuerdo* (EM) No. 804, May 1934, Ending Special Expeditions of Carlos Sanabria in El Paraíso and Tegucigalpa, Archivos, Ministerio de Guerra, Estado Mayor, Acuerdos de Mantenimiento del Orden Público, May–June 1934, Palacio de los Ministerios. Notification that contracts for commanding officers, special forces, have terminated and new ones signed; *Acuerdos* (EM), July 1941– June 1942, *Acuerdo* (EM) No. 375, 29 May 1942, *Acuerdo* (EM) No. 387, 17 June 1942.

alone, the remaining 13,290 was distributed to "special forces" commanders in Choluteca; Olancho; Yoro; Ocotepeque; Copán and its capital city, Santa Bárbara de Copán; and Comayagua.[42] Officers and enlisted personnel recruited locally for a militia were paid directly by the minister of war. A captain received 576 lempira a year, a lieutenant, 480, and a private, .075 lempira a day. For 1934, total expenditures for local "army" personnel reached 15,000 lempira.[43]

Logistical support for these special forces came from "contributions" from local merchants. For example, U.S. banana and mining companies provided housing, food, arms, and transportation for these units.[44] In return, funds for "transportation-aviation services" were paid to them for building airstrips in several departments considered strategically important to these special military expeditions. Carías wanted these landing sites finished soon after his election. He was anxious to have ammunition and materiel reach these commanders in order to consolidate his power.[45] Both Carías and Manuel Gálvez personally disbursed funds to pilots and building contractors for these sites. No "special force" commander or local government official was allowed to use these airstrips without specific permission from the president.[46]

The president was careful not to develop a cadre of local officers and enlisted men who were residents of a local department; rather, he funded the establishment of a School for Corporals and Sergeants in Tegucigalpa, under his supervision, which offered special training in artillery and infantry skills. These students were in turn sent to departments and municipalities as instructors for local units for a specified training period, then replaced. There were two reasons for this. First, sufficient funds were not always available; second,

42. See previous note; also, *Acuerdos* (EM), No. 492, 16 April 1936, No. 195, 18 October 1939; Assignments of Generals Mariano Sanabria, Juan Moncada and J. Ines Pérez; Colonels Miguel Díaz, José Barrientos.

43. *Acuerdos* (EM), Nos. 1, 25, 1 August 1934, August–December 1934, Archivos Ministerio de Guerra, Marina y Aviación, Biblioteca y Archivos Nacionales.

44. Ibid.; *Acuerdos* (EM), No. 642, 9 February 1933; No. 410, 17 May 1936; No. 503, 21 April 1936.

45. Telegrama, Ministerio de Gobernación a Gobernador Político, Departamento de Valle, 24 August 1932, Biblioteca de Telegramas. See also *Acuerdos*, No. 55, 18 September 1933, and No. 12, 5 October 1933, *Acuerdos de Mantenimiento del Orden Público*, Archivos Ministerio de Guerra, Marina, y Aviacíon, 1933–34, Palacio de los Ministerios.

46. Ministerio de Fomento to Director General de Correos, 19 April 1933, Document #695, República de Honduras, Copias de Notas, Ministero de Fomento, April 1933, No. 1701, Biblioteca y Archivos Nacionales.

Carías was deeply suspicious of a standing army with strength in numbers, training, and equipment, either at the national level or locally in departments. Decades of armed conflict apparently weighed heavily on him, and such armed units could be a potential threat to his rule.

A presidential honor guard was created in 1933. Commanded by a general, it included a colonel, lieutenant, two sergeants, four corporals, and thirty-two enlisted soldiers. The unit was led by Carías's nephew, Calixto. The head of the guard was paid from funds allocated to commanders of "special forces" for a fixed date and renewed periodically if necessary.[47]

Boosting the egos of his regional loyalists was another way Carías kept their loyalty. For example, on April 28, 1937, the pictures of two local political figures, a militia commander and political chief, appeared in La Época (Tegucigalpa). The government publication ran detailed articles on the great accomplishments of these two, Carlos Sanabria and Julián Mejía, in the departments of Colón and Ocotepeque respectively. Their lengthy achievements were enumerated, covering a wide range of activities such as building roads, airstrips, schools, and bridges and starting farming projects. These accomplishments were attributed solely to them as close collaborators of President Carías.[48] These leaders, said La Época, were the builders of modern Honduras and, like the chief executive, maintained peace and order in their respective jurisdictions. Such high visibility and praise brought them numerous benefits. Considerable sums of money were made available to the two chieftains: they were given funds to build the infrastructure of their departments, including roads, bridges, schools, and medical clinics.[49] They appointed heads of custom offices and collected a percentage of revenue from imports and exports. They managed public utilities; ran ports; supervised government monopolies in quarrying, lumber, aguardiente, and rum; operated cattle ranches; and issued licenses to explore mineral resources. As contratistas ("contractors") of the state, they owned distilleries that produced commodities and sold them to the government and the private sector. Profits from these activities were vast. For a fee they allocated government-monopoly sales of alcohol or salitre ("gunpowder") to individuals or local enter-

47. Ibid.; Acuerdos, August–September 1933, (EM) No. 54, 15 August 1933; 1941–42, (EM) No. 30, 1 July 1942; (EM), No. 31, July 1943; 1945–46, (EM), No. 376, 10 December 1945.

48. La Época, 28 April 1937, 2.

49. Bobadilla, "Município del Departamento de Cortés," 605.

prises.[50] Official lists of contratístas who brewed rum or made aguardiente were published each year by the Ministry of Finance. These reports invariably contained the names of Carísta military commanders, political chiefs of departments, and mayors of cities and towns.[51]

The government also gained the loyalty of local officials by renting buildings and storage houses for military personnel, equipment, and government-monopoly products. These were owned locally by local National Party heads who were paid rent by the state for their use.[52] Contracts for medical supplies sold by pharmaceutical companies or for clothing were regulated and disbursed by these chiefs for the maintenance of local militias. Benefits and profits for these officials were therefore varied and considerable. A "carrot and stick" system of profit for loyalty extended throughout Honduras.[53] Each year in his message to congress, Carías praised his mounted police under Tomás Martínez and his air force for their swift and effective operations traversing the unpaved roads throughout the country. These logistical operations depended on the support of local leaders.[54] The president held the purse, but his subalterns were handsomely paid, controlled by good salaries and receipts from lucrative government contracts. This entire process was watched, monitored, and reported by telegraph operators personally screened and appointed by the president. In essence, the "Lords of the House" were managed by a personalistic system of checks and balances, with salaries, perks, honors, and rewards. Their unqualified allegiance and loyalty to the nation's chief was fundamental, but in the end their loyalty to Carías brought peace to the countryside. Hipólito Pavón, the military commander of the eastern department of Olancho, long a region well beyond the control of Honduras's presidents and central government, proudly reported, after having been assigned the task of pacifying the area, "the Independent State of Olancho no longer exists."[55] That closed the book for any further regional disruption under the Caríato.

50. Decreto No. 164, 11 April 1934, *República de Honduras, Decretos Legislativos 1934–1936*, Archivos de Ministerio de Hacienda, Biblioteca y Archivos Nacionales.

51. Ibid.; contract lists in *Memoria de Hacienda, Crédito Público y Comercio*, 1935–36; 1943–44; 1944–45.

52. *Acuerdos*, No. 20–22, 1 August 1947, 6 October 1937, Archivos Ministerios de Guerra, Marina, y Aviación, August–December 1937, Palacio de los Ministerios.

53. *Memorias de guerra, marina, y aviación, 1932–1933*, Biblioteca y Archivos Nacionales, 9–11, 14.

54. *Mensaje*, 5 December 1937, 155.

55. *La Época*, 2 July 1938, 4.

A network of patronage and control emerged fairly quickly under Carías. Intimidation and compensation were the bedrock of the centralized and regional relationships. What did governing from the political capital look like? The president had a myriad of techniques orchestrated from Tegucigalpa to deepen his control. Managing local leaders was only part of his governing strategy.

Tiburcio Carías, ca. 1898

Courtesy Rafael Bardeles Bueso

Administrative divisions of Honduras during Carías's presidency

From Area Handbook for Honduras (Washington, DC: U.S. Government Printing Office, 1970)

Friends greeting Tiburcio Carías at his home in Zambrano on the occasion of his birthday, 15 March 1923. Venancio Callejas, later a bitter political opponent of Carías, is third from left. Manuel Gálvez, Carías's minister of war (1932–1948) and, later, president of Honduras (1949–1954), is to Carías's right. Miguel Paz Barahona, president of Honduras from 1925 to 1929, is standing to Carías's left.

Courtesy Rafael Bardeles Bueso

U.S. Marines on the Honduran north coast, 1924

Courtesy Rafael Bardales Bueso

Barefoot soldier on guard in Tegucigalpa

Reproduced from The Pan American Highway: From the Rio Grande to the Canal Zone, *by Harry A. Franck and Herbert C. Lanks (New York: D. Appleton Co., 1940).*

Stinson plane purchased by the Carías government in September 1933
La Tribuna, 30 May 1987

Carías with a delegation of the Guatemalan air force, 1939, Tegucigalpa
Courtesy Rafael Bardales Bueso

Villa Elena, Tegucigalpa
Photograph by author

President Carías (second from left) with a group of friends in a park in Tegucigalpa.
His longtime friend and confidant Carlos Izaguirre (third from right)
is reading a chapter from his novel *Bajo el Chubasco*.
Courtesy Rafael Bardales Bueso

5

The Hardware and Practice of Dictatorship

As presiding officer of the legislature in 1928, Tiburcio Carías was expected to respond to the chief executive's annual message. His comments seemed more like an inaugural speech, a presidential message calling for more executive authority to establish public order and end civil wars.[1] Essentially Carías's views reflected the late-nineteenth- and early-twentieth-century "ideology of progress," the tenets of positivism offered by the Frenchman Auguste Comte (1798–1857) on how to modernize and rationalize the operation of a state as it entered the world capitalist economy like Europe and the United States.

Carías's statement actually reflected a decades-old discussion by leading journalists, business exporters, and owners of industry who urged the creation of a strong executive capable of ending civil wars by instituting easily a state of siege.[2] They advocated progress, order, and efficiency through balanced budgets that would end foreign indebtedness. They were anxious to see the creation of a competent and efficient state administrative system. These views were largely expressed in leading newspapers located in Tegucigalpa, San Pedro Sula, and port cities along the north coast. Business people, entrepreneurs, and journalists were key elements in the formulation of Carías's thinking on how government should function. Many served in a kitchen cabinet, as advisers without portfolios during his 1933–1948 presidency. Among the leading proponents of positivism were Carlos Izaguirre, owner of El Debate (Cortés); Julián López Piñeda, writer and National Party treasurer; and Fernando Zepeda Durón, director of El Cronista (Tegucigalpa) and later editor of La Época (Tegucigalpa), the Carías government's official organ.[3] Durón had wide press contacts

1. *Mensaje, Presidente Miguel Paz Barahona, 1927–28* (Tegucigalpa: Tipografía Nacional, 1928), 5–9.

2. *El Cronista*, 16 December, 1923, 3; *Cartas autográficas*, Archives, Ministry of Foreign Affairs, President Vicente Tosta, prepared by Paulino Valladares (copy to president of the United States), 23 May 1923.

3. Fernando Zepeda Durón was also treasurer of the National Party fund, which collected and

throughout the Americas as a correspondent for the Associated Press, thereby becoming the sole published source of news stories from abroad.[4]

La Época was the most important propaganda vehicle of the carísta state. Along with Izaguirre's El Debate and El Norte in San Pedro Sula, it published editions in other parts of the country. Government publications, statements from the president, and stories about ministers' accomplishments all appeared in the Durón and Izaguirre papers.

Even jefes políticos and military commanders of departments wrote lengthy treatises in self praise, oftentimes competing with one another for attention. These separate reports on military security and political matters, called informes, were published in Durón's La Época. Even alcaldes ("mayors of municipalities"), often rivals of the political chief and military commander, published reports in La Época, expounding on their great achievements (all done, of course, for the glory of Carías).[5] La Época did more than report the news; it propagandized the workings of the Cariato, at all levels of the Honduran state.

Carías never held a press conference. Instead, journalists submitted written questions for interviews to be published. By 1934–38, El Cronista, which had been critical of Carías in the 1920s and early 1930s, La Época, and Izaguirre's papers in Amapala on the north coast were the only journals allowed to publish.[6]

Carías also reached a wide audience via the radio and was the first chief executive to make extensive use of this medium, extending his influence in all parts of the country. The founding of Honduran National Radio (HRN) illustrates how Carías developed an effective method for controlling and influencing a listening public. As in other areas, the president selected recognized professionals, regardless of their political persuasions, to perform tasks for his regime.

Rafael Ferrari Bustillo (1905–51) had been a broadcaster for Tropical Telegraph, La Voz de Los Trópicos, a subsidiary of United Fruit Company on Honduras's north coast, and was a pioneer in the field. Born and educated in Tegucigalpa, he studied in California, receiving a "commercial certificate in

---

administered money for National Party campaigns. Dispatch, U.S. legation, Tegucigalpa, to State Department, 25 May 1945, Confidential U.S. Diplomatic Post Records, reel 41, 1266–67.

4. William Krehm, Democracies and Tyrannies in the Caribbean (Westport, CT: Lawrence, Hill, 1984), 154.

5. El Cronista, 4 January 1938, 1, 5; 11 February 1938, 1.

6. El Cronista, 16 November 1939, 1, journalists and correspondents were often local National Party leaders, for example, Calixto Soto Rovelo in Amapala.

communication" in 1923. He traveled widely throughout the United States, México, and Central America after finishing his studies. In the mid-1920s, Ferrari became aware of radio broadcasting and its potential impact on society.[7] Returning to Honduras, he went to work in the Foreign Ministry in the administration of President Vicente Mejía Colindres.[8] Disillusioned with corruption and dishonesty in government, he resigned in 1932, joining Ángel Zúñiga Huete's presidential campaign, developing propaganda films for the candidate.[9]

Although he was well aware of Ferrari's role in Ángel Zúñiga Huete's campaign in 1932,[10] Carías wanted an expert in this new medium, so he worked out an agreement with Ferrari to start the first commercial radio station, HRN.[11] A deal was reached on May 22, 1933, whereby Ferrari could own and operate a station whose contract was renewable each year, thus allowing the government to suspend broadcasting at any time.[12] "We're on the air," Ferrari told his wife after signing the radio deal.[13]

Four radio transmission stations were started: La Voz de Atlántida (1934), Radio Sampedrana, El Eco Honduras (1935), and La Voz de La Ceiba (1936). These were not commercial stations like HRN but transmitting units in the central and northern part of the country. HRN opened its office in Tegucigalpa at the home of Carlos López Piñeda, a brother of Julián López Piñeda, treasurer of the National Party. Radio transmitters were placed on the roof of the government's Tribunal Superior de Cuentas ("accounting office") and remained there until 1956.[14] Ferrari went to work as a propagandist for Carías, inviting cabinet officers to give talks on particular subjects. The president's addresses to congress between 1933 and 1949 were heard over his La Voz de Honduras,[15] and each week on La Hora del Distrito Central for one half hour between music and

7. Ruíz and Triminio, Apuntes biográficos, 67.

8. Agustín Lagos, Los Pioneros: conversaciones con Doña Rosario S. de Ferrari (Tegucigalpa: Imprenta Calderón, 1983), 28.

9. Ibid., 33.

10. Durón interviews, January and August 1987. Jorge Fidel Durón was a one-time contributor to El Día (Tegucigalpa), lawyer, National Party ideologue, and member of the board of directors of Banco Atlántida; he was the son of Romulo Durón, subsecretary of foreign affairs in 1932, for whom Ferrari worked.

11. Lagos, Los Pioneros, 14–15.

12. Ibid., 10.

13. Ibid., 16.

14. Ibid., 142.

15. El Cronista, 9 December 1936, 4; La Época, 8 October 1937, 3.

"soap operas," time was devoted to Carías's public works, education, and housing programs. Oftentimes HRN provided a biographical sketch of the president and discussed his major bills pending in the congress.[16] La Hora de Honduras offered weekly one-hour broadcasts on cultural life—for example, progress on the excavation at the pre-Colombian site of Copán in western Honduras. Other programs described foreign cultures to listeners,[17] and stories in El Cronista became a prime news source for HRN news broadcasts. International events were sent from abroad by telegraph and read on Ecos del Mundo.[18] Children were entertained before going to bed nightly with songs played in English on "El Good Night." Close friends and collaborators of Carías were frequent guests on the radio station, some becoming permanent broadcasters, among them Carlos Izaguirre, Jorge Fidel Durón, and the chief executive's private secretary and nephew, Marcos Carías Reyes.[19]

José Albir, another assistant to Carías, regularly announced major administrative decisions on radio between 8:30 and 9:00 p.m. Known as pico de oro ("golden tongued"), Albir delivered his message in an elegant, polished style. His presentations were effusive about the chief executive's accomplishments.[20] From time to time cabinet members were singled out for praise with biographical studies or mention of some special accomplishment. From departments, even municipalities, messages were read proclaiming the great contributions made by Carías there. Local National Party leaders were recognized, and they in turn broadcast their great efforts on his behalf.[21]

Ferrari's HRN dominated the airways all through the Cariato. For example, in 1934, Carías paid Teodoro Kohncke 250 lempiras to install Radio Nacional Gráfica in Amapala, which in turn was hooked up to Ferrari's network.[22] In 1945, two Carías loyalists, Andrés Rodríguez and Filiberto Díaz Zelaya, established La Voz de Lempira and Radio Honduras San Pedro Sula respectively.[23] By

16. Informe, Ministerio de Gobernación, 1939–40, Archivos, Palacio de los Ministerios, 189–90; La Época, 5 January 1937, 1.

17. Informe, 1939–40, 49.

18. Ibid., 211.

19. Ibid., 21, 47, 211.

20. Zúñiga Huete, El desastre de una dictadura, 17; La Época, 29 August 1939, 1.

21. El Cronista, 14 August 1936, 1.

22. Acuerdo No. 1750, 2 October 1936, Ministerio de Fomento, Biblioteca y Archivos Nacionales. Contracts were concluded with other firms in the country.

23. La Época, 14 January 1938, 3. For example, "La Voz de Lempira," "La Voz de San Pedro Sula," "La Voz de Atlántida."

linking all parts of Honduras in this radio network, Carías had total monopoly of the airwaves during his tenure as president to 1949. The age of modern communication technology had arrived but under the heavy hand and tutelage of a dictator.

In addition to radio stations and a telegraph system, Vice-President Abraham Williams managed ties between departmental leaders (political chiefs and military commanders) and the central government. He also had responsibility for internal security through the national police, the only centralized paramilitary institution capable of ending uprisings by local militias. It was directed by Camilo Reina, a taciturn, hard-working administrator, personally loyal to Carías. Tomás Martínez, hated and feared, was the national police commander.[24] The police controlled the civilian population by jailing, executing, or exiling opponents and stopping contraband. When necessary, the police assisted local militias in putting down disorders, using mounted troops as reinforcements. The police force also controlled distant areas like Olancho in the eastern part of the country, which never had been governed effectively from Tegucigalpa prior to 1933. The national police also protected Honduras's borders and prevented exile groups from crossing into the country. With an "air force" (civilian pilots contracted out for services) providing aerial reconnaissance and supplies, the national police was in essence the sole effective national security element until the mid-1940s. Neither Camilo Reina nor Tomás Martínez was identified politically with a department. Their entire careers had been linked to Tiburcio Carías. In the classical style of caudillo politics, their loyalty was personal, nurtured and tested in many political crises and military campaigns. Reina, a carpenter by trade and later a building contractor, served as mayor of Tegucigalpa in 1921–22 and as vice-minister of war in the Paz Barahona administration (1924–28). He was one of Carías's closest confidants in 1924 and commanded a militia in the War of Traitors (1932–33).

When Carías created the mounted police in late 1932, it was intended to be the nucleus of a militia for assignment in and around Tegucigalpa. Once the unit was well established and secure under Tomás Martínez's command, a rural police force, serving only departmental officials, was created in 1937.[25] Until that date the mounted police force was given special missions alone ending contraband, seizing weapons from marauding armed groups, and re-

24. He was known popularly as "the Shit" for the harshness of his rule, the brutality imposed on those who violated the law.

25. *Revista de Policía*, 3 March 1941, 5; Martínez interview, 11 November 1987.

inforcing local militias. Sometimes it assisted the "special forces" that the president established to help a comandante de armas with a particular task. With airplanes carrying arms and supplies, Martínez would meet the flight, re arm as needed, then proceed with his mission. He either operated alone or with the assistance of a local militia.[26] After the mission was accomplished, these reinforcements were disbanded.[27]

Beyond the capital city of Tegucigalpa, in the rural areas, Tomás Martínez commanded the feared mounted police. He had been close to the Carías family since childhood, first as a primary school student of Carías's mother, Sara Andino. When he was sixteen, in 1919, he joined Carías in several minor tasks, calling himself and other Carías followers "the army of '24."[28] For Martínez, loyalty meant employment and prestige. At one point in the 1920s, he attended a school for corporals and sergeants, then the artillery school. He joined Carías's military forces led by Francisco Martínez Funes from Lempira, el lobo chico ("the little wolf"), who had pledged his support to Carías in 1924 and again in 1932.[29] Tall, dark, solidly built, weighing over 250 pounds, six-foot-four Tomás Martínez had dark piercing eyes, almost Asian in appearance, with huge, thick hands. He frequently and proudly showed his fourteen gunshot wounds to those who doubted his prowess and loyalty in defending Carías. Imposing, fierce, uncompromising, when asked what his task was during the president's fifteen years in office, his response was "Limpiar el país" ("to eliminate from sight Carías detractors"), adding, "I never failed to carry out a presidential order."[30]

Martínez's approximately 160 troops operated in a geographical radius as far north as San Pedro Sula, south to Amapala, and along the Honduras section of the Pan-American Highway, controlling access roads to Olancho and Yoro in the east, and west to Intibucá and Copán.[31] It was the only security force that could easily and quickly traverse the unpaved roads, mostly mere paths that crisscrossed central Honduras. Asked what his units' jurisdiction was, Martínez answered, "The whole country." Not quite, but without major geo-

26. Revista de Policía, 31 October 1935, 9.

27. Martínez interview, 11 November 1987.

28. Martínez interviews, 9 April 1987, 11 November 1987.

29. Tomás Martínez Ponce (Tomás Martínez's son), "Tomás (Kakita): el Último Gran revolucionario," La Tribuna (La Ceiba), 6 May 1993, 9-B.

30. Ibid.

31. República de Honduras, Informe de Gobernación, 1942–43, Archivos, Palacio de los Ministerios, 9; Informe, 1944–45, 13, 251.

political barriers, it could have been.[32] The mounted police evoked terror with its sudden strike force, promptly ending unrest, robbery, and civil disorder. Offenders were simply shot or sent to the penitentiary in the capital.

Martínez's mounted police were assisted immeasurably by the use of the air force, which provided information from aerial reconnaissance on the deployment of armed groups. It also carried ammunition and supplies for him when needed. The unit had a mobile security force, with arms and materiel, which could be airlifted if necessary.[33]

United Fruit and Standard frequently shipped by rail (Tela and Trujillo Railroads in the north areas) supplies to military installations for use by Martínez's troops and local militias. Airplane pilots for Pan American and Central American Air Transport (TACA) were also engaged for military transport service to points where civil disorder erupted.[34]

The national police force was divided into three sections: investigation, the mounted police force, and a traffic section assigned to control contraband and vehicular movement in the capital and along the country's many unpaved roads. Reina was given the responsibility for training the national police in the School for Officers and Sergeants. "Discipline, Obedience, and Subordination" was its motto. Its manual was adopted from the German police force of the 1930s.[35] On several occasions Reina accepted J. Edgar Hoover's invitation to have agents in the Intelligence Division receive training at the Federal Bureau of Investigation in Washington.[36] It was, in effect, Carías's sole internal security force. Political dissidents were watched and dealt with in different ways— with jail, death, or exile. The detail and thoroughness of the police force's work, chronicled in police reports, show how closely and effectively the president governed. After patrolling the streets from 11:00 p.m. to 8:00 a.m., sometimes alone and sometimes with agents, Reina prepared a report, listing people

32. Martínez interview, 11 November 1987.

33. Matthews interview, 31 May 1987. Matthews was a pilot on contract with Carías and carried out several of these missions for the mounted police.

34. *Acuerdo* No. 469, 9 May 1939, Ministry of War, Navy and Aviation, Palacio de los Ministerios: Standard Fruit, United Fruit contract payment; *Acuerdo* No. 373, 2 May 1936: 20,000 lempiras to Lowell Yerex "for military transport services."

35. *Revista de Policía*, 31 July 1934, 18–20, 31; 30 June 1937, 1.

36. *Revista de Policía*, 28 February 1941, 3–4; J. Edgar Hoover to Camilo Reina, letter printed 10 December 1940. One agent did go to Washington; see República de Honduras, *Informe*, Policía Nacional, 1941–42, Ministerio de Gobernación, 12. By executive orders in 1940, the FBI got permission to station agents throughout Latin America in response to a Nazi threat.

incarcerated and released from the Central Penitentiary. He also included the names of individuals who registered in hotels and rooming houses in Tegucigalpa and other cities.[37]

Incoming visitors to Honduras were required to register with the national police, not immigration authorities. The division's *orejas* ("ears," or spies) also reported on the activities of foreign visitors and citizens suspected of a crime or political opposition. Their observations also appeared in Reina's daily report. The apparent outwardly mundane operations of their section concealed its vast internal security functions. Checking people's identification cards at random, handling passports, and registering automobiles all assisted in compiling the daily report to the headquarters of the Intelligence Section and forwarded to the Ministry of Government.[38]

The Central Penitentiary, a large, dismal, fortresslike structure, was located in the center of Tegucigalpa. Unfortunately, but for obvious reasons, neither Reina's daily nor monthly reports give details on how prisoners were treated. One can only rely on hearsay, but according to Ministry of Government reports, prisoners committing petty crimes and political dissidents were placed together. Courts rarely, if ever, played a role in adjudicating or handing out sentences. There was no record kept of trials convened for anyone incarcerated. In sum, imprisonment was a primitive process, and inmates were left to the care and whim of the penitentiary's gatekeepers.

Inmates were assigned tasks like building bridges and roads, paving and cleaning streets. They were trained in carpentry; made hammocks, uniforms for the national police, shoes, and needlework; and learned tailoring and farming techniques. Saturday was "market day" at the penitentiary when prisoners sold their handiwork. Incarceration also meant a time for learning a trade and working when released.[39] Undoubtedly for propaganda purposes, Reina administered a correctional school for minors associated with the Central Penitentiary. Delinquents, called "students," wore a uniform and learned a trade like carpentry, toolmaking, or tailoring. Instruction was provided by people already engaged in these tasks. Primary education was offered in reading, writ-

37. República de Honduras, *Informe*, Ministerio de Gobernación, 1939–40, "Department of Investigation, Inspector General" (Policía de Investigación), 73–76, 203.

38. Ibid., Policía de Investigación, 1941–1942, 12; Correspondencia Recibida de la Policía Nacional, July–December 1935, Vol. II: "Daily Reports."

39. "Correctional School for Minors," *La Época*, 8 September 1936, 1; 23 June 1936, 3; "Edición Extraordinaria," January 1937, 12; 23 September 1938, 1; El Cronista, 23 June 1936, 3.

ing, and mathematics.[40] Each week the *Revista de Policía* published names and photos of "delinquents," youngsters who committed petty crimes and offenses who were now being trained in the "school for minors."[41] Abuse and mistreatment existed, but their practice was never recorded in Reina's daily police report. Reina made sure his image as the country's chief of police remained intact. Frequently, poems appeared in the *Revista de Policía* praising his work:

ETERNAL GRATITUDE
Alejandro Bados Murillo

We are born into the randomness of the world,
our brows hallowed in innocence,
poor people with a fruitful future
to mount the glory of being.

At the passing of life in the pestilent
dungheap of a million corrupt acts
we roll on blindly, and upon awakening,
new life shone on our hearts.

This Angel Protector [Reina], that, happy one day
full of holy ambition and triumph,
carried us to the Center that God indicated
in the golden dawn of spring mornings.

There we are in the correctional school,
teaching the mind, educating the heart,
learning the occupation, in true actions,
in the lecture hall and in the workshop with total devotion.

Every day we receive with determination,
opportunity teaches of a sure future
making us strong in the workshop that
is our hope, a happy existence.

Eternal gratitude in our hearts
shall cultivate like a flowery rosebush
for General don Camilo R. Reina,
the students of the Correctional School send you blessings.[42]

40. "Correctional School for Minors," 1
41. "Galería de Delincuentes," *Revista de Policía*, 30 June 1940, 47.
42. *Revista de Policía*, 31 August 1937, 8.

Along with Reina, Tomás Martínez could not alone have guaranteed absolute acceptance of Carías's law. Honduran history's frequent political instability made it difficult to create a permanent and professional military force. Local political figures led militias scattered throughout the country. From time to time, chief executives vainly tried to create a cadre of both politically loyal and professionally trained army officers, but failed. President Miguel Dávila (1907–11) brought in the Chilean colonel Luis Oyarzun and French sergeant Alfred Labró as heads of the Military Academy and Artillery School respectively.[43] But their leadership and training did not survive the Manuel Bonilla uprising in 1911. Consequently, no professionally trained military force existed at the national level when Carías assumed office. In fact, his assumption to power was due in large part to a personally led militia against insurgent liberals with their own armies.

Carías, ever wary of the disruptive capability of militias, took several crucial steps to minimize their growth and contain them. First, he named himself commander-in-chief of the "armed forces." Juan Manuel Gálvez took the post as minister of war and navy, and added "aviation" to his title. Comandantes de armas were appointed for each department, all Carías allies from the War of Revindication (1924) and the War of Traitors. Military commanders were named for key cities such as La Ceiba, Tela, Amapala, and Danlí. Military districts in departments would come under the direct control of the Carías-appointed comandantes.[44]

Conscripts, officers, medical personnel, and staff would be drawn from the department and kept there for training. Schools for corporals and sergeants would be established for teaching basic military skills: infantry and artillery, as well as learning to read and write. In the capital, under the president's direct control, were the Estado Mayor Presidencial ("President's Military Staff") and Presidential Honor Guard.[45] Later, in 1946, long after Carías was well entrenched, an agreement with the United States was signed providing for a Basic Arms School for enlisted personnel. In 1952, the Military Academy Francisco

43. Ropp, "The Honduran Army," 508. For a study of nineteenth-century militias, see Jesús Euclio Inestroza, Génesis y soluciones de las escuelas militares del ejército, 1831–1837 (Tegucigalpa: Talleres de Paz, 1990).

44. Informe, Comandantes de Armas, 1936–1937, Anexo #13, 1, Miguel Paz Reyes Library (Tegucigalpa).

45. República de Honduras, Memorias de War, 1934–35, August 1934–31 July 1935, Biblioteca y Archivos Nacionales, 3–4, 7, 13–16.

Morazán combined the training under North American command of both officers and recruits. Militias were phased out in 1942, replaced by the First and Second Infantry Battalions, a professional standing army.[46]

Carías was one of the first Central American leaders to understand the significance of airplanes as a strategic weapon. He had ordered the bombing of military barracks held by dissident liberal forces opposed to President Mejía Colindres in Tegucigalpa as early as 1931–32.[47] Carías became aware of the importance of airplanes in military tactics when Charles Augustus Lindbergh stopped in Tegucigalpa in January 1928. Carías personally greeted him at the airport and in his welcoming speech, as president of the congress, he spoke of a "great strategic future for aviation."[48] In 1932 when Carías purchased arms in El Salvador from President Maximiliano Hernández Martínez, he had them flown in a Stinson monoplane to Amapala to reinforce his ground forces marching north to Tegucigalpa.[49] Lowell Yerex, a contract pilot with his cache of maps, reconnoitered and spotted opposition ground troops, providing Carías with vital information for tactical operations. Even Carlos Izaguirre carried out numerous aerial missions, ferrying arms and gathering intelligence information.[50] When Yerex secured Toncontin, an airstrip outside Tegucigalpa, and key port cities along the north coast particularly in the Department of Cortés in 1932, Carías created what he called a permanent "special force" to se-

---

46. Key dates in the country's military reorganization are as follows:

    1934. Escuelas de Aviación Militar founded: Col. William Brooks, first commandant; U.S. personnel ran the school until 1947, then Hondurans took it over.

    1936. Establishment of the Estado Mayor del Ejército and Escuelas Militares.

    1946. Military treaty with the United States; the United States runs a basic army school for EMs and officers.

    1947. End of militias and establishment of the First and Second Infantry Battalions. United States fears subversion.

    1949. Treaty with the United States; first course of officer training school.

    1952. Both schools unified into the Military Academy Franco Morazán.

47. Yerex, *Yerex of TACA*, 60; Matthews interview, 31 May 1987; Franz Blom, "La Aviación Conquista a Honduras," *Revista del Archivo*, Vol. XIV, No. 9 (May 1936).

48. *El Demócrata*, 7 January 1928, 2.

49. Dispatch, U.S. legation, Tegucigalpa, to Department of State, 25 December 1932, Confidential U.S. Diplomatic Post Records, reel 5, 477, 495, 503, 521; see also Miguel Paz Reyes (archivist for Ministerio de Guerra, Marina, y Aviación), *Libro Diario de Vuelos Aviación*, in the Miguel Paz Reyes Library, Tegucigalpa.

50. Reyes, *Libro Diario*; República de Honduras, *Acuerdos*, Ministerio de Guerra, Marina, y Aviación, (EM), No. 564a 1.001, February–April, 1933; Acuerdo (EM) No. 845, 15 March 1933.

cure the sites. Shortly after, with twenty-nine men and three Stinson single-motor monoplanes, a permanent air force, (in effect, a cadre of civilian pilots) was established.[51] The aircraft had been purchased in the United States, shipped to Tela on the north coast, and flown by three pilots, Yerex and two Yankees, Harold White and Donald Griffin, to Tegucigalpa.[52]

Carías used the airplane to tip the balance of military power, thereby emerging from the pack of other politicos and their militias with a new weapon. His pilots were handsomely compensated for their work. Yerex was paid $10,000 for his "military services" up to February 1933. Payments in different amounts would continue on a monthly basis.[53]

When Carías became president in 1933, Yerex, with a five-seater Stinson named "Espíritu de Honduras" ("Spirit of Honduras"), set up a charter service employing one pilot. By late 1934, Yerex had fifteen planes and approximately eight mechanics. Carías signed a contract with him in February 1933 for a permanent mail transport service. By 1939, Yerex had expanded services to Nicaragua, El Salvador, and Panamá. Yerex received, on an average, 16,000 lempiras a month for the services of two to three planes from 1932 to the early 1940s.[54]

In addition to Yerex, Carías contracted with Empresa Dean, partly owned by Julio Lozano Díaz (president, 1954–56), and Morgan Airlines for "services." This meant shipping arms, supplies, or personnel quickly to a region where armed resistance erupted. These companies received similar but far less lucrative fees than Yerex.[55] Charles Matthews, first a mechanic then pilot and vice-president of TACA with Yerex, gave "logistical assistance" to both the Liberal and National Parties. "But," Matthews once remarked, "the Liberals ran out of money, so we became Nationalists."[56]

In early December of each year in his State of the Nation Address, Carías ex-

51. Telegrams, 25 February 1933 (Choluteca); Atlántida, Correspondencia Telegráfica, 1933, Vol. 45, Biblioteca de Telegramas. See also *Libro Diario.*

52. *Libro Diario.*

53. *Acuerdos,* Copias de Notas #1750, Ministerio de Fomento, 4 February 1933, Biblioteca y Archivos Nacionales.

54. *Acuerdos,* Ministerio de Mantenimiento del Orden Público, 1933–1934; *Acuerdos,* No. 84, 13 November 1932; No. 164, 2 February 1933; No. 130, 24 November 1933; No. 60, 18 September 1933; No. 94, 14 October 1933; No. 85, 16 October 1933, Archivos Ministerio de Guerra, Marina, y Aviación, Palacio de los Ministerios.

55. *Acuerdo* No. 94, 14 October 1933; *Acuerdo* No. 30, 24 November 1933, Archivos Ministerio de Guerra, Marina, y Aviación, Palacio de los Ministerios; see also Yerex, *Yerex of TACA,* 75.

56. Matthews interview, 31 May 1987.

pressed his "great longing to give the nation a regular army, perfectly organized, prepared and equipped . . . to maintain internal peace . . . to be an effective protector of sovereignty and territorial integrity."[57] Having made that
statement, he invariably would address the issue of strengthening "our military" by giving a litany of the great accomplishments of the air force.[58] The tedious recitation of the number of added militias, their growing ranks, and the
training they were receiving was overshadowed by glowing praise for his airplanes. The rhetoric barely concealed what the watchful observer could easily
surmise: the airplane was Carías's key strategic weapon. He also used the air
force to control local political chieftains. Party chieftains could keep their militias, but during the Cariato they could not take them outside their departments.
Carías told the country each year what his air force had done and would continue to do—cover the republic, watch for disorders, and localize and suppress
them.[59]

In late 1936, Carías's son Gonzalo and nephew Calixto were dispatched to
the United States to make arrangements for creating an aviation school.
Colonel William Brooks in the U.S. Army Signal Corps became head of the institution in 1937. With four pilots, one instructor, three mechanics, a radio operator, and four planes, Brooks ran the school until 1941 for eight Honduran
cadets.[60] Three of the planes were for flight training. One, a Curtis-Wright, was
for classroom and demonstration purposes—assembling and disassembling
motors, aerial and reconnaissance exercises. Brooks was instructed by his su-
periors in Washington not to conduct any military operations, but he assisted
Carías immeasurably in carrying out reconnaissance and military supply missions.[61]

Honduras's first officially commissioned pilot was Luis Alonso Fiallos,
who joined Carías's army at Toncontin air base in 1924 at age fourteen. Later, he
was sent to the Ryan School of Aviation in Englewood, California, for training.
He was licensed as a pilot by the North American Corporation there and flew

57. *Mensaje*, 5 December 1937, 153, Biblioteca y Archivos Nacionales.

58. *Mensaje*, 1936, 99.

59. *La Época*, 3 March 1940, 3; see also República de Honduras, *Memorias de guerra, marina, y aviación, 1935–1936* (1 Aug. 1935–31 July 1936), Biblioteca y Archivos Nacionales, 4–6.

60. Matthews interview, 31 May 1987; see also Dispatch, U.S. legation, Tegucigalpa, to Department of State, 29 December 1936, Confidential U.S. Diplomatic Post Records, reel 12, 719.

61. U.S. legation, Tegucigalpa, to Department of State, 4 March 1936, Confidential U.S. Diplomatic Post Records, reel 12, 715.

back to Tegucigalpa in a plane Yerex had purchased there. His first military campaign took place in the fall of 1932 when he strafed and bombed Amapala and the capital.[62]

Fiallos worked closely with Yerex and flew several supply and reconnaissance missions for him.[63] He became interim director of the Aviation School in 1941, serving one year. Two Yankee lieutenant colonels, Harold White and Malcolm Stewart, served as directors from 1942–44.[64] By 1942, the Honduran Air Force had twenty-two planes with pilots trained in the United States. Between 1941 and the end of his term in 1949, Carías spent 62 percent of "lend-lease" funds on buying airplanes and equipment. In 1941–1945, he received $368,000 in arms transfers and paid only 9.23 percent of the cost of material delivered.[65] By 1942, he had purchased twenty-two planes in the United States for service in Honduras.[66] Building his air force was based on emerging Western Hemisphere security issues during World War II, a subject he repeatedly raised with Washington.

Casting his eyes outside Honduras, looking for ways to obtain arms for security assistance, Carías seized on a threat to U.S. interests in Nicaragua. The Nicaraguan rebel Augusto Sandino had mounted a campaign to expel Yankee troops who had invaded his country in 1927 (and remained until 1933). After becoming president, Carías asked Washington how he could assist in defeating Sandino since the Nicaraguan rebel forces frequently operated from bases in eastern Honduras. In 1933, Yerex was hit by Sandino snipers in Octotal, Nicaragua, when flying reconnaissance missions for Carías. This incident was reported to the U.S. legation in both Tegucigalpa and Managua. In response, the president's requests for security assistance, meaning more planes and arms, were received favorably by Washington.[67]

Izaguirre enlisted Yerex, along with Carías's son Gonzalo in New York City and nephew Calixto in Washington, to purchase aircraft and arms in the United

62. El Cronista, 24 February 1932, 1.

63. Ibid.

64. Rafael Heliodoro Valle, "La aviación en Honduras," Honduras Rotaria, No. 33/34 (April–May 1954): 12.

65. Euraque, "Industrialists and Merchants," 352.

66. Valle, "La aviación en Honduras," 13; also see Dispatch, U.S. legation, Tegucigalpa, to Department of State, 3 March 1938, Confidential U.S. Diplomatic Post Records, reel 10, 380.

67. Dispatch, U.S. legation, Tegucigalpa, to Department of State, 30 December 1932, Confidential U.S. Diplomatic Post Records. Charlie Matthews described the incident in an interview, 31 May 1987.

States.[68] Speed was of the essence in early 1933 as insurgent militias were still resisting Carías's assumption to power. The "team" in the United States acquired three Stinson single-motor monoplanes in mid-1933 for $2,500 each. They also purchased six machine guns and three gun racks.[69] Whenever new planes arrived in Tegucigalpa, Carías would assemble his entire cabinet, congress, and judiciary to meet them.[70]

Leasing and purchasing planes, which numbered fifteen by 1938, continued unabated all through the 1930s. Gonzalo Carías, the Honduran consul general in New York, also bought bombs, rifles, and machine guns from Federal Laboratories in Pittsburgh, Pennsylvania.[71] In May 1936 alone, he acquired one hundred bombs for $864 and fifty machine guns for $8,360.[72]

All of TACA's planes, many running from Guatemala City to Panamá, were headquartered at Toncontin air base in Tegucigalpa. Yerex and Matthews operated out of Tegucigalpa principally because Carías gave them lucrative leasing contracts. The arrangement was purely financial for the airline entrepreneurs but fulfilled strategic military needs for the president. Said Matthews, vice-president of TACA, "We had to help Carías. If he got thrown out, we would have to go as well."[73]

Both TACA and Dean Airlines carried presidential messages directly to the headquarters of departmental governors and military commanders. The sheer volume of these documents increased dramatically from 1933 on. Most of the messages and cargo, including rifles, ammunition, food, and clothing, were for Carías loyalists in the interior.

---

68. Carlos Izaguirre, Honduran legation, Washington, DC, to Foreign Minister, Tegucigalpa, *Correspondencia Recibida del Ministerio de Relaciones Exteriores*, Archivo, Comisión de Soberanías y Fronteras (Comayagua), 14 March, 10 April, 12 April, 27 April, 28 April, 16 May, 22 May 1933; U.S. Department of State to Honduran Minister, Washington, DC, 31 March 1933; Minister of War Manuel Gálvez to Foreign Minister, 3 May 1933.

69. Julian Lay, U.S. Minister, Tegucigalpa, to Minister, Foreign Relations, 18 April 1933, *Correspondencia Recibida del Ministerio de Relaciones Exteriores*.

70. *Datos cronológicos de la comprar de aviaciones de la Fuerza Aérea de Honduras, 1933–1934*, Miguel Paz Reyes Library.

71. Izaguirre to Foreign Minister, 16 June 1933, *Correspondencia Recibida del Ministerio de Relaciones Exteriores*.

72. *Acuerdos*, Ministerio de Intendencia, 1936–38, Acuerdos, No. 564, 13 May 1936, No. 588, 26 May 1936, No. 702, 31 July 1936, *Acuerdo* (no number) June 1938, Archivos Ministerio de Guerra, Marina, y Aviación, Palacio de los Ministerios.

73. Matthews interview, 31 May 1987.

TACA undertook these logistical missions under specific contracts signed personally by the president. For example, in 1934, Yerex was paid 3,120 lempira to transport government correspondence, personnel, and military supplies to and from Comayagua and 3,600 lempira to El Salvador.[74] Equipment for setting up the elaborate telegraph system was also delivered by air to cities and towns in western and eastern departments, areas where considerable unrest and opposition to Carías existed in the spring of 1933.[75]

An 11 April 1935 contract illustrates TACA's responsibilities and benefits. TACA agreed to establish a regular domestic airline service in Honduras with its headquarters in Tegucigalpa for ten years. TACA would use other designated landing sites for its three planes and pay a tax (to be set later). In return, the airline agreed to construct service buildings at Toncontin and other landing strips around the country. Eighty percent of TACA employees were to be Hondurans. Finally, in a concluding section of the agreement, TACA agreed to place at the service of the Carías government use of its aircraft when, according to the contract, "it was asked to do so."[76] By 1934, Carías had sixty-seven airstrips and was leasing twelve to fourteen planes regularly from TACA.[77] Aerodrums (buildings for storage) were built in several department capitals, but no aircraft ever was permanently stationed in these regional airports, only in Tegucigalpa.[78]

General administration of aircraft deployment was overseen by Carías, Minister of Defense Manuel Gálvez, and Vice-President Abraham Williams. Yet the president was involved in every detail from drawing up general terms of contract agreements to the distribution of oil and supplies to depots throughout the country. Comandantes de armas, jefes políticos, and municipal govern-

---

74. República de Honduras, Acuerdos, No. 117, 15 August 1934, August–September 1934, Ministerio de Fomento, Biblioteca y Archivos Nacionales. For 3,120 lempiras annually, "air services" Tegucigalpa to Comayagua, Yoro; doc. 116, San Pedro Sula to Ocotepeque, 3,600 lempiras annually; doc. 115, 14 August 1934, Tegucigalpa to San Salvador, 1,980 lempiras annually; doc. 290, 4 September 1934, Tegucigalpa to Puerto Cortés (no amount given); doc. 1750, 3 October 1934, 280 lempiras, TACA "mission" to Occidente.

75. Telegram, 9 February 1933, to Abraham Williams, Correspondencia Telegráfica, Biblioteca de Telegramas.

76. Acuerdo, 9569, No. 176, 11 April 1935, Republic of Honduras, Gaceta, Biblioteca y Archivos Nacionales.

77. Blom, "La aviación conquista a Honduras," 632.

78. Memorias de guerra, marina, y aviación, 1936–37, Biblioteca y Archivos Nacionales. See also Copias de Oficios, April–June 1934, Vol. 1709.

ment officials were excluded entirely from managing any aspect of aircraft deployment or shipment of supplies.[79]

Soon after taking office and securing the central part of the country, Carías began to lease and purchase Stinson, Fokker, and Ballanea aircraft.[80] They were assigned to track down armed vigilante bands, "reconnoitering" Nicaraguan and Guatemalan borders with Honduras for dissident rebel groups, and, when necessary, shipped supplies to local militia commanders to suppress these gangs.[81]

By 1937 the minister of government could confidently say that "no one speaks of revolts," as the entire republic was criss-crossed with a vast and secure aerial network. Local militias continued to parade on Saturdays in their department capitals but performed few tactical exercises. A newspaper in San Pedro Sula ran the headline: "The Honduran People Are [using English] 'Air Minded.'"[82] Carías would have agreed, having spent his first term of office consolidating power via the airplane, telegraph, and radio and promoting rivalries at the department level between political and military chiefs. No political leader in Honduras had managed to govern and control the Honduran political landscape as efficiently and thoroughly as Carías. Besides the military hardware that secured the Carías regime in its first term, the National Party would provide the organization and mechanisms for deepening and extending the president's dictatorial hold on the country. At a certain point, Carías and his apologists would lay claim to an extended term based on the need to prolong the nation's domestic peace and, of course, the chief executive's tenure.

79. *Copias*, doc. 535, 5 April 1933; doc. 677, 18 April 1933; doc. 695, 19 April; doc. 165, 20 August; doc. 269, 30 August, 1934. See also Julian Lay, U.S. minister, to Foreign Minister, Tegucigalpa, 31 January 1934, *Correspondencia Diplomática Recibida, de la Legación de Estados Unidos de América en Honduras, 1934.*

80. *Libro diario de la escuela militar de aviaciones*, Vuelos, 24 December 1933. See also *Gaceta*, 9569, Republic of Honduras, Decreto 176 April, 1935; Valle, "La aviación en Honduras," 11.

81. *Informe*, Comandante de Armas de San Pedro Sula, 1936–37, *Memorias, Minister de Guerra*, Miguel Paz Reyes Library; see *Notas Vuelos Diarios*, 1936, 16 March, 11, 14, April, 1936, Miguel Paz Reyes Library; *La Época*, 31 July 1936, 1.

82. *El Diario Comercial*, 1 April 1933, 1.

III

"God Is Also a Continuísta"

6

Prolonging Power Extends the Peace

Unlike any of his predecessors, Tiburcio Carías entered the presidency with a well-organized political machine, the National Party. Its foundations, even its functions, typically rested on the personalism and localism of politics in Honduras.[1] It was a political force held together by regional leaders and their personal loyalties to Carías. He had spent the years since 1919 shaping the rudiments of a following, which through electoral victories and defeats made him the undisputed leader of the party well before 1933.[2] The party provided him with the popular support he needed in elections, but it also contained the administrative and organizational structure at all levels of the state for mobilizing followers, promoting his message, and giving him the electoral triumphs he wanted.[3]

The National Party, while dominated by Carías, was run locally by loyalists, his longtime associates in past civil conflicts. These were cohorts during his days as a civic chief and military commander in different parts of the country reaching back to 1907. It resembled a political force in an authoritarian state, creating a cult of Carías the leader—"the Benefactor of the Country," "the Father of Peace and Order." The party also disseminated through its local communities a vast amount of propaganda extolling the accomplishments of the chief executive. Local committees at the departmental and municipal levels selected candidates for office, and party headquarters in Tegucigalpa kept membership records and administered its financial affairs throughout the country. When Carías gained control of the nation's administrative apparatus, National Party members assumed greater roles at the local levels of government.

The 1932 elections marked the successful culmination, not the beginning, of this party as a major force in the country. Starting in 1923, the party propa-

1. El Nacionalista (Tegucigalpa), 2 May 1919, 3; 7 February 1919, 2.
2. La Época, 4 February 1978, 2.
3. Libro de Oro (Tegucigalpa), n.d. [1939], 3.

gandized more an agenda than an ideology for governing the country: namely, ending civil wars and tackling a growing domestic and foreign debt. It was a simple but compelling appeal for peace and order, to build a nation-state that had an effective administrative structure. With an influential press and Carías at work locally, then nationally, as a political leader, the party was a truly major force by 1932. But its leaders were basically Carías loyalists whose allegiance went back to 1919. Personalism in politics was merely institutionalized by the new president in 1932.

When the journalist and writer Paulino Valladares organized the National Party administratively in the fall of 1922, he created a provisional governing junta. Later it was reorganized into a central committee with seventy people from different parts of the country. Local committees became primarily Carías organizations by 1923. They did so through the 1932 elections and beyond.[4] Their attention was directed at electing National Party candidates to congress as well. In 1928 the party changed its governing statutes to allow Carías to hold the posts of party director and candidate for president at the same time.[5]

Venancio Callejas, a prominent lawyer who had briefly been Carías's vice-presidential running mate in 1928, withdrew from the ticket, objecting to the lack of a National Party convention as a vehicle for selecting candidates.[6] He also challenged the fusion of the posts Carías now held: party presidential contender and head of the organization running the campaign. Rather than begin his own presidential campaign or launch a revolt in the customary fashion in Honduran politics, Callejas maintained his loyalty to the party. He continued to express his differences with Carías and became a vocal dissident at the time when plans were set to continue the president's term in 1936.[7] Fearing for his life, he arranged a quick and secret departure from the country before the police reached him.[8] Other members of his family who had suffered harassment while living in Honduras followed.

The National Party had well over 500 clubs around the country ready to gear up for a Carías campaign in 1932. They were principally located in departments and districts, others in villages. The central committee, with Carías at its head,

---

4. Stokes, *Honduras*, 242; *Libro de Oro*, 4 October 1932, 3.

5. *El Pueblo*, 25 February 1932, 1, 8.

6. *Vanguardia* (Tegucigalpa), 13 October 1947, 2.

7. *El Cronista*, 4 February 1936, 1.

8. Dispatch, U.S. embassy to Department of State, National Archives, Record Group 59, 815.00/4658, 17 January 1936.

ran local organizations through regional partisans. While departmental and municipal campaigns were exclusively run by the National Party leadership, the central committee in Tegucigalpa provided immeasurable help. Planes flown by Carías partisans and loyalists like Carlos Izaguirre were rapidly dispatched throughout the country to provide funds and campaign materials for departmental and district party organization.[9]

Carías never barnstormed around the country. He let political campaigns run locally.[10] The head of a local, departmental committee varied from a jefe politico to a military commander to a member of congress. Regardless of the person's official title, ultimate party authority went to the person designated by Carías. Frequently that person was a longtime, trusted collaborator whose loyalties had been tested in 1923, 1924, 1928, and 1932. A few extended back to 1907–11 when Carías had been a political chief and military commander in Copán and Cortés. But even those with a long history of political loyalty did not receive Carías's unqualified trust. For example, Martínez Funes of Choluteca, although a Carías ally since 1924, changed posts from military commander to political chief according to the need at the time, ensuring his loyalty to the president. Carías's nephew, Calixto Carías, was named comandante de armas in Amapala as a guarantee to stop efforts organizing political clubs opposing the government's moves to promote the president's continuation in office in 1936. And General Pedro Triminio of the Department of Paraíso in southwest Honduras alternated posts as jefe político, comandante de armas, and National Party chief.[11] Sometimes Carías merely identified himself with a local, popular political leader and over time acquired that person's support, like the populist Gregorio Ferrera, who was killed in 1931. In the latter case, Carías offered the backing of his followers for local candidates who were partisans of the late political leader.[12]

Carías controlled National Party chieftains by providing them with funds from his central committee coffers. The source was a tax deducted from the pay of public employees. This was explained as "expenses for national defense by

9. Velásquez interview, 27 October 1987.

10. Ibid.

11. Dispatch, U.S. legation, Tegucigalpa, to Department of State, 1 June 1935, National Archives, Record Group 59, 815.00/4615. See also Dispatch, U.S. legation, Tegucigalpa, to Department of State, 1 November 1936, Record Group 59 815/4636, 2. See also La Época, 10 January 1938, 2, for Triminio's job shifts after 1936 to ensure loyalty to Carías.

12. Dispatch, 1 June 1935.

the Chief Executive." Carías personally controlled this money and saw to it that local National Party leaders received a salary for their efforts.[13] Sometimes money was raised by extracting amounts from "local fat cats," as one loyalist in San Pedro Sula explained it.[14] The amount was sent directly to Carías and the central committee. Rarely, if ever, did a local party leader collect and spend funds. Control was always maintained at the top.

In addition to the tax deducted from bureaucrats' salaries, ten lempiras were charged to citizens for a certificate that indicated the person had registered to vote. In addition, the certificate recognized a voter as a member of the National Party in good standing. Another National Party source of funding was concessions such as liquor sales or a construction contract, granted by the government to local party loyalists.[15]

By 1933, the National Party was capable of mobilizing the faithful in campaigns as far down as the municipal level. The party had been making substantial gains in local and congressional elections since 1924.[16] Even Liberal president Mejía Colindres (1928–32), facing armed rebellion within his own party, took note of the National Party's superb organization. Election procedures in 1932, and for most of the Carías era, were geared to favor the incumbent. Election ballots were printed by political parties and distributed to voters. People often were forced to show their ballots before actually casting their votes.[17]

National Party members during the Carías era had a set of beliefs rather than an ideology. People vividly recalled civil wars, participated in them, and saw their homes and property destroyed. National Party leaders backed Carías because he proposed ending these conflicts. But more than that, these local and regional leaders from different walks of life—soldiers, schoolteachers, business exporters and importers, landowners, and small farmers—wanted an efficient state to manage order and keep the peace.[18] Liberal Party hegemony from the 1890s to 1932, so long advocating the politics of constitutionalism

13. Gabriel Mejía interviews, San Pedro Sula, 25–26 February 1987, November 1987. Mejía was administrator of tax revenues for Cortés, 1940–49.

14. Luque interview, 10 September 1987.

15. Luque interview, 14 September 1987.

16. La Época, 9 December 1933, 1; 15 December 1933, 3.

17. Telegram to Ministerio de Gobernación, 19 October 1932, Correspondencia Telegráfica, 1932, Vol. 1, Biblioteca de Telegramas.

18. La Época, 14 March 1936, 3. See also Julián López Piñeda, La reforma constitutional (Paris: Ediciones Estrella, 1936), 7, 8, 15, 19.

and economic growth, had lost the confidence of people by the 1930s. The Bonillas, Policarpo and Manuel; Francisco Bertrand; and Rafael López Gutiérrez had failed to create order, and the Liberal-controlled congresses were unable to select chief executives, as they were supposed to do in election stalemates. Worse still, many strongly criticized the concession system during the Liberal era which granted land and tax exemption to North American banana companies in return for loans.

Carías and his Nationalists offered different approaches and solutions to perceived failures of traditional Liberal doctrine. For example, he added to economic growth the need for financial probity, no armed movements for political gain, reorganizing government finances (then in total disarray), and restoring public credit, which was almost nonexistent. By adopting the word "National," Carías partisans wanted to reach beyond the narrow exploits of local warring politicians and lure old-time Liberals to their cause in creating an efficient bureaucratic state.[19]

Liberal president Trinidad Cabañas (1852; 1853–55) was celebrated by the National Party as a successful chief executive because he came close to creating a stable, unified state that promoted economic development. Carías displayed Cabañas's picture in public buildings, naming parks, bridges, and schools after him. Carías also took themes from Cabañas's speeches, quoting excerpts that claimed government should protect and serve the national interests first, then individual rights. The National Party leader was helped immeasurably by a cowed press. By 1936, some editors devoted the bulk of their issues to propagandizing the National Party program.[20] With a more cooperative and compliant press, Liberal Party journalists became more defensive of the organization's old principles, once advocated in the 1880s. But as expected the National Party gained power under Carías.[21]

The Carías-controlled press, like La Época and El Cronista, preached the National Party dogma of peace, order, and fiscal conservatism. These newspapers published the Carías government's economic and financial agenda and commemorated anniversaries of the party and its political chieftain. Through the local party apparatus, they advertised the "public" demand for his election in 1928 and 1932. Beginning in 1936 the propaganda focused on the need for Carías to remain in office past the legal end of his term. The national radio net-

19. "Manifesto of the National Party," *Tegucigalpa*, 23 October 1932, 14–16.
20. *La Época*, 19 November 1937, 1; *El Cronista*, 23 May 1923, 2; 24 May 1923, 2; 23 July 1923, 2.
21. *El Pueblo*, 25 February 1932, 1, 8.

work, HRN, which had been utilized as a party mouthpiece since 1932, was also used to promote the continuance of the president's rule.²² Planes dropped campaign leaflets all over the country. Deputies in the party-controlled congress extolled their chief's personal virtues. As with "manifestations" (petitions for support) for his 1932 election, a *libro de oro*, or party honor book, displayed at all party headquarters was signed by those who wanted him to stay in power after 1936. Each department had a *"continuista* committee."²³ With expanded lists of National Party stalwarts, this was perhaps the best campaign for extending a term of office by "popular" demand in Honduran history, and the president maintained party discipline at all levels.²⁴

The full measure of the party's organization and electoral successes became clear by 1935. Liberals were gradually losing seats in the congress and in major municipalities. No Liberal sat in congress after 1936. Meanwhile, Carías had taken dramatic steps to stem the country's economic collapse even though revenues continued to drop during his first term. He halted government expenditures that exceeded income. He cut budgets and began major administrative reforms on fiscal management by consolidating accounting procedures in several ministries. For example, he abolished "development boards" established in the 1920s in several departments for the distribution of central government funds locally. By 1930, these administrative units were consuming about 35 percent of total government revenue.²⁵

La Época declared that Carías would be reelected "by a unanimous count," saying "everyone, even God, was a *continuista*" (one who backed a second term for the president).²⁶ It was one thing for Carías's National Party to proclaim an extended presidential term,²⁷ but it was quite another to find a clear justification and a legal basis for such a move. The 1924 constitution and its predecessor in 1894 prohibited reelection of chief executives. Even Carías, as president of the congress in 1928, had extolled the virtues of this constitution calling for elections as means for legally transferring presidential power.²⁸ In

---

22. *Libro de Oro*, 1939, 10.

23. *La Época*, 11 July 1939, 1.

24. *El Heraldo*, 28 June 1982, 2.

25. Euraque, "Industrialists and Merchants," 239.

26. *La Época*, 29 November 1939, 2.

27. Ibid.

28. For Carías's response as president of congress, see *Mensaje*, *President Miguel Paz Barahona* (Tegucigalpa: Tipo Litografía Nacional, 1928), 9.

1935 the party mustered the full measure of its organization, in the press, radio, and a profusion of writings by intellectuals, and embarked on a campaign to change the single-term provision.

Like many of his dictatorial contemporaries in Latin America, Carías faced the fundamental dilemma of how to prolong his term of office beyond the constitutional limit yet maintain legitimacy. The common approach was *continuismo*—or amending a constitution to extend a president's term. Carías and his partisans offered three reasons for their amendment: the need to reorganize the administrative structure of the state, to deal with the economic crisis, and to resolve security issues, such as the growing threat from Nazi Germany. Later, the communist challenge to the nation-state would replace the German threat.[29] The party set out to mobilize the public and cultivate nationwide support of the president. Its basic premise was if the people willed it, if the country wanted Carías to extend his term by amending the constitution, then it was his duty and responsibility to respond to this demand.

Carlos Izaguirre, Carías's closest confidant, ready to undertake any task for the president, led the journalistic campaign. He was joined by Julián López Piñeda, a deputy like Izaguirre and editor of *La Época*, who wrote numerous essays explaining why the no-reelection principle impeded social and economic development in the country. Izaguirre's writings in the 1920s, which deplored the lack of national unity, were published once again.[30]

Both López Piñeda and Izaguirre maintained that what was needed first was order, political peace that would allow the creation of administrative efficiency. They argued that the constant cycle of revolutions and obstructionist legislatures had left Honduras a landscape of divided and weak institutions, a prey to foreign enterprises like banana companies. A framework for building a nation-state had to be sustained and continued so that democracy and voting rights would emerge.

Izaguirre and others pointedly referred to European trends toward fascism in the 1930s, particularly in Italy, as models for establishing order.[31] Izaguirre made distinctions between Europe's repugnant dictators, like Hitler, Stalin, and Mussolini, and the Western Hemisphere's strongmen who wielded vast power but not in a totalitarian fashion, men like Plutarco Elías Calles in México, Jorge Ubico in Guatemala, and Maximiliano Hernández Martínez in El Salvador. Latin

29. Fitzgibbon, "Continuísmo," 210–17.
30. El *Cronista*, 9 December 1936, 3.
31. Izaguirre, *Readaptaciones y cambios*, 53.

American dictators were good models for a carísta government. Izaguirre also cited Franklin D. Roosevelt and Britain's prime minister Ramsey McDonald as strong leaders justifiably exercising considerable executive power in time of economic crises. Together, Izaguirre and López Piñeda, along with Marcos Carías Reyes, the president's nephew and private secretary, argued that partisan politics—so divisive, so destructive in the country's past—needed to be placed below the interests of the state under an extended term for Carías.[32]

Many of Carías's partisans believed liberal democracy had failed Honduras. They scornfully ridiculed incompetent presidents who did not know their own government's income and expenses. Even Liberals like the well-known writer Luis Mejía Moreno (1878–?) condemned anarchy in Honduran politics, calling for order, peace, and administrative efficiency over a congress that under the constitution in force had greater powers than the chief executive.[33] López Piñeda suggested that associations (corporate groups, as he described them) of different economic and social entities like labor, business, and professionals, while encouraged to remain organized, active, and to exert influence, should be managed by the nation-state or a corporate state. Their supervision would in turn, he said, protect each one from exploitation by the other.[34] In sum, these writers all maintained that the 1924 constitution was out of date and had to be rewritten to give more power to the president and to reduce the existing vast prerogatives of the legislature.

Rather than concentrate on European fascist models for the reconstruction of Honduras, La Época writers focused on the Mexican Revolutionary Party and its constitution of 1917 as an excellent model for a future carísta state. That document made references to several interest groups within that party, including campesino urban workers, government bureaucrats, and organizations, each representative of special sections of Mexican society and all controlled by a powerful president. The Mexican state's role in economic development as "sovereign" over its subsoil was viewed as a model for future economic planning in Honduras.[35] Specifically, agrarian cooperatives in México, with credit banks and a central bank with partial public ownership, were mentioned as institutions for stabilizing future currency fluctuations.[36]

32. Ibid., 157.
33. See Mejía Moreno, El calvario de un pueblo.
34. López Piñeda, La reforma constitutional, 3.
35. La Época, 25 September 1933, 3.
36. Julián López Piñeda wrote several articles on the need for a central banking system run by

Other Central American dictators were extending their terms in the mid-1930s. In Guatemala, Nicaragua, and El Salvador, governments assumed vast powers in like-minded regimes in face of world depression. Carías moved quickly to gain support from his neighbors. Jorge Ubico of Guatemala, who expected Carías to be around for some time keeping his neighbor domestically quiet, assured the president of his full support.[37] Ubico felt it would be easier to deal with a like-minded incumbent regime in Honduras than to be troubled by the need to promote a new government through subversion. Moreover, the controlled press in Guatemala City made note that Carías once had been a Liberal Party member like Ubico.[38] President Maximiliano Hernández Martínez of El Salvador gave his full and unqualified backing too. In a public gesture of support, he docked all government salaries by one half day's pay and sent the funds to flood victims in southern Honduras in 1935. Carías's newspapers gave the story full coverage, pointedly explaining that the Salvadoran's tenure as chief executive had no term limits.[39] Nicaragua's minister in Tegucigalpa, Alberto Baca, spoke for his country's commander of the National Guard (later president) Anastasio Somoza García, offering unqualified support to Carías's continuismo.[40] Honduras's relationships in Central America and its need to manage the internal financial crisis, which required Washington's help, meant that the country would not turn into anything akin to a fascist state. Carías's participation in inter-American conferences throughout the 1930s and 1940s preparing a Western Hemisphere defense against Axis aggression attests to this view. Carías wanted very much to fit into the political landscape of contemporary Central America, a region of dictators, and continuismo would make this happen.[41]

Shrewdly, Carías and his party, through its newspapers and writers, drew parallels for continuismo with Franklin Roosevelt's reelection in 1936, and

---

the public and private sectors: *El Cronista*, 14 October 1936, 7; 15 October 1936, 7; 19 October 1936, 7.

37. *Cartas autográficas*, Presidente Jorge Ubico a Presidente Tiburcio Carías, 16 Mayo 1936, Archivos del Ministerio de Relaciones Exteriores, 1935–1936, n.p.

38. Grieb, *Guatemalan Caudillo*, 99, 197.

39. Dispatch, U.S. legation, Tegucigalpa, to Department of State, National Archives, Record Group 59, 815/4640, 15 November 1935.

40. *La Época*, 18 March 1936, 1.

41. Plutarco Muñoz, "Mensaje," *Boletín Legislativo*, 3 August 1946, 13–14, Biblioteca y Archivos Nacionales.

later in 1940 and 1944. Similarities in severe economic conditions in both countries were cited as reasons for assuming "dictatorial powers" handling these crises. La *Época* published selected correspondence between Carías and Roosevelt, which attested to their cooperation as tensions with the Axis powers grew. Precedents in North American history for seeking "second terms" were also mentioned, among them, Thomas Jefferson looking for a successor, Grover Cleveland's nonconsecutive second term, Teddy Roosevelt's unsuccessful bid as a Bull Moose Party candidate in 1912, and Woodrow Wilson's second term (1919–23). Franklin Roosevelt's emergency legislation in the 1930s prompting calls for his re-election in 1936 was also cited.[42]

Carías presented his plan for extending the term before the United States Legation staff in Tegucigalpa. He noted that the U.S. Constitution did not preclude a second term for a president. Citing grave economic conditions in both nations, he suggested that a crisis in Honduras required his "continuance" in office as Roosevelt had done in 1936.[43]

Washington concluded that since similar dictatorial regimes had been established in El Salvador, Guatemala, and Nicaragua, no exceptions could be made by withholding recognition of Carías if he chose to extend his term. For the United States, the 1923 Central American Treaty of Peace and Amity, which did not recognize a government coming to power by a coup or revolution, was a dead issue in 1935. Added to this, President Franklin Roosevelt's Good Neighbor Policy precluded meddling in the internal affairs of Latin American countries. In Washington's view, the Carías regime was providing political stability and dealing with fiscal problems wisely.[44] Perhaps Franklin D. Roosevelt's often quoted comment that "Anastasio Somoza (1936–56) may have been a SOB but at least he is our SOB" could be applied to Carías in Honduras.

Saturnino Medal, a Carías loyalist, National Party leader, and onetime minister to Costa Rica, followed up on Carías's interview with U.S. embassy staffers by laying out the party's strategy for continuismo after 1936. The plan was to mobilize popular support through petitions by the National Party committees at all levels in the country from the capital to municipalities. This would

42. La *Época*, 12 February 1936, 1.

43. Dispatch, U.S. legation, Tegucigalpa, to State Department, 10 December 1935, Confidential U.S. Diplomatic Post Records, reel 10, 388.

44. Dispatch, U.S. legation, Tegucigalpa, to State Department, 30 April 1936, Confidential U.S. Diplomatic Post Records, 1, 15–16. See also Dispatch, U.S. minister, Tegucigalpa, to Department of State, 30 April 1936, Confidential U.S. Diplomatic Post Records, reel 1, 917.

be followed by a proposal made for the convocation of a constituent assembly to revise the 1924 constitution and extend Carías's term. The U.S. diplomats responded cautiously to the proposal and suggested that Carías either pick a figurehead and rule through him or force the constituent assembly to call an election for a second term, making all but certain that he would be elected. Essentially, the legation wanted the inevitable accomplished by a legal procedure. Saturnino Medal pointedly warned that there was opposition to Carías's plan within the National Party, which could lead to confusion and even failure in this strategy. He suggested that the president might not win another election. Worse, he added, touching a nerve, if the election were thrown open, the president's chief rival, Ángel Zúñiga Huete, "a close friend of Mexico, no ally of Washington's in Central America, might win the election."[45]

As a precautionary measure, responding to a rumor of possible revolts in the eastern department of Olancho and elsewhere, Carías dispatched airplanes with small arms for distribution to loyalists.[46] Moreover, the United Fruit Company manager in Honduras, Walter Turnbull, supported an extended term for Carías.[47] The banana enterprise had already made loans to the government in exchange for lucrative concessions in reduced taxes and land concessions. The U.S. legation reported to Washington that UFCO had given Carías $200,000 in July 1936, a portion of which he used as "political expenses," laying plans for continuismo.[48] Thus, North America's largest private enterprise had officially given its approval to an extended Carías term.

The National Party organization launched its campaign for a Carías second term on two fronts in mid-1935. First, it arranged public manifestations from municipalities all the way to the central committee. Second, the outcry for continuismo was expected to move the party-controlled congress to act on a con-

45. Dispatch, U.S. minister, Tegucigalpa, to Department of State, 7 March 1935, Confidential U.S. Diplomatic Post Records, reel 1, 3. Also see Dispatch, U.S. minister, Tegucigalpa, to Department of State, 7 March 1935, Confidential U.S. Diplomatic Post Records, reel 10, 908.

46. *Libro diario de la escuela militar de aviación* (lista de vuelos), Ministerio de Guerra, 16 May 1936. A flight for the same purpose to the Department of Paraíso with arms was also logged on 11 April 1936. Biblioteca, Miguel Paz Reyes, Director, Oficina de Historia Militar, Fuerzas Armadas.

47. Dispatch, 15 November 1935, Confidential U.S. Diplomatic Post Records, reel 10, 1–2; see also Dispatch, U.S. minister, Tegucigalpa, to Department of State, 15 November 1935, Confidential U.S. Diplomatic Post Records, reel 10, 363.

48. Dispatch, U.S. minister, Tegucigalpa, to Department of State, 18 December 1936, Confidential U.S. Diplomatic Post Records, 2. See also Dispatch, U.S. minister, Tegucigalpa, to Department of State, 18 December 1936, Confidential U.S. Diplomatic Post Records, reel 12, 131.

stitutional revision extending the presidential term. A flood of proclamations from all kinds of groups and organizations poured out from the pages of *La Época* and *El Cronista*. Several departmental party committees issued proclamations with signatures reading "General Carías: the Exemplary Patriot," "Humble Peasants overjoyed at Carías's continuation in office," "Carías's work is national reconstruction," "Carías will continue in office, thanks to popular demand." On and on the "manifestos" poured in.[49]

The Catholic Church even welcomed and supported plans for continuismo. Pope Pius XI through his papal nuncio issued a long letter congratulating Carías on his widespread support. It thanked the president for his unqualified assistance in its role in education and society as a whole. But the Church's power and authority had been sharply reduced in the 1880s during the Liberal era with enactment of laws separating church and state, withdrawing financial support from the government, authorizing civil marriages, and legalizing divorce.

Carías never attempted to restrict the Church's efforts in its pastoral work. When the German-born bishop Agustin Hombach died in 1934, congress passed a law making it a requirement that his successor be a naturalized citizen. This decree merely enhanced Carías's popularity with his country's clergy.[50] In 1939, the Vatican appointed Monsignor Emilio Morales Roque, a Honduran, as apostolic administrator of the Archdiocese of Tegucigalpa. Two other nationals, Monsignors Ángel María Navarro and José de la Cruz Turcios y Barahona, were named titular bishops of Santa Rosa and Copán respectively. They both served currently through Carías's term.[51] Yet many of the president's closest associates were members of the Masonic Order, such as Zepeda Durón, director of *La Época*, a grand master of the Honduran Masonic Lodge. Doña Elena, the first lady, however, kept close ties with the Catholic Church in charitable activities.[52]

Like clockwork, National Party deputies, dominant political figures in their respective departments who were all longtime Carías backers and fellow veterans in revolutions, took steps to revise the 1924 constitution. The document was more than simply an impediment to a president's extended term; it em-

49. Dispatch, U.S. minister, Tegucigalpa, to Department of State, 29 July 1935, National Archives, Record Group 59, 815/4618.

50. Rómulo Durón to Cardenal Gasparri, secretary of state of the Vatican, 30 August 1923, *Cartas diplomáticas, 1923–1935*, Archivos del Ministerio.

51. *Revista del Archivo*, Vol. XII, No. 5 (1933): 308.

52. Ruíz and Triminio, *Apuntes biográficos*, 27.

bodied everything in their view that weakened and debilitated government in its management of public affairs. For years, Paulino Valladares, Carlos Iza-guirre, Zepeda Durón, and others deplored its provisions, which created a par-liamentary government, not a modern, authoritative, executive system. Now was their chance to change all that.

Plutarco Muñoz, a Carías loyalist, the president of congress, a member of the legislature since 1926, and a lawyer for the United Fruit Company, from Yoro, was considered the shrewdest parliamentarian in Honduras.[53] He was someone who could revise the constitution and see to it that Carías's presi-dency was extended "legally." Supporting another Carías term, he said "Tam-bién Dios es continuista" ("God is also a continuista")[54] and drove a resolution through the legislature convoking a constituent assembly. Called "the Lord of the House," Muñoz ran congress single-handedly as his fiefdom. For example, the unicameral chamber convened at 9:30 each weekday when in session. Two sets of matters were required for discussion, administration business and leg-islation introduced by members. Frequently cutting off debate, he rarely allot-ted time for discussion on congressional issues.[55]

Two longtime carísta National Party deputies, Zepeda Durón, editor of La Época, and Rodolfo Velásquez, the party chieftain in Intibucá who would serve forty-nine years in congress, introduced the resolution for a new constituent assembly on January 4, 1936. Liberal Party members argued against the pro-posal, saying that the constitution limited the president to a fixed four-year term. There also were dissidents in the National Party on the issue, but their op-position was not serious. Former president Miguel Paz Barahona (1924–28), writing a letter for publication from his diplomatic post in Washington, doubted the legality of calling a constituent assembly to change the constitu-tion. He deplored the departure of his party from its traditional position reject-ing continuismo.[56] Three National Party deputies, Rómulo Carvajal, Mariano Bertrand Anduray, and Venancio Callejas, openly criticized the proposed change. They were summarily ousted from congress and sent into exile.[57]

53. Revista del Archivo, Vol. XII, No. 5 (1933): 308.

54. Krehm, Democracies and Tyrannies, 152.

55. Boletín Legislativo, 11 December 1946, 7, Biblioteca y Archivos Nacionales.

56. Copy of letter, Miguel Paz Barahona, Honduran Minister to the United States, February 1936, Notas, Library Roman Oquelí, Tegucigalpa.

57. Dispatch, U.S. legation, Tegucigalpa, to Department of State, 15 May 1936, 18 October 1935, National Archives, Record Group 59, 815.00/469.

Callejas later organized the Partido Nacional Legalista, and from Costa Rica opposed the Carías dictatorship. A fourth party dissident, José Funes from Cortés, stayed in Honduras and refused to leave the legislature. He stated he was "being faithful to the republic, carrying out [its] laws and faithful to that promise" and voted against amending the constitution. He got his final say, but it was his last vote. He was summarily ousted from office.[58]

On February 26, elections were held for the constituent assembly. No Liberals or dissident National Party members were elected. The new body consisted only of deputies who sat in the legislature.[59] By the end of March a new document was written. It would go into effect on April 15. Its basic provisions were the same as the one it revised, but there were some major changes, all suited to the Carías dictatorship and its plans for continuing his term and adding powers to the chief executive. Major changes included extending the president's and deputies' terms from four to six years. Congress could no longer censure a cabinet officer. The legislature was denied the right to decide the outcome of an election if no one received an absolute majority. The new constitution stipulated that if the legislature did not select a president within twenty days, the supreme court could do so (Act 101).[60]

Henceforth, by law, the national budget could not exceed the average income of the past five years by more than 5 percent, unless new levies were set. The congressional commission, which functioned as a legislative body when congress was not in session, was abolished. The secret, direct vote provided in the 1924 document was replaced with, "voting shall take place in a form under conditions prescribed by law" (article 28); women were denied citizenship and not given the vote (article 24).[61] Last, indicating the influence of the 1917 Mexican constitution, the state was given a new role and several additional powers; among them were sovereignty over the subsoil and waters from the twelve-mile limit of its territory. The state could impose regulations on the "use of private property" (articles 130, 152, 153) and utilize public lands for agricultural production.

58. Fonseca Zúñiga Guatama, *Cuatro ensayos sobre la realidad política de Honduras* (Tegucigalpa: Universidad Nacional Autonoma de Honduras, Editorial Universitaria, 1984), 61.

59. Ibid., 66.

60. Ibid., 61; [Constitution, 1936], National Archives, Record Group 57, Box 5495, 1930–1939, 815.011/31.

61. *La Época*, 19 March 1936, 3, editorialized that women as yet had not demonstrated political skills.

The new constitution was a curious blend of late-nineteenth-century lib-eralism calling for peace, internal order, and liberty within the law, and a more active, interventionist stance on economic issues. Drawing on the roots of Ibero-American centralism, the revised constitution recognized the powers of separate branches of government—executive, legislative, and judicial—but said they were to be subordinated to the "general will" determined and defined by the president. Ironically, when the National Party later published a history of its organization, it called Carías "a genuine Liberal."[62] This was only partially correct, as his 1936 constitution contained both the old principles of a turn-of-the-century Honduran Liberal Party and indications of a centralized, activist state designed in the modern era to deal with a broader constituency faced with a number of economic crises.

From now on, all jefes políticos of departments were required to distribute copies of Carías's legislative proposals to mayors of municipalities in their ju-risdiction. In turn, these mayors were to inform their constituents of the pro-gram's contents.[63] Carías, through his National Party organization, and public officeholders in all departments and municipalities fulfilled the designs of Paulino Valladares and others, who years before had urged a new Honduran state, centrist in the exercise of its constitutional authority and with a powerful chief executive.[64]

Security issues in the Western Hemisphere came to the fore after 1936. As war loomed in Europe, Carías declared his country's full cooperation with the United States. Noting Franklin Roosevelt's third victory in 1940, he made plans that year for extending his own term beyond 1943. He justified this move by stressing the need to continue maintaining internal peace and international co-operation with Washington.[65] La Época faithfully publicized "continuismo" again in 1939–40, again citing Roosevelt's 1940 victory: "one term is tradi-tional [in the United States] but in these times . . . the welfare of the people in Washington and here [in Honduras] requires continuance in office."[66] In 1940 the task for congress and its National Party deputies was simple; they merely

62. Abel Villacorta Cisneros, Reseña história del Partido Nacional de Honduras (Tegucigalpa: Im-prenta Nacional, 1966), 10.

63. La Época, 27 April 1936, 1.

64. La Época, 19 July 1939, 1.

65. Dispatch, U.S. legation, Tegucigalpa, to Department of State, 9 December 1941, Confiden-tial U.S. Diplomatic Post Records, reel 22, 985.

66. La Época, 27 April 1936, 1.

decreed in December that Carías would govern until 1949; they also gave him a new title, "benefactor and reformer of Honduras."[67]

Carías's Liberal rival, Zúñiga Huete, and his National Party critics, Venancio Callejas and Mariano Bertrand Anduray, remained in exile. A U.S. diplomat in Tegucigalpa, reflecting on the Carías era, spoke of Honduras as "a wonderful country . . . no volcanoes, no earthquakes, no tornados, no army, no navy, no revolutions, no elections, no communists, no labor unions, no wage or social security laws, no income tax—no doubts about whose [sic] boss."[68] Most would probably have agreed, some enthusiastically, others with resignation.

67. Dispatch, U.S. legation, Tegucigalpa, to Department of State, 8 and 12 November 1940, Confidential U.S. Diplomatic Post Records, reel 20, 978. See also El Cronista, 8 January 1936, 2, and La Época, 15 July 1939, 3.

68. Thomas M. Leonard, The United States in Central America, 1944–1949: Perceptions of Political Dynamics (Tuscaloosa: University of Alabama Press, 1984), 109.

7

Crisis Management and Reform

Always dressed in formal attire, a cutaway, Carías entered the chamber of deputies each December for fifteen years to give his annual message to congress. Called la buchona ("the big one"), he dominated the small assembly hall with his size. He was a dignified, patricianlike figure and stood stolidly before the microphone that broadcast his message. Dispassionately and resolutely he delivered his address, with its oft-repeated refrain of paz y orden ("peace and order"), declaring, "I am the incarnation of the nation's interest and well being."[1]

In a flat, monotone voice, Carías recited a litany of his government's accomplishments during the past year. He methodically and deliberately covered each ministry's tasks and goals achieved; roads and bridges constructed; schools, hospitals, medical clinics, and orphanages built; the rise in literacy; farmers receiving land; and towns obtaining water and electricity for the first time. All through his fifteen-year presidency, he pointedly emphasized the progress taking place due to the peace and order he gave the nation.

He spoke before assembled deputies and to listeners across the country through Radio Honduras Nacional. (He was the first chief executive to use this media to reach all parts of Honduras.) The figure who appeared before congress seemed vastly different from the homey, tieless country farmer in boots and floppy hat who often talked to peasants in Zambrano. But these contradictory personas reflected the essence of Tiburcio Carías. He was two people in one, a man of the city and town, a role none of his contemporaries or predecessors emulated. As president in Tegucigalpa, he extended the power of the central government to all parts of the country. The substance of his annual messages revealed his personality. Never an individual given to introspection, he devoted full attention to action, directing even the minute administrative affairs of government. He thrived on details, governing his state with a surgical indifference to emotions or feelings. He wanted to integrate this mountainous

1. Mensaje, Primera Parte, 1936, Biblioteca y Archivos Nacionales, 133.

country of villages, tied together almost entirely by dirt paths and unpaved roads, with its urban centers. His messages were also delivered in a fashion and style to gain the respect and support of his fellow citizens rather than winning their adulation and love.

The economic crisis facing Honduras in 1933, made worse after the outbreak of a revolt in 1931–32, contributed to Carías's rise to power. The president emphasized repeatedly that he symbolized the peace and order the country needed, which he said was the best hope for economic recovery. As a member of the legislature in 1930, he frequently referred in a complimentary way to the era of Liberal political leadership under Presidents Marco Aurelio Soto (1876–83), Luis Bográn (1883–90), and Policarpo Bonilla (1893–99), whose platforms all called for fiscal responsibility. These chief executives' agendas and Carías's in 1924, 1928, and 1933 were strikingly similar.

Among the similarities between them were creating a central bureaucratic administration, identifying territorial boundaries and effectively governing remote areas, building a police force, writing a constitution as a legal framework under which codes and laws would be faithfully adhered to, and establishing an effective public educational system with a curriculum that emphasized practical courses for employment. Carías reintroduced and updated President Luis Bográn's administrative structure, which gave the office of the president extensive accounting and budget authority. Carías wanted to show the continuity of his reforms with the work of his late-nineteenth-century predecessors by repeating his goal, "to promote a vigorous and active government intervention to direct society and initiate and maintain progress."[2] Carías's first address to congress in December 1933 was an exact replica of a speech he delivered in 1930, as president of the National Assembly. It referred to the need first to restore order and peace, then to address critical economic issues caused by unending civil strife.

Honduras had been experiencing a relatively peaceful era in the 1920s, until the Mejía Colindres administration (1928–1932) faced an outbreak of civil strife along with an accelerating economic and budget crisis made worse by a world depression. These conditions demonstrated that yet again a government could not keep order and manage its finances. As presiding officer of the congress in 1930, Carías had called for the creation of an economic plan to deal with the financial crisis—balancing the budget, cutting salaries, and reducing

2. *La Gaceta*, 28 February 1891, 8.

the number of government workers. He also urged the centralization of administration from the capital on down through municipalities. "Civil strife," Carías said in 1930, "totally disrupted our financing, forcing government to make expenditures that in other circumstances would have been unnecessary."[3] Each December from 1933 to 1948, in his end-of-the-year messages, President Carías would say that his mission was "to keep the peace and balance income with expenditures."[4]

The presidential addresses viewed over a period of time offer insights into the political makeup of this leader and the elements of his economic agenda. In his speeches he frequently referred to some of the founding fathers of Honduran liberalism, including Terencio Sierra (1899–1903) and Marco Aurelio Soto, and the contributions they made to the creation of the Honduran state. He praised them for their economic development plans, the roads they constructed, and their careful management of fiscal and financial matters.[5] He also lavished praise on the Liberal president of Central America, Francisco Morazán (1827–1830), a Honduran, about whom he wrote a testimonial for his regional state-building efforts.[6] Carías, once a Liberal Party member, referred to the collapse of this party and the failure of its leadership to continue the work of its founders, who unfortunately resorted to civil wars as a means to gain power and govern. As a token of his respect for these Liberal Party chieftains and their short-lived reforms, he constructed bridges, roads, and public buildings in their names. For example, the central plaza in Comayagua, outside the capital district was called Justo Rufino Barrios, after the nineteenth-century founder of Guatemalan liberalism.[7]

But during an "interregnum," as Carías called it, the period of almost constant strife from 1902 to 1933, Honduras stumbled from one political crisis to another with mounting economic problems under Liberal presidents.[8] In his 1933 message, Carías promised to end armed domestic conflicts and to man-

3. *Mensaje*, 5 December 1934, 14, 16.

4. *Mensaje*, 9 December 1947, 9.

5. Ibid.

6. *Homenaje del gobierno que preside el Doctor Tiburcio Carías al General Morazán*, in *Mensaje*, 5 December 1942, 237.

7. *La Época*, 5 June 1936, 1; 6 February 1937, 1.

8. *Mensaje, Segunda Parte, 1937–1945*, 5 December 1946, 5; Joseph Thompson, "An Economic Analysis of the Public Expenditure in Honduras, 1925–1963" (Ph.D. diss., University of Florida, 1968), 164.

age government more efficiently. In sum, he wanted his administration to re-store the nineteenth-century Liberal agenda of administrative reform and sound fiscal policies with an efficient, free, secular public educational system. But civil wars had forced administrations to direct whatever income they had for defense expenditures.[9] Revolutionary activity made it difficult to maintain sound public administration begun in the 1880s and 1890s.[10] By the 1920s, there were no central government budget procedures, not even within ministries. At the local level, district and municipal units had no means to determine income and expenditures.[11] Oftentimes governments lacked funds to meet even basic costs such as paying public officials' salaries. The deficit was due in large part to payments for destroyed property.[12] The Supreme Tribunal of Accounts, responsible for overseeing all government budget expenses, never monitored spending activities and had no idea how ministries actually handled their budgets.[13] In 1931 and 1932, projected budget allocations compared to incoming revenue was over-estimated by as much as 50 percent.[14]

Carías took steps to centralize budget operations for the first time in modern Honduran history. Never in the past had any serious effort been undertaken to review or supervise the state's fiscal operations. For all practical purposes, each ministry had its own "special treasurer" managing its financial matters. Presidents merely estimated budgets each year. It was precisely this dilemma that caused critics for decades to bemoan the lack of any efficient state machinery to give the government a responsible role in the way its economy was managed. Rightfully, they blamed fruit companies for their influence on the country's fiscal operations.[15] They also sharply criticized political figures who carelessly, and indifferently ignored the importance of centralized administration. The Casa Moneda ("Treasury House," established in the 1880s) was still closed in 1933 with a poignant and telling sign on its door that read, "Closed—the government has no funds to guard it."[16]

9. Thompson, "An Analysis of Public Expenditure," 164.

10. Ibid., 18.

11. Ibid., 5.

12. Ibid., 35–36.

13. Darío Euraque, "San Pedro Sula, la capital industrial de Honduras: su trayectoria entre Villorio Colonia y emporio bananero, 1536–1936," Mesoamerica, No. 26 (December 1993): 217–52.

14. Ibid.

15. Mensaje, December 1935, 60–61.

16. Informe, Ministerio de Fomento, Agricultura y Obras Públicas, 1921–23, 37.

Added to the inefficient and weak administrative infrastructure of the state, and inextricably linked to it, was the preponderant influence of the banana industry. By the 1920s, Honduras was the world's largest exporter, its gross domestic product reaching 90 percent of the country's exports by 1933. Seventy-five percent of the country's banana lands were held by United Fruit or Standard Fruit and Steamship Company. Since the turn of the century, and accelerating into the 1920s, vast tracts of land had been given to these Yankee enterprises in exchange for building railroads. Concessions were also granted for free importation of materials to construct and maintain these track lines. Close to 65 percent of these lands were actually acquired between 1910 and 1920. As concessionary contracts were negotiated and signed by the country's chief executives and authorized by congress, Honduras became more dependent on world prices for bananas. Just as critical, the government had to wait and see what fruit companies planned to do from year to year on production planning. In 1930–31, as fruit prices began to fall, companies began to cut wages and lay off large numbers of workers.[17]

Overall, the value of imports started to fall in 1932 as the world depression widened. The price of needed imports dropped along with customs duties. At one point, when the Honduran government ended the sale of public sector lands, United and Standard Fruit stopped making investment plans entirely.[18] Earlier, in 1927, Standard reported profits of $250,000 to $500,000 after taxes and depreciation on equipment. In 1930, profits fell to $10,000, forcing a draconian reduction in the work force and banana production.[19] Twenty-eight thousand stems were exported in 1930, dropping to 12,000 by 1935.[20]

The dominant role fruit companies played in the Honduran export economy reflected their powerful influence in all governments regardless of party affiliation since the turn of the century. A U.S. legation report from Honduras bluntly stated that "no fruit company . . . ever exercised a more powerful influence and control on a Honduran government (with the possible exception of the government of Manual Bonilla [1912–13], created out of a revolution aided by Cuyamel [Fruit Company], than does the company [United Fruit] on the

---

17. Leslie Bethel, ed., *History of Latin America since 1930: Mexico, Central America, and the Caribbean* (Cambridge: Cambridge University Press, 1990), 7:196–97.

18. Ibid.

19. Thomas Karnes, *Tropical Enterprise: Standard Fruit and Steamship Company in Latin America* (Baton Rouge: Louisiana State University Press, 1978), 183.

20. Memo, Department of State, National Archives, Record Group 59, 815.00/3223.

government of President Carías."[21] Oftentimes banana enterprises competed amongst themselves for land and railroad concessions by supporting one side or another in the fratricidal civil wars plaguing the country. Carías was consistently viewed as sympathetic to United's economic interests. His political rise from the 1920s on was based on the financial backing of the company. Most of his cabinet members in 1933 had worked for United Fruit. In fact, many in the National Party hierarchy were on the company's payroll. For example, President Miguel Paz Barahona (1924–28), a medical doctor by profession, had drug store concessions all along the north coast, all tied to United Fruit's enterprises. Plutarco Muñoz, president of the congress, and Juan Manuel Gálvez, minister of war under Carías, were lawyers for United.[22]

Fruit companies literally financed the operations of government itself. Probably the first instance of this took place when President Francisco Bertrand (1911–12, 1913–15, 1916–19) turned to the banana companies, not international financial institutions, to finance his administration's budget operations. He received $50,000 from Samuel Zemurray's Cuyamel and from Standard Fruit's Banco de Atlántida. The loans' provisions were simple and straightforward. Atlántida would open an account of 200,000 pesos silver at 6 percent for one year. The bank in addition would lend Bertrand's government 500,000 pesos silver at 7 percent using income from La Ceiba's custom house as guarantee for the loan.[23]

During the 1920s, Carías had close ties to the United Fruit Company, known in Honduras as *el pulpo* ("the octopus"). Rafael López Padilla (1875–1962), a banana grower, was a business associate of Samuel Zemurray, president of Cuyamel Fruit Company (and later head of United). Padilla had lost land to United in the Department of Colón in 1932. Writing to his friend Zemurray in 1934, he recalled their earlier association when Zemurray had fought hard to keep United from monopolizing the north coast banana industry. Padilla noted the company's enormous influence, immorality, and rapaciousness. He also recalled that he and Zemurray had both feared in the 1920s that if Tiburcio Carías, United's friend, ever reached the presidency, "would not the octopus in fact, control the Honduran state?"[24]

21. Argueta, *Tiburcio Carías*, 296.

22. *Sufragio Libre*, 28 July 1923, 4, offers a brief biographical sketch of Barahona and his campaign style.

23. Karnes, *Tropical Enterprise*, 75.

24. Rafael López Padilla, San Pedro Sula, to Samuel Zemurray, Boston, 24 October 1934. Padilla, a longtime adviser of Zemurray, had lost land to the United Fruit Company in the Declaration of Colima in 1932; Euraque, "San Pedro Sula," n. 76.

A substantial amount of evidence links Carías with United's interests over the years. For example, Cuyamel's manager, Joseph Montgomery, told the U.S. minister that his enterprise supported General Vicente Tosta, a contender for the presidency in 1924, giving him $25,000 to buy arms. United, he said, financially backed Carías.[25] In the same period, Cuyamel wanted to extend its railroad lines in San Pedro Sula and other areas in the north near its banana plantations. In violation of an earlier concession, it wanted the track to be built within 40 kilometers on either side of the national railroad. Carías successfully blocked the concessions.[26] In 1925, Venacio Callejas, a Carías rival in the National Party and a member of congress, wanted to raise export duties to 30 percent for bananas shipped out of Honduras by United. Although the decree was passed, Carías again sided with United Fruit and opposed the higher import duties.[27]

When civil war erupted in 1931, Carías, then a presidential candidate, supported the incumbent Liberal president Mejía Colindres. The National Party standard bearer wanted to ensure a peaceful transfer of power in the 1932 elections if he won. Consequently, United Fruit gave Mejía Colindres $50,000 to buy arms for Carías's use.[28] In 1933, shortly before Carías took office, "the octopus" gave the president-elect an additional $25,000 to pay military personnel who were loyal to him in defending the besieged regime from Liberal dissidents. Two years later, in 1934, United gave Carías $75,000 to buy three airplanes.[29] Other examples abound showing Carías's sympathy for United Fruit and its operations.

Standard Fruit Company's influence was displayed more discreetly than that of its rival United. While it made cash payments to revolutionary groups and government sympathetic to its interests, its resources were considerably smaller. Yet Standard owned Banco de Atlántida. It therefore had considerable clout when negotiating contracts with governments. In 1920, Honduras owed $1,711,500, a third of that lent by Standard's bank. These funds actually kept the central government functioning.[30] A year later, President Rafael López Gutiérrez asked for $375,000 from Banco Atlántida; in return, Stan-

25. Argueta, Tiburcio Carías, 240–41.

26. Ibid., 245; Memo, Department of State, 10 October 1924, National Archives, Record Group 59, 815.00/3508.

27. Argueta, Tiburcio Carías, 253.

28. Ibid., 254.

29. Dispatch, U.S. legation, Tegucigalpa, to Department of State, 16 July 1934, Confidential U.S. Diplomatic Post Records, reel 7, 5464.

30. Ibid., 77.

dard could operate the customs houses of north coast towns at La Ceiba, Trujillo, and Tela.[31] An additional $225,000 was borrowed from United Fruit in 1922.[32] However, it was United Fruit that provided Carías with the largesse he needed to balance his budgets—bringing expenditures in line with income and purchase military hardware. United reaped benefits too from this relationship.

Shortly after taking office Carías announced that his government would recognize all debts incurred by his predecessors. This earned him the gratitude of both Standard and United.[33] The former had recently loaned the Mejía Colindres government $250,000. Repayment typically was made by deducting customs collections from Standard's imported material for banana operations. Carías paid off this debt by 1936.[34] In addition, he negotiated a $300,000 loan from the New Orleans Canal Bank and Trust Company. President Mejía Colindres had stated in the fall of 1932 that he had no idea what the country's income was or an estimated figure on forthcoming expenditures. Consequently, Carías's first concern was resolving a grave financial crisis. The $300,000 presumably was a start. He gained the confidence and trust of the banana companies by demonstrating his capacity to control most of the country's militias and by promising to honor previous debts. United became the trustee and agent for the amount guaranteeing payment. In return, Carías promised no increase in customs duties or taxes on the company until 1943.[35] The $300,000 was further secured by allowing United to collect customs receipts at the northern ports of Puerto Cortés, Tela, and Puerto Castilla. United would guarantee, collect, and make the loan repayments.[36]

Favors poured forth from the Carías regime. In April of the same year, the Trujillo Railroad, a subsidiary of United, was allowed to build rail lines and a bridge across the Ulua River. In exchange for returning unused land to the government, the company would build a railroad from the north coast port of

31. Ibid., 78; Euraque, "Industrialists and Merchants," 269.

32. Euraque, "Industrialists and Merchants," 163.

33. Carías recognized all the debt obligations of his predecessors.

34. Karnes, Tropical Enterprise, 183.

35. "General Conditions, February–March 1933," U.S. legation, Tegucigalpa, to Department of State, Confidential U.S. Diplomatic Post Records, Honduras 1930–1945, n.d., file 815.00/615, Record Group 59, 17; Argueta, Tiburcio Carías, 263–64.

36. U.S. legation, Tegucigalpa, to Department of State, 1933, Confidential U.S. Diplomatic Post Records, reel 38, 874–84.

Trujillo to Juticalpa and a line to Tegucigalpa. Later that same year, the Carías-controlled congress relieved the Trujillo Railroad from its obligation to build track from Juticalpa to Tegucigalpa.[37] The U.S. minister, shocked at the benefits acquired by United, was flabbergasted by the swiftness of the debt's approval. "The United Fruit Company," he said, "probably never had a Honduran congress more acquiescent in its [United's] desires."[38]

Loans from United continued at a rapid pace. They came in small amounts, but several were substantial, including one in 1936 for $200,000, $75,000 of which was to go for "opening congress." The remaining $125,000 was for "emergency purposes." In fact, it went to pay back governmental employee salaries.[39] Again in 1937, United provided Carías with $105,000 against payments due it (by January 1938).[40] Between 1936 and 1938 United Fruit loaned the Carías government $875,000.[41] On one occasion, in September 1937, the U.S. minister to Honduras along with Minister of War Juan Manuel Gálvez and Finance Minister Julio Lozano met Walter Turnbull, United's manager, regarding a $100,000–$150,000 loan needed by the Carías government. Turnbull said he would report the request to company officials in New Orleans but expected them to wait until the president made an official report on the country's revenue and expenses.[42] A detailed account of the regime's fiscal situation was presented in December as anticipated. A $200,000 loan, substantially larger than requested, was made in the spring of 1938.[43] The financial loan arrangement was typical in the manner it was set by the Honduran government, a pattern begun in the first decade of the twentieth century. Deficits were bolstered by banana company beneficence. Noticeable,

37. U.S. legation, Tegucigalpa, to Department of State, 28 April 1933, Confidential U.S. Diplomatic Post Records, reel 7, 218.

38. Dispatch, U.S. legation, Tegucigalpa, to Department of State, 22 April 1933, National Archives, Record Group 59, 815.032/1229, 2.

39. Dispatch, U.S. legation, Tegucigalpa, to Department of State, National Archives, 31 July 1936, Record Group 59, file 815.00/4711, Record Group 59, 2.

40. Dispatch, U.S. legation, Tegucigalpa, to Department of State, 2 April 1937, Confidential U.S. Diplomatic Post Records, reel 14, 298.

41. Euraque, "Industrialists and Merchants," 238; Dispatch, U.S. minister John Erwin, Tegucigalpa, to Department of State, 9 December 1938, National Archives, Record Group 59, 815.51/953.

42. Dispatch, U.S. legation, Tegucigalpa, to Department of State, 24 September 1937, National Archives, Record Group 59, 815.00/19.

43. Dispatch, U.S. legation, Tegucigalpa, to Department of State, 16 April 1938, National Archives, Record Group 59, 815.00/253.

however, was the speed with which money flowed from United Fruit to Carías. The longstanding relationship between the two was an important factor in making these cash subsidies possible. There were more telling reasons by the 1930s.

The country's deepening economic crisis in 1933 was caused largely by the precipitous and continuing drop in world prices on banana exports. In 1943 banana production was a mere 10 percent of what it had been in 1929–30. In his first message to congress, and repeatedly afterward, the president said that his chief concern was the income and expenditures of the government, as well as the status of its internal and external credit.[44] The president tackled the economic crisis from a revenue and expenditure approach. He began with cuts in government salaries by 20 percent. At the same time, cash from the New Orleans Canal Bank and Trust loan of $300,000 gave him funds to meet basic expenses in the first year of his administration.[45]

In 1934 he introduced exchange controls and appointed a commission composed of representatives from the commercial sector to oversee foreign exchange supplies.[46] Congress enacted a new tariff to regulate duties on imports more closely and effectively The tariff was also designed to protect small domestic production from competitive imports.[47] The following year Honduras negotiated a reciprocal trade agreement with the United States. It removed all the protections the 1934 tariff bill had enacted. The government willingly made tariff concessions in the negotiations in order to get Washington's approval for constitutional changes that would give Carías vast powers and extend his term in 1936. In any case, the agreement accepted more import competition against local manufacturing and considerably reduced import revenue.[48] The plain truth of the matter was that factory workers were of no significance either in numbers or as union organizers all through the Carías era. No more than 1,500 people were employed in manufacturing-related jobs in any major city except Tegucigalpa in the late 1940s. Cumulatively, between 1935 and 1950, factory-based manufacturing in the country's major cities never exceeded more than

44. Ibid.

45. *Boletín del Congreso Nacional Legislativo,* 1934–1936, 4 April 1934, no. 19, 10.

46. Euraque, "Industrialists and Merchants," 229, 245.

47. Ibid., 241–42, 245–46.

48. *Memoria,* Ministerio de Hacienda, 1938–1939, Archivo, Palacio de los Ministerios, Tegucigalpa, 3.

4,000 per year. A minimum wage (1967) and labor code (1959) would not be enacted until the well after the president left office.[49]

Honduras was the only country in Central America not to default on its foreign debt in the 1930s. The domestic debt was another matter, however. Carías tried to reduce it by giving creditors only 7 percent in cash at the face value of their bonds. However, borrowing funds to pay public employees actually increased indebtedness through 1937. From then on, the government had a fiscal balance in its revenue and expenditures.

Always the fiscal conservative, Carías each year began his annual report on finances to congress with the words, "Unfortunately we lament the budget deficit in our finances but it has not increased as it did last year." He explored ways to increase revenue by supervising more closely the state rum monopoly, which had usually provided anywhere from 10 percent to 15 percent of revenue (as it did in 1923–24 and 1932–33). By 1933 the state-operated rum concessions accounted for as much as 85 percent to 95 percent of the monopoly enterprise.[50] There were wide fluctuations from the rum industry earnings. After 1943 it produced sizable revenue for the government. Efforts to increase production in tobacco, corn, rice, wheat, and wool, and even trade with El Salvador from the western department of Intibucá, achieved only marginal results.[51]

Efforts to curtail smuggling were assisted by United Fruit Company launches, which proved somewhat helpful in stopping the illegal importation of arms, opium, liquor, and other merchandise. A lingering crisis in the export sector overshadowed any real hope for economic recovery well into 1937. The collapse of foreign exchange earnings due to a drop in banana prices, crop disease, and hurricanes forced Carías to reduce imports sharply. This meant a radical decline in government revenues from taxes on its external trade. These administrative reforms were undertaken immediately after Carías took office.[52]

All special treasury accounts, the finance offices in each ministry, were merged under the Office of General Treasury of Justice and Roads. The special

---

49. Euraque, "Industrialists and Merchants," 310–12; U.S. Embassy, "Military Intelligence Report," 15 April 1944, Confidential U.S. Diplomatic Post Records, reel 39, 53; 22 December 1944, reel 39, 66.

50. Euraque, "Industrialists and Merchants," 242.

51. La Época, 19 July 1937, 1.

52. Dispatch, U.S. legation, Tegucigalpa, to Department of State, 21 February 1936, Confidential U.S. Diplomatic Post Records, reel 12.

treasuries had channeled funds directly to "development boards," which in turn funded projects as established by a municipality. Actually these boards became nothing but spoils-distribution centers in exchange for favors rendered in presidential and congressional elections. Carías abolished the development boards in 1933 as part of his administrative budget reforms.[53]

The Supreme Tribunal of Accounts was revived, though it never actually performed its statutory function. The tribunal was created by the constitution of 1894 to approve or disapprove executive expenditures. It was also to present a post-government audit to congress. The entity was to be independent of any direct control by the chief executive or the legislature. In reality, though, it was supposed to be a check on the executive.[54] In 1930, when Carías was elected a deputy from Tegucigalpa and president of congress shortly thereafter, he initiated a move to activate the functions of the tribunal. In an effort to check the financial management of the government headed by the Liberal president Mejía Colindres, the National Party leader gave it some statutory authority. Specifically, it was authorized to examine, approve, or reject the financial accounts (budgets) of all offices in the administration. It could also sanction, or not, executive expenditures. Until Carías became chief executive, the tribunal never really had a defined status in relation to congress or the presidents. The body never met during the Mejía Colindres presidency because National Party members appointed to it constantly feuded with the chief executive.[55]

Soon after taking office in 1933, Carías staffed the tribunal with eight accountants, considered "specialists," but who were also National Party loyalists. The congress continued to select its members. Ostensibly the president wanted it to operate as originally envisioned, as an agency independent of congressional and executive meddling—providing post-audit reports on government expenditures. But with a pliable, National Party–dominated legislature, the tribunal oversaw budget operations and rubber-stamped Carías's budget directives in all ministries. Under the president's close supervision and strict fiscal management, it decided how revenue receipts would be allocated to the various government departments throughout the country. The chief executive in effect kept expenditure levels the same from 1933 to 1943. He also concluded his fiscal reform by establishing an "office of central accounts" where former sections of income and expenditures in ministries were removed and placed under his supervision.

53. Euraque, "Industrialists and Merchants," 239.
54. El Demócrata, 19 January 1938, 2. See also Tegucigalpa, 9 July 1927.
55. Ibid.

Municipal reorganization was another step in conjunction with Carías's fiscal and budget reforms, but it also had political significance. The undertaking was designed to make local government more efficient in the allocation of spending and revenue collection. More importantly, municipal administrative reforms were designed to extend the power of the central state. Historically, municipalities were the basic units of local representative government. Yet they never truly developed as autonomous entities. Personalism and caudillo politics had consistently dominated public affairs from the seat of presidential power to the smallest aldea (town). Law did not coexist with political reality. The legal tradition of centralism grew as the dictates of a chief executive were faithfully followed. By 1936, the president dictated the selection of candidates from municipal offices and congress.

Before the enactment of municipal reform in 1940, the country was governed through fourteen departments. Districts under them were composed of two or more municipalities. By law, the minister of government had jurisdiction over these districts and the municipalities within them. In time, departmental governors loyal to the president exercised considerable power over these districts. Often these governors appointed individuals to council seats in the municipalities who came from different parties. Yet constant civil wars in the early twentieth century contributed to the development of truly autonomous, even totally independent municipalities throughout the country. Presidents rarely controlled their fiscal operations.

Carlos Izaguirre in his book *Redaptaciones y cambios* (Readaptations and Changes) called for major reform in the administration of the municipalities. He urged the abolition of municipal government in favor of superintendents appointed by the president. He also proposed that the positions of comandante de armas and jefe político be fused into one post to be named by the chief executive. Izaguirre's proposals were aimed at creating an efficiently run administrative structure for Honduras. "Development" to him meant managing and properly handling revenue and expenditures at all levels of government. This had never been done. As a member of congress in 1937, he introduced a plan for administrative-municipal reform. It was an exact replica of the Carías plan to make a more efficient state at all levels, and enhance his power.[56]

After 1935, Carías gradually exerted his influence over municipal governments. As the National Party gained a monopoly of power, the president was

56. *Tegucigalpa*, 11 January 1937, 2.

able to enforce his policies more effectively and directly through departments, districts, and municipal governments. Municipalities traditionally had their own budgets and negotiated loans with entrepreneurs and banana companies. For example, in May 1934, the municipality of Cantarranas in the department of Francisco Morazán negotiated a loan with the New York and Honduras Mining Company for 20,000 lempiras to meet "operational expenses."[57]

By the mid-1930s, Carías was distributing the basic outlines of his economic program in all parts of the country. Department governors—National Party members and Carías loyalists—were required to provide government circulars to mayors of all municipalities in districts under their department. In turn, mayors of cities were obliged to explain the details of the president's programs to the public. By 1938, town magistrates were frequently asking the president directly for financial assistance, namely for funds to meet local operational expenses.[58] This practice indicated the extent to which the National Party was effectively organized rather than the efficient operation of a public administrative system. Caudillo politics and a patronage system functioned smoothly.

The economic depression of the 1930s hit local governments hard. Deep in debt, they could not administer their fiscal affairs effectively. At the president's behest, Carlos Sanabria, comandante de armas of the Department of Colón, called for a meeting of all mayors within his jurisdiction to work out a plan for cooperation on several issues, including development of a rural credit bank and an economic development board comprised of representatives of each municipality. The board's purpose was to make plans for centralizing finances, initiate road construction, and create an economic strategy for developing Colón's resources.[59]

The 1936 constitution did not include provisions for municipal reform. It gave the chief executive minor functions vaguely referred to as "promoting economic development, undertaking a census from time to time and ending vagrancy."[60] But the government newspaper La Época editorialized the effective way President Jorge Ubico of Guatemala (1931–44) and Maximiliano Hernández of El Salvador (1932–44) ably handled their countries' economic crises and

57. "Notas Varias, January 1934," Ministerio de Fomento, Sección Agricola y Trabajo, 18 January 1934, 156, Biblioteca y Archivos Nacionales.

58. Ibid., 166.

59. La Época, 7 October 1936, 1.

60. La Época, 31 October 1936, 3.

financial woes by administrative centralization that abolished municipalities altogether.[61] It was an attempt to justify Carías's steps in this direction.

By late 1937–early 1938, Carías, now in his extended term and going beyond the 1936 constitution's restraints, was taking over municipal government operations on fiscal matters like Ubico and Hernández had done. Since separate ministerial treasury agents were consolidated into one office under the Finance Ministry, local treasury officials looked to the central government for assistance to build roads, schools, and other new construction projects, as well as to pay salaries. For the first time in the nation's history, Carías was including "municipal revenue and expenditure" figures in his Ministry of Government's annual reports.[62] Similarly, as mentioned earlier, this newfound executive administrative authority was based on the effective National Party organization, which had reached down to the municipal, even alcalde, level by 1937. Carías's party was electing majority seats in municipal councils as well.[63]

The first steps toward administrative centralization, ending all local authority, began in 1938 with the creation of the central district. Carlos Izaguirre proposed it, obviously reflecting Carías's wishes.[64] Tegucigalpa and Comayaguela were administratively combined on March 15, the president's birthday. Tomás Quiñonez, former mayor of the capital and a member of congress, was appointed as the municipality's first magistrate presiding over a council of four people. Article 179 of the 1936 constitution had to be amended to give Carías appointive powers, canceling the electoral process.[65] A public drinking water system was installed, and in the new central district streets were paved for the first time. Books, pamphlets, and signs appeared praising Carías for creating the "most modern metropolis" in Central America. "Paving a city creates a civilization," said one; "like Rome, when one takes a walk on Avenida Paz Barahona [in Tegucigalpa], it is like walking the Unterden Linden, Paris or Brooklyn."[66]

Two years later, in 1940, Carías ended municipal government autonomy in many cities. He substituted directly appointed, local, salaried officials for the traditionally elected municipal and department councils in the country's most im-

61. La Época, 30 January 1936, 3.
62. Informe, 1937–1938, Ministerio de Gobernación, 8–9.
63. La Época, 21 January 1937, 1.
64. Carlos Izaguirre, "El distrito central," Tegucigalpa, 12 December 1937, 1.
65. Ibid.
66. Ibid.

portant urban centers.[67] Powers of departmental governors would therefore be sharply reduced. Through his vice-president, Abraham Williams, who
was also minister of government, Carías would administer directly municipalities that were once under their departmental jurisdictions. The newly appointed
municipal councils would henceforth name mayors for towns located in their
municipalities. By 1940 Carías was personally deciding all budget disburse-
ments, allocating expenditures, and supervising taxes at all government levels.[68]

The once-autonomous municipal functions, particularly fiscal matters
such as budget allocations and taxation, would be overseen by "inspectors" appointed by the minister of government. As expected, municipal authorities, of
course Carías partisans, cheered the measure. The municipal council in San Pedro Sula celebrated the move by constructing a "Boulevard Carías." It also
erected a bust of the president in front of the government palace that stood until 1958, ten years after Carías left office.[69]

The president's municipal reorganization included the Bay Islands of Roatan, Guanaja, and Utilia off the north coast. They had been ceded formally to
Honduras by the British in 1859. The islands, largely populated by blacks,
whites, and mestizos, engaged in self-sufficient agriculture, fishing, and shipping. By tradition, the governor of the Bay Islands was from the area. Carías recalled that when he was governor of the Department of Cortés, their interests
were far more a part of the Caribbean with economic ties to the United States
and Belize than with Honduran development.[70]

Under his policy of direct administration from Tegucigalpa, the islands
would have one council under government-appointed "inspectors" to oversee
finances. The president required, among other things, that schoolteachers be
bilingual (English and Spanish). Typically, as in other areas, he extended his
control by building an airstrip, to be used exclusively by his chartered pilots,
and a government house on Roatan Island.[71] In 1937, for the first time, the
Honduran flag was displayed on all government buildings and the "National

---

67. *Informe, 1940–1941*, Ministerio de Gobernación, 3.

68. Euraque, "Industrialists and Merchants," 222; and *Libro de actas del Congreso de distrito departa-
mental de Trujillo*, 1941, 2 January 1941, Archivos del Departamento de Colón. The council received
the first direct instructions on the management and regulation of its finances from the Ministry of
Government.

69. *La Época*, "Edición Extraordinária," 7 January 1937, 1.

70. Ibid., 89.

71. *La Época*, 19 November 1936, 3.

Hymn to Peace" sung in schools each day.[72] The objective, Carías said, was to make them "culturally Spanish, and Catholic, as well as English speaking and Protestant."[73] Standard and United Fruit Companies were instrumental in helping Carías take direct control of the islands, building an airstrip on Roatan, and transporting supplies for a militia and equipment for road construction.[74]

Governors of departments where municipalities were now administered directly from Tegucigalpa made regular publicized visits to cities in their jurisdictions examining their management. During these sojourns the local chief executives effusively praised Carías's leadership, attesting to his complete control of all local governments.[75]

Beneath the surface of public expressions of praise to Carías was a profound change in the relationship between the president and local political leaders. Now under municipal reorganization, councils of Carías appointees were exercising more influence than the departmental governors, many of them old political allies of the president. For example, the municipal council of La Ceiba in 1941 consisted of merchants, physicians, and professionals, often with ties to the banana companies—a more diverse group than the appointed pals of a local leader had been. Both the governor and the military commander of Colón chafed under the "independence" of these new councils. For example, Miguel Moncada, a customs administrator and Carías's appointee as La Ceiba's "city manager," paid no attention to the directives of General Justo Rufino Solís, the comandante de armas there. In fact, Solís even tried to discredit Moncada by accusing him of being pro-German in 1941.[76]

U.S. vice-consuls in La Ceiba all through the 1940s reported the municipal council's competent, efficient, and honest management of the city's finances. They observed that a general lack of interest in politics contributed to the overall improvement in the economy, an activity more to their interests than national politics.[77] Carías had created a new economic-political force in munici-

72. La Época, 13 May 1935, 1, 4.

73. La Época, 7 January 1937, 1.

74. Acuerdos, 27 February; 9 May; 24 May 1939, no. 444, Oficina del Oficial Mayor, Ministerio de Guerra, Marina, y Aviación, Archivo, Palacio de los Ministerios.

75. El Cronista, 4 January 1939, 1.

76. "Political Report," U.S. consul, La Ceiba, to U.S. legation, Tegucigalpa, n.d., Confidential U.S. Diplomatic Post Records, reel 24, 2–3.

77. U.S. consul, La Ceiba, to U.S. legation, Tegucigalpa, 20 September 1943, Confidential U.S. Diplomatic Post Records, reel 32, 42; 24 January 1941, reel 24, 311.

palities, fostering local competition between military commanders, governors, and municipal chiefs.

In February 1939, in an innovative step, congress initiated a long-term "Plan for National Reconstruction." Julio Lozano Díaz, minister of hacienda and public credit, and the Carías government's financial wizard, was the proposal's chief architect. The states' financial and fiscal structures were to be studied with recommendations for reforms made by foreign advisers. Basically, it was a blueprint for agricultural-industrial growth to promote economic development. A part of the plan was devoted to ways the country's land could be better utilized for greater production.[78]

Carías was not interested in the social and economic conditions of campesinos (farmers) or laborers in cities and on banana plantations. First and foremost, as in all matters, he wanted order established and peace maintained in the countryside. "We must protect agriculture and people must work to protect it," he said, adding, "we will combat indolence and punish loafers."[79] His views on labor were paternalistic.

Honduras had very liberal and progressive land laws on paper. But the reality was quite different. In 1829, soon after independence, a decree provided for the sale of former crown property. Sales were limited to twenty units per purchaser. Perfunctory efforts were made in the nineteenth century to prohibit land grabs by individuals. In 1835, a law took into account the plight of people who were not able to purchase land and a statute was passed a year later to make it easier for people to buy it. People were supposed to receive plots free from the government ostensibly to create cooperative farming communities (*ejidos*). Later, in 1888, 1898, and 1902, rural communities were granted land if they needed it, but few did. A 1924 agrarian law allowed donations of 50-acre family plots free of charge and exempt from municipal taxes but, again, was not enforced.[80]

When Carías issued a decree in 1935 creating a rural colonization plan offering 50-acre plots at no charge, the government offered to supply animals, tools, seeds, and other supplies for farmers to begin crop production. In addition, a person could rent national land from 5 to 20 cents per acre per year. Limitations were imposed on the size of land holdings, allowing only 250 acres a person for

78. El Economista Hondureño, 2 February 1939, 42–43; and La Época, 1 February 1939, 3.

79. La Época, 6 July 1933, 1.

80. La Gaceta, Decreto, no. 34, 8620; La Época, 19 August 1938, 1. See also William Stokes, "The Land Laws of Honduras," *Agricultural History*, Vol. 3 (1947): 148–54.

agriculture and 1,000 acres for cattle. For a time, there was no undue pressure to own large tracts of property, no effort to push campesinos off the land to enhance the production of a cash export crop like coffee. Since Honduras was a country of excess land in relation to the size of its population, labor unrest and clashes between landless farmers and landowners were rare. Yet when they did occur, Carías's views of workers' rights were clear and unequivocal.

He had no interest in legislation improving the lot of banana workers. His main preoccupation was putting down intermittent strikes on United and Standard Fruit plantations. When Manuel Calix Herrera, one of the country's earliest labor leaders, organized a "syndical" league for banana workers in 1932, he attacked both National and Liberal Parties as bourgeoisie with no interests in the worker. His program was radical, calling for revision of all concessions granted to fruit companies, reclaiming the railroads they built, and returning lands sold or leased to them. Moreover, he demanded increased wages for workers and unemployment relief with social insurance.[81] Carías's response to Herrera's plan was to urge workers not to adhere to disruptive propaganda that called for economic and social upheaval.[82] The syndical league was never organized, as Herrera was arrested and imprisoned. He suffered from tuberculosis in prison and died in Juticalpa, Olancho, in July 1939.[83]

In 1942, the U.S. War Shipping Board ordered banana companies to stop their east coast operations from Puerto Cabezas, Nicaragua, north to La Ceiba, Honduras, as a precaution against German U-boat attacks. This meant a sharp drop in employment, from 7,000 down to 4,000 workers around La Ceiba alone that year. Efforts to strike and prevent layoffs proved useless. Carías was able to quell the unrest with, in his words, "the generous cooperation of the United States and the fruit companies."[84]

Carías's principal interest in agrarian affairs was exclusively in education on crop experimentation and production, not the social and economic issues affecting small farmers and landless campesinos.[85] A basic textbook, *Elements*

81. Dispatch, U.S. legation, Tegucigalpa, to Department of State, 11 June 1932, Confidential U.S. Diplomatic Post Records, reel 4, 966.

82. *Mensaje*, 5 December 1936, 116.

83. Rina Villars, *Porque quiero seguir viviendo habla Graciela García* (Tegucigalpa: Editorial Guaymuras, 1991), 337.

84. *Mensaje*, 5 December 1944, 235–236.

85. *Informe, Ministerio de Fomento, Agricultura, Trabajo y Comercio*, 1936–1937, 52–55, Archivo, Palacio de los Ministerios.

of Agriculture, written by Emilio Pinel, a well-known agronomist who focused on ways to cultivate certain plants and how to grow them, was based entirely on research done at Carías's farm in Zambrano.[86] Agrarian subjects and issues were left exclusively to the academic and research interests of the regime. For example, in 1937, the government purchased a 2,800-acre estate from Arturo Fortín in Zamorano for 45,000 lempiras ($45,000). The land was located some 30 kilometers east of Tegucigalpa. Samuel Zemurray of United Fruit Company put up $500,000 for the construction and maintenance of a private, autonomous national agriculture school, now called the Pan American School for Agriculture, as a "hands-on educational experience." The hacienda already had a substantial number of buildings, hydroelectric power, and good land for crop production. It also had a good water supply, an excellent climate, and an ideal site near Tegucigalpa. The school opened its doors in 1941 and graduated its first class of 155 students in 1946.[87]

In 1944, with the help of the Inter-American Institute for Agricultural Affairs, three centers were opened for crop experimentation and production in Comayagua, Danlí (south), and one in Toncontin outside the capital for the training of future teachers in regional schools. These were smaller and less demanding academically than the Pan-American Agricultural School in Zamorano. The regional centers specialized in rice, bean, corn, and sugarcane production, all for export. They also taught farmers grain production, cattle raising, and how to operate wool plantations.[88]

For Carías, reform and reconstruction of the country meant institutional changes that would make central government more efficient. Interest groups were effective and important only insofar as they reflected his will. Recovery came gradually after 1937, but it did not mean the transformation of Honduran society or raising people's standard of living. It was never the president's intention to mobilize new economic and social groups and make them participants in the political process. His main goal was the establishment of domestic peace and an orderly administration that made things work.

Actually, Carías's daily and meticulous attention to revenue expenditure supervision and hiring people with accounting experience made a notable difference in the way government managed its finances. Urbano Quesada, the in-

86. *La Época*, 21 July 1939, 1.

87. *Revista Tegucigalpa*, 10 February 1942, 1.

88. *Mensaje*, 5 December 1944, 287. See also *Informe, Ministerio de Fomento, Agricultura, y Trabajo*, 1945–1946, 92–95.

spector general of finances for the Office of Accounts and Public Credit in the Ministry of Hacienda, worked directly with the president. Fluent in English, he had lived in the United States for years. He had no political interests, no allies or enemies in the country's political landscape. The inspector gave his full effort to overseeing budgets in each ministry. Without fanfare, Quesada gave an account of his stewardship in 1947, near the end of Carías's term, reporting that surpluses could be shown in the area of general government income, public credit, and commerce.[89] In the same year, salaries and pensions of public employees were paid. "There is," he said proudly, in his typically understated fashion, "a favorable margin in the treasury."[90] Overall, the inspector general's positive report was correct, as economic recovery was clearly evident by the mid-1940s. For example, production and the diversification of new export crops increased, including fruits, vegetables, expanding forestry for lumber and wood products, and cotton. The United and Standard Fruit Companies also converted several of their banana plantations to the production of rubber, basil, fat oils, hides, and medicinal herbs.[91] There was even a boom in gold and foreign exchange reserves, allowing the government to reduce its old public debt faster than it contracted new ones.[92] Income from state monopolies such as aguardiente and rum reached 33.5 percent of total government income.[93] Coffee production became a new foreign exchange earner in the mid-1940s after Honduras signed a coffee agreement (1940) to compensate for the loss of exports to German markets. Actually, other Central American states also were given quotas by Washington. Honduras's overseas coffee sales doubled by 1945, and as a percentage of total exports, they went from 5.1 percent in 1945 to 16.1 percent in 1955. Capitalizing on this gain, the president did not impose export duties on coffee until 1947, allowing substantial profits for exporters.[94]

New capital was available for investment by entrepreneurs, but manufacturing remained a very small sector.[95] Commercial recovery in the mid-1940s motivated merchants in San Pedro Sula, Tegucigalpa, and the northern department of

89. Joseph Thompson, "An Economic Analysis of Public Expenditures in Honduras, 1875–1950" (Ph.D. diss., University of Florida, 1963), 11.

90. Ibid.

91. Bethel, History of Latin America, 7:201.

92. Karnes, Tropical Enterprise, 95.

93. Mensaje, 5 December 1944, 285.

94. Euraque, "Industrialists and Merchants," 295.

95. Ibid., 305.

Cortés to form Rotaries (1946–47). Later, in 1949, several chambers of commerce met in a national assembly and made recommendations for future economic development to Carías's successor, Juan Manuel Gálvez (1949–54). They proposed that under the direction of the state, the collective interests of commerce, industry, and agriculture be promoted. The chamber would have headquarters in Tegucigalpa and in the departments of Atlántida, Cortés, and Copán.[96]

All these factors contributed immeasurably to the economic recovery and growth of government revenues. This meant that Carías could spend more cash and time on public works, building an infrastructure to facilitate the movement of goods to markets at home and abroad. Road building in mountainous Honduras was a slow and tedious process. Only 478 kilometers, all unpaved roads, were constructed from 1899 to 1932. An additional 2,300 kilometers would be completed by 1963, fourteen years after Carías left office.[97]

Carías had several objectives in his road-building projects. Aside from increasing farm products' access to markets, he wanted to link all municipalities to make administration from the capital quicker and more efficient. Just as important, he wanted to connect traditionally remote regions like the department of Olancho and its cattle industry in the northeast with other urban centers. Even Tegucigalpa was far and not accessible to key ports and commercial locales. It took about eleven hours to travel the north-south road joining the capital to San Pedro Sula (246 kilometers).[98] Travel by land was done in stages. First, one went from Tegucigalpa to Pito Solo, located at the south end of Lake Yojoa (five hours) and then by ferry to Jaral at the north end of the lake (two hours). From Jaral, one would travel overnight to Potrerillos (two hours). The final leg from Potrerillos to San Pedro Sula also could be covered in two hours. A road connecting Potrerillos, located at the southern terminus of the National Railroad, and Pito Solo was not completed until the mid-1940s. An airplane could make the trip in one-and-a-half hours.[99]

To address road-building tasks, Carías typically turned to administrative procedures first. How a project was managed and by whom were key to the successful outcome of the effort, at least as far as Carías's political interests were concerned. First, he merged the Treasury Accounts Offices of the several min-

96. Ibid., 319; *Boletín del Congreso Nacional Legislativo*, 29 April 1946, 1.
97. *Mensaje*, 5 December 1944, 9.
98. "Entrevista con Benjamín Henríques," *La Época*, 16 August 1940, 1.
99. *Mensaje*, 5 December 1948, 4.

istries into the single General Treasury of Justice and Roads under the Ministry of Government, headed by Vice-President Abraham Williams. Second, he placed one of his closest friends, Benjamín "Black Beard" Henriques, in the post of director of roads.[100] Williams, the well-known and highly respected engineer, took charge of overall road and bridge construction, but Henriques handled the funding and budget of this vastly developing enterprise in the mid-1940s. Henriques, a swarthy-looking figure, casually, even sloppily dressed, with a white towel always wrapped around his neck, became rich and influential. He never put money in a bank but collected and spent funds for road construction projects with cash. Carías did not monitor his friend's work with the same scrutiny he gave other ministries. Henriques once boastfully described his influence in the country by saying, "We are like the Holy Trinity. God is the father in Honduras, Carías is the son, and I'm the Holy Spirit."[101]

Henriques's budget operations were run quite simply. He ordered political governors of departments to raise money locally for the construction of roads or bridges in their locale. These chieftains in turn "taxed" individuals, businesses, and property owners, by compiling names and the amount due on what were called listas de capitalistas contribuyentes al fondo de caminos ("Lists of Business Contributions to the Road Fund").[102] Frequently, mayors of municipalities were also directed to tax people, raising funds for construction projects in their jurisdiction.[103] Henriques then personally contracted out construction projects and paid people for the materials they provided for a road project.[104] Sometimes foreign, but mostly U.S., firms were engaged in bridge and road building.[105] Henriques also paid individuals in a department or municipality

100. Dora Henriques (daughter of Benjamín Henriques, director general of roads), interview, Tegucigalpa, 4 August 1987. Henriques had been mayor of Comayagüela before it joined with Tegucigalpa and governor of the Central Department of Tegucigalpa.

101. Ibid.

102. Lista de capitalistas contribuyentes al fondo de caminos para el año 1938, vol. 19, Ministerio de Fomento, Agricultura, y Trabajo, Bibliteca y Archivos Nacionales. Benjamín Henriques received funds from political governors of departments. See Abraham Williams to the Ministerio de Fomento, Agricultura, y Trabajo, 25 January 1940; Notas, 1940, vol. 1528, Ministerio de Gobernación, Biblioteca y Archivos Nacionales.

103. Ibid.

104. Acuerdos del Ministerio de Fomento, 15 October 1934; 24 January 1938, no. 828–31, Biblioteca y Archivos Nacionales.

105. Acuerdo del Ministerio de Fomento, 28 January 1938.

for storing and maintaining equipment and for housing personnel engaged in local construction projects.[106] Often airstrips would be built on the property of a Carías partisan, and an appropriate sum of money would be paid as rent for the use of the land for the airstrip.[107]

The construction of the Pan-American Highway in the 1940s was undertaken by the United States as part of the "Inter-American Cooperation for Defense." The project provided extraordinary benefits to the Honduran road-building program. Aside from the considerable employment utilized, the Carías government also received vast quantities of equipment for other construction projects.[108] The road ran along the country's south coast, leaving Tegucigalpa isolated from the main artery. As a consolation to the disappointed Carías, Washington provided funds and material for the construction of two bridges in the capital over the Goascorán (in central Tegucigalpa), as well as over the Guacerique (Comayaguela) and Choluteca Rivers.[109]

In 1942, Carías received a million-dollar loan from the Import-Export Bank for the construction of an Inter-American Highway. A year later, 13.5 percent of the budget, $765,924.00, was spent on road construction.[110] At the same time, the president's overall plan to link several parts of the country to the north-south artery were under way; some links were even completed. For example, there were in progress at this time roads from Tegucigalpa south to San Lorenzo on the Pacific coast, stretching 184 miles; one to Yuscarán, capital of the southwest department of El Paraíso; a third, linked Santa Barbara de Copán in the west to San Pedro Sula. Last, a road connected Potrerillos at the southern terminus of the National Railroad to Pito Solo on the south end of Lake Yojoa, making overland travel possible for the first time from Tegucigalpa, 165 kilometers north to San Pedro Sula.[111]

106. *La Época*, 16 August 1939, 3.

107. "Informe de Olancho, 1937," *Memoria*, Ministerio de Gobernación, 7, 12–14; *Libro diario*, 1 October 1937, 12–13, Miguel Paz Reyes Library, Tegucigalpa. These records were kept by pilots who were contracted to deliver materials to departments where road construction was underway.

108. *Libro diario*, 12–13.

109. U.S. Minister John Erwin to the Honduran Foreign Minister Salvador Aguirre, 11 September 1935; 9 November 1939; *Correspondencia diplomática recibida de la Legación Americana en Honduras durante el año económico de 1935–1940*, no. 6697, Archivos, Ministerio de Relaciones Exteriores, Comision de Soberanía y Fronteras, Comayaguela.

110. Stokes, *Honduras*, 12.

111. Ibid.

Carías's public works projects accelerated during the period following economic recovery in the 1940s. Funding from the United States, collections from local entrepreneurs, and help from the Import-Export Bank made this happen. Approximately 126 bridges were built. Tegucigalpa's streets were paved for the first time; several new parks were added and old ones fixed up; and a national baseball stadium and housing for tuberculosis patients, the elderly, and infirm were also constructed.[112]

Since the pressing fiscal crisis was gradually coming under control and the economy was reviving somewhat by the mid-1940s, Carías turned to education. Although far less critical than other issues, it was of paramount interest to him personally. "I am a teacher at heart," he reminded congress as he launched an elaborate plan for revising the public school curriculum at all levels.[113] As an educator in the late 1890s to 1907, Carías faced the chaos and upheaval of civil wars that disrupted education and, as he said, forced him out of the profession. Many of his generation had left the classroom to join sides in civil wars, sometimes going into exile.

In the late 1930s, many former educators entered his administration and began again the changes started by their mentors and heroes, the Liberal presidents of the 1880s–1890s. The doctrines and principles of education reform, like Carías's fiscal policies, had their origin in the late nineteenth century in the vision of chief executives like Marco Aurelio Soto, Luis Bográn, and Policarpo Bonilla. Public education offering practical subjects to promote free enterprise was reinstated under Carías. A school like the National Institute of Commerce, which had begun in the late nineteenth century with North American teachers, was created to train students in accounting and bookkeeping.[114]

Some of Carías's followers proposed a state-run educational program, advocating the subordination of the individual into groups such as unions, professional organizations, and athletic associations. None of these "clubs" were to exist outside the state but were to be mobilized around a hierarchical structure.[115] Carías emphasized discipline as the core of the academic and co-cur-

112. *Mensaje*, December 1947, 10, 12.

113. *Mensaje*, December 1944, 238.

114. Florencia Leiva Sansores, "Armonía docente," in *Aspectos culturales de Honduras* (n.p., n.d.), 67.

115. Abelardo Fortín (subdirector, Instituto Normal Central de Varones, 1937–44; director, 1944–47, 1951–54), interview, Tegucigalpa, 21 November 1987.

ricular programs.[116] Honduran presidents in the first three decades of the twentieth century never offered principles underlying their educational goals. Yet in 1933, pedagogical doctrines similar to Liberal programs of the 1880s and 1890s reappeared in Carías's end-of-the-year reports to congress.[117] For example, a new code of instruction was introduced similar to the one offered by President Marco Aurelio Soto in 1878.[118] The organizers of the president's educational system were graduates of special training institutes created by Liberal figures in the 1880s and 1890s. Vicente Cáceres Hernández, "El Tunco" ("the Arm Stub," 1882–1944), was a graduate of the Colegio Nacional de Ensenanza (National Teachers College) established by President Soto.[119] He became director of the Instituto Nacional y Escuela de Comercio (National Institute and Business School), also founded in the 1880s. However, civil wars in 1909 and later in the 1920s forced him to give up teaching and directing schools. He fled to México and there worked with the renowned educator José Vasconselos.[120] When Carías became president, Cáceres returned and was again named director of the Instituto Nacional y Escuela de Comercio. At the same time, in 1933, he became head of the "flagship" school, La Escuela Normal Central de Varones (Central Normal School for Boys), where a core of the earlier Liberal education programs was adopted. At Cáceres's suggestion, the two schools were combined.[121]

Cáceres, the education "czar," assembled a core of educators, believers in the doctrine of order, discipline, and study of practical subjects.[122] As a graduate of the Colegio Nacional de Ensenanza, staffed in the 1870s by North Americans, he grew to dislike the permissiveness of schools in the United States.[123] Therefore, he embarked on a rigorous academic program for the school. Working closely with the president, he inaugurated a curriculum of "practical subjects," as he called them, emphasizing mathematics, English, the natural sci-

116. Ibid.

117. "Educación Pública," *Mensaje*, 5 December 1933.

118. Rafael Bardales Bueso, *Biografía del Profesor Rodolfo Velásquez* (Tegucigalpa: Imprenta Cettna, 1985).

119. Fortín interview, 12 November 1987.

120. Ibid.

121. Rafel Jerez Alvarado (member of the faculty, Instituto Normal Central de Varones, 1938–44; editor of *La Época*, 1954), interview, Tegucigalpa, 3 November 1987.

122. *El Cronista*, 29 August 1936; *Mensaje*, December 1936, 107; Alvarado interview, 3 November 1987.

123. *El Cronista*, 29 August 1936, 3; Fortín interview, 3 November 1987.

ences (mineralogy, chemistry, and so forth), accounting, and commerce.[124] Honduran, not Central American, history was taught.[125] Military uniforms were worn, and strict training to instill discipline was provided by officers from the Tegucigalpa-based militia.[126] Women at the separate Escuela Normal Central de Señoritas wore uniforms, too. Like their male counterparts, they carried wooden rifles for drill each day. A National Federation of Sports was established in the Ministry of Education with "committees for specific sports." Everyone had to participate in one of them, either baseball, soccer, hiking, or some form of calisthenics.[127]

Faculty for the Escuela Normal Central de Varones was drawn from the medical, legal, and engineering professions. They provided the basics in practical subjects, offering skills specifically for future employment; "all," said a teacher, "in the interests of growth and progress."[128] The curricula in public schools from Manuel Bonilla to Mejía Colindres in 1932 generally were less technical in nature. They included courses such as geography, political economy, sociology, commercial geography, history of education, and medieval history. Under Carías, in addition to a regular academic classroom program, students were required to take two months of practical work outside of school in occupations such as accounting or engineering.[129] The entire budget for the institution was financed by the government. Other schools, like the Commercial Private School, were not.[130]

The overall structure of the educational system began typically, as in the past, with a focus on primary and secondary schools (*colegios*) in cities and in rural areas. With about 121,000 children in 1933,[131] these institutions through-

124. Alvarado interview, 3 November 1987.

125. "El Vicente Cáceres, cien años de sabidura para millares de Hondureños," *La Prensa*, 25 October 1964, 6–7, 14; *Acuerdo*, 6 July 1936, No. 880, *Libro de Acuerdos*, Vol. 61, Archivo, Ministerio de Educación.

126. *Programa para la instrucción militar, Instituto Normal Central de Varones*, n.d., Ministerio de Educación, Archivo, Palacio de los Ministerios.

127. *La Época*, 29 May 1935, 3; *Revista de Policía*, Vol. 4, No. 38, August 1936, 2; *República de Honduras: Informe de educación pública, 1939–1940*, 7, La Federación Nacional de Cultura, Fisica y Deportes, Ministerio de Gobernación, Archivo, Palacio de los Ministerios.

128. *Informe de educación pública*, 7.

129. *Acuerdo* No. 420, 31 January 1929, 238, Ministerio de Educación, Vol. 30, Archivo, Palacio de los Ministerios.

130. *Acuerdo* No. 558, 16 May 1934, 289.

131. *Informe*, 1941–1942, Ministerio de Educación, 31, Archivo, Palacio de los Ministerios.

out the country were named after nineteenth-century Liberal Party chief executives.[132] Carías also added a correctional school for the national penitentiary in Tegucigalpa to provide delinquents with primary education and secondary school training in vocational courses such as carpentry, sewing, shoemaking, and "engineering" (skills for building roads and bridges).[133]

As with the other ministries, Carías closely supervised the Ministry of Education's budget. He personally approved monetary allocations and salary contracts for teachers.[134] He deposited funds in Standard Fruit Company's Banco de Atlántida, which in turn distributed the money to northern departments for their education expenditures.[135] He took great pride in the efficiency of his managerial skills in this area, often bragging, "We paid salaries regularly and promptly at all levels of the system."[136]

Carías's preoccupation with detail was legendary. For example, he scrutinized the competence of people who were to administer exams in primary and secondary schools, assigned scholarships to needy students, and approved or disapproved the transfer of credit from one school to another.[137] He made special funds available to people who needed to continue taking courses for job skill training. He examined and approved salaries for teachers from abroad,[138] working out the details for transporting school materials and instructors by TACA (Lowell Yerex's Central American Airlines) to all parts of the country.[139] He even scheduled an hour a week on Honduran radio for la hora de los maestros ("teachers' hour"), to discuss education issues of particular interest to him.[140]

In an effort to bolster Honduras's cultural history and draw attention to its indigenous past, the minister of education, Jesús María Rodríguez, was instructed in 1935 to restore the ancient Mayan city of Copán in the western part of the country. In February of that year, arrangements were made with the Carnegie Institution in Washington, DC, for funding and professional assis-

---

132. *Memoria, Ministerio de Educación, 1933–1934*, 58, Archivo, Palacio de los Ministerios.

133. *Tegucigalpa*, 30 December 1945, 9; *Revista de Policía*, 31 October 1935, 19.

134. *Libro de Acuerdos*, 23 September 1931–27 October 1931, Vol. 44, 3–13, Archivo, Ministerio de Educación.

135. *Libro de Acuerdos*, 11 May 1934–31 July 1934, Vol. 54.

136. *Mensaje*, 5 December 1943, 246.

137. *Libro de Acuerdos*, 11 May 1934–31 July 1934, Vol. 54.

138. *Libro de Acuerdos*, 1937–1938, 30 August 1937, Vol. 65, 4–5.

139. *Acuerdo No.* 381, 21 December 1933, 66.

140. *El Cronista*, 24 September 1936, 7.

tance in the project.[141] Noted archaeologists Sylvanus Morley and Gustavo Stromsvik began excavating the site. An archaeological museum at Copán was inaugurated on Carías's birthday, March 15, 1939.[142]

The Copán project, like other aspects of Carías's educational reform, was designed to include landmarks of cultural significance as central to the nation's renovation through education. Similar to his financial restructuring and administrative reorganization, he tried to give meaning to the place of Honduras's indigenous past and pre-Colombian heritage in Central American history. He referred to this, as his Liberal Party predecessors often had, as "cultural integration."[143] Although education was important, it was not an immediately pressing issue. The economic crisis needed attention first as a top priority. Yet putting all these reforms together was in effect restoring the nation-building agenda of late-nineteenth-century Liberals. Carías was proud of this program and of his place in history as a regenerator, a practical reformer casting his regime as a continuation of an earlier age when nation building was a top priority. In essence, Carías felt he was continuing the Liberal agenda of the 1870s, which had been interrupted by civil war and economic collapse in the 1920s and 1930s only to be resumed under his rule.

Tiburcio Carías used the same remedies for dealing with economic and financial crises as his Liberal Party predecessors had: financial reorganization of the central government, with a corresponding emphasis on fiscal expenditures and income. This required taking the operations of the banana industry seriously, for they provided the country with its main source of foreign exchange income. But the price paid for this benefit was huge. Loans the banana companies made to the central government permanently attached the Honduran fiscal structure to a foreign enterprise. Carías's reforms, while important for organization purposes, did not win financial independence for his country, nor did they improve the lot of its people. The principles of classic nineteenth-century liberalism prevailed, and the state apparatus was to be an institution for buttressing the economy and strengthening a dictatorship, not an engine for social change.

Toward the end of his presidency, after the laborious task of making economic and financial changes had gotten under way, Carías was giving his usual

141. La Época, 24 February 1935, 1.

142. La Época, 28 January 1939, 1.

143. El Cronista, 24 September 1936, 2.

bland recitation before congress of statistics on numbers of schools, roads, and bridges constructed; this time, however, he announced with little fanfare that the internal and external debt had been paid. "And," he added, "the government paid them promptly." This consummate politician and tireless administrator, a manager of details, offered the straightforward observation that under his stewardship, "expenditures were in balance with revenue."[144] He would have been proud when a Yankee diplomat who was observing the proceedings and reporting the contents of the speech noted that "the national budget is balanced . . . the country is on a pay as you go basis, accomplished through old-fashioned, orthodox virtues of hard work and frugality, without recourse to screwball economics."

In firm control of government with a blueprint for its economic recovery, Carías turned to a subject in which he was not well versed but that needed attention, foreign affairs. Although his early political career involved the politics of neighboring states, the bulk of his time and interests were in Honduran domestic politics. Of one fact he could be certain, the internal peace of his country depended greatly on friendly neighbors. Honduras's central location in the region often pulled it into conflicts with neighbors. He was therefore determined to engage his fellow chief executives to establish a stable and peaceful Central America, and to work with the preponderant influences of Washington in the area as well.

144. *Mensaje*, December 1948, 283–84. The debt to British bondholders was not paid until 1953.

IV

Central America's Senior Caudillo

8

Ties That Bind

Central American Neighbors and the United States

President Carías had three foreign policy objectives: first, keep peace with his four Central American neighbors, three of which had borders contiguous to Honduras; second, develop and maintain close ties with the United States; and third, participate in the international conference system in the Americas.[1] Each of these goals conveyed basic realities Honduras faced in the community of Western Hemisphere states. Carías needed political stability at home guaranteed by nonintervention in his country's internal affairs, and economic, financial assistance only Washington could provide.

Historically, Liberal or Conservative governments in Central America viewed regimes of the opposite party as a threat to their own existence. Borders were frequently used as staging areas by exiles for toppling their own government. Honduras's boundaries were unmarked and mainly in uninhabited areas. These regions allowed rebel chieftains to cross back and forth to neighboring states for security and logistical support ousting a regime. Carías began his political career participating in these excursions, finding refuge in José Santos Zelaya's Nicaragua as he worked to keep Manuel Bonilla from the presidency. The president's early political experience was set in these transnational allegiances of parties, Liberals and Conservatives, each one looking for supporters in neighboring states.

Honduras's location in the middle of Central America frequently made it a battleground of feuding political groups. Its neighbors, Nicaragua to the east, Guatemala to the west, and El Salvador in the south, were headed by Liberal regimes at the time Carías became chief executive in 1933. Consequently, the new president, a Nationalist (conservative), was somewhat vulnerable. Although the country's official neutrality had been recognized in the Washington

---

1. *Memorias del Congreso Nacional, 1939–1940*, 13–14.

Treaties of Amity and Peace in 1907, and again in 1923, borders with neighbor states had not been fixed. Worse, they remained centers for rebel movements challenging both the Mejía Colindres (1931–32) and Carías governments in the War of Traitors (1931–33). Pledges not to interfere in the internal affairs of another state made in the same accords did not make Carías's regime immune from meddling by dispirited Liberal exiles in the 1930s or any time thereafter.

Asked in an interview, several months after taking office, how he perceived relations with other Central American states, Carías described Presidents Juan Bautista Sacasa of Nicaragua, Maximiliano Hernández Martínez of El Salvador, and Jorge Ubico of Guatemala as strong leaders capable of maintaining stable regimes. That is exactly what he needed with porous borders on all sides.[2] Guardedly and diplomatically he said, "We have no historical enemies, but neighbors with similar problems as Honduras." He based these assumptions largely on his earlier experiences witnessing and participating in interventions in neighboring states with his father and other Liberal partisans in Honduras, Nicaragua, and El Salvador in the early twentieth century.[3] Like his neighbors, Carías faced a severe economic crisis and tackled it, as they did, with fiscal austerity measures. Honduras was linked with other Central American states on several foreign policy goals, too. They also had to deal with world depression, noninterference in the internal affairs of states, and Central American integration.

As in all other matters involving the management of public affairs, Carías (who lacked experience in international relations) appointed competent and experienced people to direct his foreign ministry. He set the basic diplomatic objectives and let able people carry them out. Salvador Aguirre, Antonio Bermúdez, and Silverio Laínez each headed this ministry during the fourteen years of Carías's presidency. They were well-traveled figures and fluent in several languages. Unlike Carías, they moved easily and comfortably in international circles with friends in many capitals in the Western Hemisphere and Europe. Moreover, as lawyers they practiced international law and participated in arbitration and mediation cases.[4] All three were good administrators. Julian Lay, a Washington emissary to Honduras, at one point appreciatively observed that during the Carías regime "messages to the foreign office are answered

2. Dispatch, U.S. legation, Tegucigalpa, to State Department, 7 December 1933, Confidential U.S. Diplomatic Post Records, reel 7, 435.

3. *Mensaje, 1936,* Biblioteca y Archivos Nacionales, 93.

4. *Memoria Presentada al Congreso Nacional, 1943–1944,* Biblioteca y Archivos Nacionales.

more promptly and replies are prepared with more care, skill and consideration than ever before."[5] These foreign ministers were responsible for increasing the country's diplomatic representation abroad beginning in 1933. At that time only five states had legations in Tegucigalpa. By 1947, there were fifteen.[6]

Honduras barely exercised effective claim over much of its territory in the early 1930s. The Bay Islands off the north coast, recovered from Great Britain in the 1860s, were administratively autonomous. Sovereignty over the Swan Islands in the same area was disputed by the United States. El Salvador, Nicaragua, and Honduras contested claims to islands in the Bay of Fonseca.[7] Far more dangerous to Carías were border problems to the east and west with Guatemala and Nicaragua, and El Salvador to the south.

In the early months of his presidency Carías was deluged with dispatches from his emissaries in Guatemala City, San Salvador, and Managua relaying protests against the presence of Honduran Liberal groups and dissidents along contested borders. None of these areas had boundary marks, nor were they peaceful or safe. For example, from Honduran diplomats in Guatemala came messages that "criminals roam the Honduran-Guatemalan border." The dispatch added that to maintain peace and order, "Guatemalan "troops had to move into the western department of Ocotepeque" (in Honduras). The Guatemalan foreign minister issued a formal protest.[8] From Managua came charges that some 200 Honduran rebels had crossed from the south and southeastern departments of Choluteca and El Paraíso into that country, disrupting communities.[9]

In the 1930s, Nicaraguan rebel Augusto César Sandino and his partisans operated from staging areas in the eastern Honduran region of Danlí and freely moved back into Nicaragua conducting military campaigns against the government.[10] Managua's foreign minister, Leonardo Argüello, also objected to incursions of Honduran troops further east to the Atlantic coast town of Puerto Cabezas.[11]

5. Dispatch, U.S. legation, Tegucigalpa, to Department of State, Confidential U.S. Diplomatic Post Records, reel 38, 874–84.

6. *Mensaje*, 5 December 1947, 23.

7. Bethel, *History of Latin America since 1930*, 191.

8. *Correspondencia recibida de Ministerio de Guerra, Marina, y Aviación por el Ministerio de Relaciones Exteriores, enero–julio*, 25 May 1933, Comisión de Soberania y Fronteras, Comayaguela.

9. *Correspondencia recibida de Ministerio de Guerra*, 17 January 1933, no. 143.

10. *Correspondencia recibida de Ministerio de Guerra*, 23 February 1933.

11. *Correspondencia recibida de Ministerio de Guerra*, 29 April 1933.

Faced with these sharp protests from all his neighbors, Carías took steps to remedy the growing crisis. First, he dispatched special expeditionary forces led by trusted loyalists like General Martínez Funes to the troubled frontiers.[12] Then he used aviation to transport arms and equipment to support them. To inaccessible areas he deployed Tomás Martínez's mounted police, and he arranged joint border patrols with Guatemala and Nicaragua.[13]

Having shored up the Mejía Colindres regime against its armed detractors, barely securing his new government, Carías sought immediate recognition from his neighbors. He sent "special agents," loyal confidants and personal representatives, to Guatemala, El Salvador, and Nicaragua, assuring each president that the Honduran government was in control of its internal affairs; he would dispatch troops to the troubled borders, and if need be, do so in a joint effort with their governments.

Fortunately, Carías's neighbors had good reasons to recognize his regime and see it control its internal affairs effectively. Jorge Ubico of Guatemala wanted to extend his country's influence throughout Central America, so he supported Liberals for president, not an unusual strategy in that country's role in the region. For example, he sent $30,000 to Liberal presidential candidate Ángel Zúñiga Huete in his unsuccessful 1932 campaign against Carías.[14] The Liberal Juan Bautista Sacasa, elected chief executive in Nicaragua in 1932, wanted close ties to México, Guatemala's northern and sometimes hostile neighbor. This did not make him a promising ally. A realist, however, the Guatemalan president endorsed both the Sacasa and Carías elections, to gain friends against his next-door neighbor and rival Maximiliano Hernández Martínez of El Salvador. Ubico essentially wanted to neutralize El Salvador's influence while dominating Honduras and Nicaragua in Central American politics.[15]

Ubico sent his private secretary, Antonio Najera Cabrera, as special emissary to his fellow Liberal Honduran president Mejía Colindres, assuring him of Guatemala's continued interest in maintaining good relations in the succeed-

12. Salvador Aguirre, Foreign Minister, Honduras, to Sub-Secretary of War, Tegucigalpa, 18 August 1924, *Correspondencia recibida de Ministerio de Guerra*.

13. *Memoria, Ministerio de Gobernación, 1935–1936*, Archivo, Palacio de los Ministerios, 17.

14. *El Cronista*, 23 May 1932, 1. Ángel Zúñiga Huete received $150,000 from President Jorge Ubico of Guatemala. Grieb, *Guatemalan Caudillo*, 98.

15. Grieb, *Guatemalan Caudillo*, 82–83.

ing national government of Carías.[16] Soon after sending reassurances to Mejía Colindres, and before Carías took office, Ubico offered a warm greeting expressing his desire to have close and friendly relations with Honduras.[17] Diplomatic exchanges continued and accelerated. Carías's strategy for gaining approval and recognition for his government was based in part on exploiting the Ubico–Hernández Martínez rivalry in the northern tier of Central America. His special agent and longtime confidant Edgardo Valenzuela provided glowing reports from Guatemala of his private meeting with Jorge Ubico, establishing personal contacts between the two presidents. Even before formal diplomatic recognition was accorded to Carías, in somewhat of a diplomatic anomaly, the Guatemalan president made Valenzuela an "honored guest" and received him unofficially.[18]

Similar special agents were sent to San Salvador and Managua. The everloyal, discreet, and competent Silverio Laínez, sent to both states, was instructed to be especially careful not to give any notoriety to his mission, fearing it would antagonize El Salvador's rival, Guatemala.[19] Carías's instructions, like Valenzuela's in Guatemala, were to propose the creation of a joint commission to settle border claims. Laínez also proposed the creation of a regular air mail service. This latter suggestion implied closer military-logistical cooperation as Carías recalled the munitions he received from El Salvador during the War of Traitors. Of course, Carías wanted diplomatic recognition in order to be a Central American player in the El Salvadoran and Guatemalan rivalry.

Maximiliano Hernández Martínez had come to power in December 1931 as vice-president succeeding President Arturo Araujo, who was ousted by a coup. He had not gained recognition from the United States or his neighbors because this action violated the Central America Treaty of Peace and Amnesty, which prohibited recognition of a government coming to power by force. Now he needed the Honduran leader's concurrence to break his diplomatic isolation.

16. President Jorge Ubico, Guatemala, to President Vicente Mejía Colindres, Honduras, 28 January 1933, *Cartas autográficas, 1932–1933*, Ministerio de Relaciones Exteriores, Archivo, Palacio de los Ministerios.

17. Ubico to Tiburcio Carías, Tegucigalpa, n.d., *Cartas autográficas*.

18. Special delegate Edgardo Valenzuela (later foreign minister, Guatemala) to foreign minister, Honduras, 2 April 1933, *Diplomática Recibida: Varias, 1932–1933*, Ministerio de Relaciones Exteriores, Comisión de Soberanía y Fronteras.

19. *Memoria de Relaciones Exteriores, 1933–1934*, Archivo, Palacio de los Ministerios, 23.

Carías's first gesture was to let the new president know of his friendship and desire to deal with border issues.[20] Then the Honduran chief executive personally welcomed Concha de Martínez, the El Salvadoran president's wife, who visited Tegucigalpa in late 1933 to attend a wedding. Carías made a special point to greet her, and as a personal gesture of friendship he sent his private secretary, José María Albir, to escort her back home.[21]

The dispatch of an emissary to Managua in 1933 was particularly important, as border disruptions were taking place on the north coast and along the eastern areas contiguous to Nicaragua. In pointed fashion, Horacio Fortín, a relative of President Sacasa living in Honduras, went to Managua as the Carías emissary. In fact, he had at one time been the Honduran minister there. He and President Sacasa were on good terms.[22] Shortly after reaching the Nicaraguan capital, Fortín received assurances from Sacasa that anti-Carías rebels, some already incarcerated, would continue to be watched. Later in 1933, the Honduran envoy reported that Sandino and the Sacasa government were negotiating a peace agreement that included ending border crossings to and from Honduras.[23] The Guatemalan minister in Managua at the time assured Fortín that his government also would not allow dissident political exiles to receive visas or passports to enter or leave his country.[24] Cooperation with Ubico proved useful, too. Justo Umaña, a Liberal Party dissident who hated President Mejía Colindres and condemned Carías for supporting him, conducted his military operations in the western department of Copán, bordering Guatemala.[25] Carías wanted to end that rebel activity, so with Ubico's help in 1937, Umaña was captured in Guatemala and "shot while trying to escape."[26]

Based on a 1930 agreement to set a boundary between Guatemala and Hon-

20. Dispatch, U.S. legation, Tegucigalpa, to Secretary of State, 9 September 1933, Confidential U.S. Diplomatic Post Records, reel 7, 333.

21. La Época, 21 July 1933, 1; Dispatch, U.S. legation, Tegucigalpa, to Department of State, 18 August 1933, Confidential U.S. Diplomatic Post Records, reel 7, 503.

22. Correspondencia Diplomática Recibida de la Legación de Honduras en Nicaragua, 1933–1934, 23 November 1933, Archivos, Comisión de Soberanía y Fronteras, Tegucigalpa.

23. Cable, Legación Managua, Tegucigalpa, 29 April 1933, Correspondencia Diplomática: Varias, 1932–1933.

24. Agente especial, Nicaragua, to Ministro de Relaciones Exteriores, Tegucigalpa, 23 April 1933.

25. La Época, 7 December 1933, 1.

26. Dispatch, U.S. legation, Tegucigalpa, to Department of State, 24 March 1937, Confidential U.S. Diplomatic Post Records, reel 14, 790.

duras, Charles Evans Hughes, Chief Justice of the U.S. Supreme Court, announced in January 1933 that the Río Motagua would be the demarcation line. Hughes had been asked by both countries to study the border issue.[27] Carías and Ubico then established a Joint Technical Commission to place markers on agreed sites from aerial photos taken by the Honduran air force.[28] The Honduran chief executive wanted to confirm his boundaries and was anxious to delineate boundaries with Guatemala, so he promptly accepted the commission's report.[29] The demarcation line was completed in August 1938.[30] In the meantime, Carías sent a special military expedition into the recently designated Honduran territory and explicitly cautioned his minister in Guatemala and military commander in the newly confirmed Honduran region to be extremely careful not to encroach on any contested territory.[31]

Formal diplomatic relations were established with all Honduran neighbors except El Salvador by the summer of 1933. Although questions over the legitimacy of Hernández Martínez's presidency delayed immediate recognition,[32] Carías wasted no time doing so. As the Carías regime was recognized by each state, contentious issues were promptly dealt with and, in turn, assurances were given by neighboring governments that border questions would be taken up with Tegucigalpa. Moreover, all promised that Honduran dissidents moving back and forth across state lines would be promptly interred. For example, Ángel Zúñiga Huete, defeated in the 1932 election, left for Guatemala after the election and wanted to return home in the fall of 1933, but his efforts to do so were thwarted by the cooperative President Jorge Ubico.[33]

No special emissary was sent to Costa Rica as it was not a border state, and there were few contentious issues between the two countries. However, Hon-

27. La Época, 15 February 1938, 1.

28. Ibid.; Memoria al Congreso Nacional, 1935–1936, Relaciones Exteriores, Archivo, Palacio de los Ministerios, 19A.

29. Grieb, Guatemalan Caudillo, 100.

30. Alfredo Skinner Klee, Guatemala, to Antonio Bermúdez, foreign minister, Honduras, 23 August 1933, Correspondencia Diplomática Recibida, 19A; Rodolfo Gálvez Molina (Guatemalan minister to Honduras) to Honduran foreign minister, 28 February 1933.

31. Honduran foreign minister, Honduras, to Honduran minister, Guatemala, 20 August 1933, Correspondencia Diplomática Enviada a la Legación Hondureña Guatemala, 1933–1934, 196.

32. "Relaciones con vecinos, 1934–1935," Memoria, Ministerio de Relaciones Exteriores presentada al Congreso Nacional, Archivo, Palacio de los Ministerios, 4–5.

33. Honduran minister, Guatemala, to foreign minister, Honduras, Correspondencia Diplomática, 23 October 1933.

duran Liberals, even some anti-carístas in the National Party, fled to San José. They mounted a press campaign in 1933, denouncing the Carías dictatorship from abroad in Costa Rica, and continued to do so for many years thereafter.[34] As a result, diplomatic relations between the two countries remained cool and correct, but this was not of immediate concern to Carías.

The president was concerned about his three porous borders and the lawlessness and unrest evident in each area. As a security precaution, he sent militias to maintain order in areas along the borders and simultaneously dispatched personal envoys to assuage his neighbors' fears. He assured them that cooperation on the joint commissions could end these disruptions or at least minimize difficulties. Fortunately his neighbors had good reasons to develop cordial relations with him as well. Guatemala's Ubico was a pragmatist. His Honduran Liberal ally, Ángel Zúñiga Huete, had lost the 1932 election, but stability in Honduras and peaceful relations with this new ally against El Salvador were far more important than backing a defeated Liberal abroad.[35]

Hernández Martínez had been recognized by all his neighbors as the president of El Salvador, yet his country's ill-defined borders with Honduras enabled Liberal Party rebel groups considerable freedom in those areas.[36] Since 1932, when the El Salvadoran legislature had elected him president, Hernández Martínez consistently detained several Honduran anti-carístas.[37] Moreover, President Sacasa of Nicaragua, who wanted to end the military conflict with Augusto César Sandino, felt that settling the Honduran border issue was of major concern, as the Nicaraguan rebel freely moved back and forth between each country. Therefore, for practical reasons which Carías exploited, each of his neighbors wanted peace with him and good diplomatic relations. Carías also emerged as a pivotal figure in the power struggle between El Salvador and Guatemala in the northern tier of Central America. He enjoyed his newfound prominence but was wary too of its implications insofar as it might draw him unnecessarily into the region's embroilments.[38]

Central American states split over the issue of recognizing Hernández Martínez in 1931. Both El Salvador and Costa Rica adhered to the Estrada Doctrine, which called for immediate recognition of a new regime. In 1923, a re-

34. La Época, 10 September 1933, 3.

35. Grieb, Guatemalan Caudillo, 99.

36. Honduran minister, Guatemala, to foreign minister, Honduras, 12 January 1934.

37. Honduran minister, Guatemala, to foreign minister, Honduras, 23 October 1933.

38. La Época, 18 May 1936, 1.

gional Treaty of Amity and Peace prohibited the recognition of a state coming to power by revolutionary means. Washington at this time had wanted to impose arms limitations in Central America. Yet by 1933 the 1923 agreement was virtually ignored. Its advocates felt that the principle of de facto recognition made revolutions less possible than testing the legitimacy of a government before recognition, a policy supported by Washington. Consequently, both states repudiated the 1923 treaty. This left Guatemala and Nicaragua backing a new accord. Ubico launched an initiative seeking to enhance his country's influence in Central America. He called for the Central American Conference as a strategy in this diplomatic offensive. His plan was to draw Honduras and Nicaragua closer to Guatemala and make himself the major diplomatic player.[39]

With no certain ally in Nicaragua under President Juan Bautista Sacasa and failing to isolate Hernández Martínez in El Salvador diplomatically, Ubico assiduously cultivated the Honduran chief executive. Because Honduras bordered El Salvador as well, Ubico felt he could better monitor events in that country by having an ally in Tegucigalpa and Managua.[40] The test for leadership in this power struggle came in 1934 when the Guatemalans called for a conference to change some sections of the 1923 Central American Treaty of Amity and Peace.

Ubico urged that several aspects of the old accord be kept in place: the abolition of tariffs, a free trade agreement, one monetary unit, and a regional educational system. The proposed new treaty, similar to the earlier one, also would promote economic cooperation rather than mandating a political union and the standardization of all legal codes.[41] When a regional conference convened in Guatemala on March 15, 1934, separate Guatemalan and Salvadoran diplomatic interests were tested. Both El Salvador and Costa Rica disavowed the 1923 convention, thereby creating a bloc. Ubico courted Honduras and Nicaragua, and both endorsed Ubico's proposal.

Honduras, aware of its pivotal role in the two-bloc feud, carefully weighed its economic, political, and strategic interests. Carías was concerned that an arms buildup anywhere in Central America, particularly in Nicaragua, his eastern neighbor, might upset the balance of power in the region.[42] Moreover, the

39. Grieb, Guatemalan Caudillo, 105.

40. Ibid., 197.

41. Ibid., 106.

42. Correspondencia Diplomática Recibida de la Legación de Honduras en Nicaragua, 1933–1934, 8 February 1934.

alluring prospect for trade with Managua made a regional commercial agreement an attractive project.[43] Actually, the Tegucigalpa delegation was skeptical of any progress a conference could make, given the intense rivalry between El Salvador and Guatemala, and, more telling, it was certain that Guatemala, with its economic resources, would dominate the proceedings anyway.[44] Carías believed that if a Central America conference were convened in Panama, Washington, or Mexico City, animosities between states could be modified and prospects for a new convention would improve.[45] Above all, he wanted all Central American states represented at a meeting, avoiding the formation of subregional power blocs forcing Honduras to take sides.[46]

The Guatemalan foreign minister, Alfredo Skinner Klee, organized the agenda, with discussion points for a new agreement. He kept in contact with Ubico by telegraph. Dispatching a plane to bring the Honduran delegation to Guatemala City, thus bolstering his position and reinforcing his president's wish to play the central role, Klee convinced Honduras that a regional peace with the Guatemalan draft was more in Tegucigalpa's interest given its numerous borders. As the conference convened, Guatemala had secured the support of Managua and Tegucigalpa for a new Treaty of Amity and Peace.[47] Carías sent two able and experienced diplomats, Silverio Laínez and Saturnino Medal, with his nephew Marcos Carías Reyes to the meeting. He instructed his emissaries to reach an accord on a general Central American treaty.[48] The Honduran president wanted both Ubico and Hernández Martínez as friends, but he did not wish to antagonize El Salvador or Costa Rica. Consequently, his position was a bit awkward, but it provided opportunities as well.[49]

Although El Salvador, Honduras, and Nicaragua accepted Ubico's plan as a working document, other drafts of a new treaty also were presented. Basically, all states called for the maintenance of peace and rejection of force in settling differences. In effect, the principle of nonintervention was recognized. As in the 1923 accord, several practical ways to promote union were suggested,

43. Ibid.

44. Grieb, *Guatemalan Caudillo*, 110–11.

45. Ibid.

46. *Correspondencia Diplomática Enviada a la Legación de Honduras en Nicaragua, 1933–1934*, 10 February 1934.

47. Skinner Klee, Guatemala, to foreign minister, Honduras, 26 February 1934.

48. "Conferencia Centroamericana: Guatemala," *Mensaje*, December 1935.

49. *Memorias, Ministerios de Relaciones Exteriores, 1933–1934*, Archivo, Palacio de los Ministerios, 20.

among them creating a regional elementary, secondary, and professional education program. Arguing and bickering went on during the entire meeting, most of it over legalistic points. The principal antagonists were Guatemala's Carlos Salazar and Costa Rica's Octavio Beeche, both of whom were described as "aging, irascible lawyers who favored rigid arguments and legalistic principles."[50] Honduras, by contrast, took sides on votes more with Guatemala than Costa Rica but consistently promoted the adoption of compromise language.[51]

The issue of procedures on arbitration and mediation was hotly debated. Honduras wanted each state bound by arbitration and mediation. Costa Rica and El Salvador proposed an "honor reservation" in an effort to thwart Guatemala's influence. It would have allowed a country to disavow compulsory arbitration and settle a dispute alone with another state. Honduras viewed this as a dangerous departure from the need to involve all countries in a peacekeeping process should the need arise.[52] The Honduran delegation, playing the pivotal role between the two blocs (El Salvador and Costa Rica; Guatemala and Nicaragua), reworked the language of this dispute.[53] It suggested that Costa Rica and El Salvador's objection to compulsory arbitration could be met by stipulating that cases not currently subject to mandatory mediation as set by the 1923 accord would remain for ten years. In effect, Honduras joined Guatemala and Nicaragua in rejecting the "honor reservation" but gave Costa Rica and El Salvador a way to resolve pending disputes by placing them on hold. Carías's delegates enjoyed this key player role.[54]

The Guatemalan, Costa Rican, and El Salvadoran representatives bitterly debated major points on a new Treaty of Central American Fraternity and a Convention of Extradition of Fugitive Criminals.[55] New articles on arbitration procedures, nonintervention in states, and exchange of information on education and trade were included, but not without rancor and testy arguments, especially between Costa Rica and Guatemala.[56] Ever searching for ways to exert

50. Ibid.; Grieb, *Guatemalan Caudillo*, 109.

51. Grieb, *Guatemalan Caudillo*, 110.

52. Silverio Laínez (head of the Honduran delegation, Central American Peace Conference), Guatemala, to Antonio Bermúdez (foreign minister of Honduras), 13 March 1934, *Correspondencia Diplomática Recibida de la Delegación de la República de Honduras a la Primera Conferencia Centroamericana, 1934.*

53. *Memorias del Ministerio de Relaciones Exteriores, 1933–1934,* Archivo, Palacio de los Ministerios, 20.

54. Ibid., 19.

55. Grieb, *Guatemalan Caudillo*, 109.

56. Ibid.

his influence regionally, Ubico proposed a Free Trade Agreement with Nicaragua and Honduras, but Carías rejected the idea,[57] offering instead a less potentially contentious proposal to have Guatemala offer scholarships to citizens of other states to its polytechnic school, the Instituto Nacional, in the fields of medicine, engineering, and aviation training.[58] But Ubico persisted in urging the Honduran and Nicaraguan diplomats to join him in a free trade agreement. Nicaragua agreed, but Honduras claimed it was not ready to make such a commitment.[59] Very little of President Ubico's draft language appeared in the final text of the treaty. Carías showed his cautious hand in limiting his country's role in regional affairs. The final text was vague and general, leaving the principle of nonintervention intact, along with arbitration and a proposed single educational system for Central America. The treaty was never ratified by all the signatories. El Salvador was left diplomatically isolated by Ubico, who convinced Honduras and Nicaragua that a new agreement would have weight only if all states signed the accord. For joining Ubico, Carías gained full partnership with Central America's Liberal Party chief executives.

Carías studiously worked in other ways at home to consolidate good relations with his neighbors. The government-backed newspaper La Época continuously touted praise for Ubico, Hernández Martínez, and Somoza. Extensive coverage was given to their activities regarding birthdays, addresses in their respective congresses, national holidays, and independence day celebrations, sometimes jointly celebrated with Honduras.[60] Citations, awards, and medals were exchanged among the four dictators. For example, the Order of Quetzal was given to Carías from Guatemala and, in turn, the Order of Morazán for Ubico.[61] Special missions from Tegucigalpa traveled to Managua, San Salvador, and Guatemala to commemorate the centenary of President Francisco Morazán's birth, celebrating the anniversary of the 1871 Liberal revolution of Justo Rufino Barrios, Ubico's hero, in Guatemala.[62]

57. Ibid., 110–11.

58. Ibid., 6–15, 21.

59. Ibid., 111.

60. La Época, 14 July 1938, 1. This government paper gave extensive coverage to Ubico, Martínez, and Somoza on their public works projects, national holidays, addresses to Congress, and tours through their respective countries.

61. Tegucigalpa, 28 February 1937, 1. President Ubico of Guatemala awarded President Carías the Order of the Quetzal. Later Carías bestowed the Order of Morazán on Ubico; see Memoria Presentada al Congreso Nacional, 1941–1946, Ministerio de Relaciones Exteriores, Archivo, Palacio de los Ministerios.

62. El Cronista, 2 July 1937, 1.

Carías further engaged Honduras in regional diplomacy by upgrading missions to the rank of full minister in all Central American countries.[63] Honduran military cadets enrolled in Guatemala's polytechnic school.[64] Joint technical commissions placed markers to indicate boundaries between Honduras, El Salvador, and Guatemala. "We are," Carías confidently said in 1935, "united in a sincere and loyal friendship."[65] The United States viewed Carías's diplomatic craftsmanship regionally as tantamount to creating a security pact, in effect keeping peace, minimizing revolutions, and reducing meddling in each other's internal affairs.[66]

From time to time Carías celebrated "continuismo," the extension of his colleagues' terms in office. In turn he won their unqualified support when he did the same in 1936. On that occasion, Ubico sent his support and warned Guatemalan residents in Honduras not to participate in any political activity criticizing Carías.[67] Hernández Martínez also backed Carías's plan for an extended term in 1936[68] and, as he saw the emergence of communist activity in his own country and the region, called for close cooperation with all his neighbors.

Nicaragua's Anastasio Somoza, who ousted Juan Bautista Sacasa in June 1936, had supported Carías since his 1932 election. As National Guard commander in 1934–35, he imprisoned Honduran Liberals in Managua and sent troops east to his neighbor's border to quell antigovernment unrest there. After becoming chief executive, Somoza expelled Ángel Zúñiga Huete from Nicaragua and sent a personal representative to Carías in 1936 congratulating him on his "new term in office."[69]

Costa Rica greeted continuismo in Tegucigalpa with restraint, less enthusiastically than its neighbors.[70] The country's record for holding free elections—re-

63. President Jorge Ubico to President Tiburcio Carías, 11 December 1936, *Cartas autográficas, 1920–1923*, Ministerio de Relaciones Exteriores, Archivo, Palacio de los Ministerios.

64. *Memoria, Ministerios de Relaciones Exteriores, 1934–1935*, Archivo, Palacio de los Ministerios, 6–7.

65. *Tegucigalpa*, 17 July 1938, 1.

66. *New York Times*, 20 July 1937, 6.

67. Dispatch, U.S. legation, Tegucigalpa, to Department of State, 21 February 1936, National Archives, Record Group 59, 815.00/4678.

68. Dispatch, U.S. legation, Tegucigalpa, to Department of State, 21 February 1936, 20 April 1936, National Archives, Record Group 59, 815.000/Revolutions.

69. *La Época*, 8 August 1936, 1.

70. *Memoria al Congreso Nacional, 1935–1936*, Ministerio de Relaciones Exteriores, Archivo, Palacio de los Ministerios, 9.

flecting a literate population with substantial participation in government—while not perfect, was far superior to its Central American neighbors. Hence distancing itself from Carías was not unexpected. Several Honduran exiles fled to San José after severely criticizing Carías's efforts to change the country's constitution in 1936. While they roundly condemned their fellow Hondurans for permitting a dictatorial state to emerge,[71] Carías viewed Costa Rican criticism of his government more with contempt than concern.[72] Cooperation among Central America's dictators in the "northern tier" of the region (Honduras, Guatemala, and El Salvador) continued after each president pledged noninterference in the internal affairs of the others. Each head of state had to contend with exiles living abroad plotting for the overthrow of an authoritarian regime at home. For example, Carías backed Ubico by supporting Guatemala's claim to Belize, calling the British-held territory "colonialism similar to its occupation of the Malvinas [Falkland] Islands in Argentina and Guyana in South America."[73] In fact, he appealed to all Latin American countries to act jointly in conflicts of this kind dealing with non-American states' claims to territory in the Western Hemisphere.

The enormous stretch of boundary along the Honduran-Nicaraguan border in the east was always a potential source of conflict. In 1906, both countries accepted King Alfonso XIII of Spain's proposed boundary in the northeastern area of Mosquitia, but Nicaragua rejected it in 1910 after President José Santos Zelaya left office.[74] In 1937, Nicaragua printed a postage stamp showing a large part of the territory claimed by Honduras as part of its territory. Carías issued a decree affirming his country's sovereignty over the area and ordered all mail using the stamp returned to the sender.[75] However, he promised not to send troops to the disputed area. Nicaragua agreed to a similar position.

Carías asked the United States, Venezuela, and Costa Rica to mediate the issue.[76] The significance of the choices did not go unnoticed. The first two countries were outside Central America, and Costa Rica, to Nicaragua's south, had frequent border conflicts with Managua. The Costa Rica–Nicaragua border was marked in 1902 and not seriously challenged after that, even though there

71. Ibid.
72. Ibid.
73. *Tegucigalpa*, 29 October 1939, 1.
74. *Memoria Presentado al Congreso, 1939–1940*, Ministerio de Relaciones Exteriores, Archivo, Palacio de los Ministerios, 8–9, 11.
75. *La Época*, 3 September 1937, 1, 4.
76. *Mensaje, Segunda Parte, 1937–1945*, 5 December 1938, 180.

were conflicts at the border in 1948 and 1954. By early 1938, both nations agreed to allow a resolution of the conflict by the Carías proposed mediation commission,[77] and "to refrain from any act preliminary to war and from mobilization and assembly of troops."[78]

The territorial issue remained unresolved until 1961 when the Organization of American States settled it, affirming the 1906 territorial boundaries that were acceptable to both countries. The Honduran president was careful to see that it did not get out of hand during his tenure. The continuing mediation process he called for helped to maintain cordial relations with Managua from then on. For example, in 1947, when President Anastasio Somoza García (1936–56) held elections, Carías promptly recognized the new president, Somoza's choice (his uncle), Victor Román y Reyes.

The collapse of the Ubico and Hernández Martínez regimes in 1944 changed the diplomatic equation in Central America for Carías. But the Honduran president pursued his longtime foreign policy goal of keeping peace with neighbors, accepting change of regimes with noninterference in his neighbors' internal affairs. After trying to extend his term in 1944, Hernández Martínez was toppled in May. Carías refused to give asylum to enemies of General Andrés Ignacio Menéndez, the new head of state.[79] Carías remembered vividly the United States' meddling in Honduran presidential politics in 1924, preventing him from running for chief executive.

Washington was concerned about stability in Central America in the post-Ubico and Hernández Martínez era. It felt that Honduran exiles would find more receptive responses in efforts to topple Carías from Guatemala and El Salvador now that new governments had been installed.[80] For example, revolutionary forces from the latter took the southern Honduran town of Mercedes de Ocotepeque in late 1944.[81] Similar exile units from Guatemala attacked Honduras's western department of Copán.[82] In both instances, Carías sent his air

77. Ibid.

78. *Memoria de la República de Honduras y Counter Memoria República de Nicaragua*, c. 1938.

79. Dispatch, U.S. legation, Tegucigalpa, to Department of State, 21 August 1944, Confidential U.S. Diplomatic Post Records, reel 38, 29.

80. Dispatch, U.S. legation, Tegucigalpa, to Department of State, 12 May 1944, Confidential U.S. Diplomatic Post Records, reel 37, 882.

81. Dispatch, U.S. legation, Tegucigalpa, to Department of State, 14 October 1944, Confidential U.S. Diplomatic Post Records, reel 38, 52.

82. Dispatch, U.S. legation, Tegucigalpa, to Department of State, 12 April 1945, Confidential U.S. Diplomatic Post Records, reel 41, 989; reel 38, 67–68.

force and pushed these groups back across the Salvadoran and Guatemalan borders.[83] But the era of close collaboration with neighboring dictators was over.

These two border incursions and rising unrest at home prompted quick action. Carías was especially distrustful of the Juan José Arévalo reformist regime in Guatemala, so he moved on two fronts. First, he gave assurances to the United States he would not intervene in either country. Second, he met with Salvadoran military officers in November and discussed mutual security concerns, namely exile groups opposing both regimes and communist party activities.[84] The new basis for cooperation appeared to be succeeding when Ángel Zúñiga Huete was denied entry to El Salvador.[85]

More troublesome were the changes in Guatemala. There, Ubico's fall ushered in a popular reform government under Juan José Arévalo (1945–48), a former university professor. The initial revolutionary junta declared in November that it would not interfere in the internal affairs of neighboring states. Carías recognized the Arévalo regime, and Honduran exiles rushed there from México and Costa Rica.[86] Equally worrisome, President Arévalo called for a Union of Central American States in an effort to "avoid," in his words, "rising imperialism in Central America."[87] In response to this declaration, Washington diplomats in Tegucigalpa, supporting the stable, predictable Carías dictatorship, called on other states in Central America to put an end to the Arévalo anti-Yankee effort. The United States viewed the reformist Guatemalan chief executive as an extension of a Mexican ploy to exert its influence in Central America.[88]

Honduran and Salvadoran military leaders, distrustful of the Arévalo regime, met again in the spring of 1945. They issued communiqués calling for the suppression of exile groups and ending Arévalo's union effort.[89] They were

83. Dispatch, U.S. legation, Tegucigalpa, to Department of State, 2 November 1944, Confidential U.S. Diplomatic Post Records, reel 38, 68.

84. Dispatch, U.S. legation, Tegucigalpa, to Department of State, Confidential U.S. Diplomatic Post Records, reel 67, 1036.

85. La Época, 20 July 1944, 1.

86. Dispatch, U.S. legation, Tegucigalpa, to Department of State, 1 November 1944, Confidential U.S. Diplomatic Post Records, 67.

87. Dispatch, U.S. legation, Tegucigalpa, to Department of State, 21 May 1945, Confidential U.S. Diplomatic Post Records, reel 41, 739, 749; 23 May 1945, reel 41, 747.

88. Ibid.

89. John M. Cabot, State Department [to U.S. legation, Tegucigalpa], 17 January 1945, Confidential U.S. Diplomatic Post Records, reel 41, 955.

both concerned about exiles from both countries in Guatemala organizing to oust their governments.[90] Anastasio Somoza also joined Honduras and El Salvador to stop Guatemala's proposed anti-imperialist pact.[91]

The Costa Rican Civil War of 1948 tested Carías's diplomacy of realism and pragmatism. The conservative Rafael Ángel Calderón's Guardia (1940–48) National Republican Party attempted to manipulate the 1948 presidential election by installing Teodoro Picado (president, 1944–48). Utilio Ulate, candidate of the National Opposition Coalition, claimed fraud. Military forces led by José "Pepe" Figueres, the prominent democratic reformer, defeated government troops. Carías was told by his minister that the revolutionary government in Guatemala had supplied planes and ammunition to Figueres.[92]

Initially Honduras was reluctant to recognize the Figueres junta over the conservative Calderón Guardia. The Calderón Guardia regime had earlier assured him that it would never allow Honduran exiles to organize or to leave and coordinate their efforts with other dissidents in El Salvador or Guatemala. Carías accepted the Calderón Guardia's probable electoral defeat,[93] but at the same time he refused to recognize the new government, preferring to await a decision by a mediation commission (composed of the Apostolic Nuncio, México, the United States, Panamá, and Chile). He was particularly fearful that the Caribbean Legion, a loosely organized, ad hoc army of leftists led by José Figueres, might invade Honduras. His concerns were well founded, as the Honduran plot leader in 1943, Ribas Montes, had gone to Costa Rica to join the Caribbean Legion hoping to oust Carías. The mediation group proposed Santos León Herrera, the former minister of government whom Carías liked, as interim president. The choice eventually paved the way for the installation of Utilio Ulate as chief executive sixteen months later.[94]

The Honduran minister in San José provided Carías with a detailed and pes-

90. *Military Intelligence Report*, Confidential U.S. Diplomatic Post Records, reel 41, 1273.

91. Dispatch, U.S. legation, Tegucigalpa, to Department of State, 6 June 1945, Confidential U.S. Diplomatic Post Records, reel 41, 807.

92. Honduran legation, Costa Rica [to Foreign Minister, Honduras], 18 May 1948, *Correspondencia Recibida Ministerio de Relaciones Exteriores, Honduras, 1947–1948.*   .

93. Dispatch, U.S. legation, Costa Rica, to U.S. legations, Tegucigalpa and San Salvador, 7 June 1944, Confidential U.S. Diplomatic Post Records, reel 38, p. 30; Dispatch, Foreign Minister (Honduras) to Honduran Minister (Costa Rica), 16 February 1948, Correspondencia Despachada, Honduras, 2334.

94. Honduran Minister, Costa Rica [to Foreign Minister, Tegucigalpa], 20 April 1948, *Correspondencia Diplomática Recibida, 1947–1948,* no. 180.

simistic report on José Figueres's probable political agenda and its leftist lean-
ings. Among the National Liberation Party's plans the diplomat noted were
"nationalization of all banks, socialization of agriculture, a socialist federation
of Central American Republics adding Panama and the Dominican Republic,
withdrawing recognition of all dictatorial regimes."[95] But Carías was less concerned with Figueres's radical platform than with the presence of Costa Rica's
communist party, Vanguardia Popular, headed by Manuel Mora, in Rafael
Calderón's camp with Teodoro Picado. He therefore cast his lot with the new
democratic left and took his chances with Utilio Ulate, who was installed as
chief executive in 1949 and remained in office until 1953.[96] Central to Carías's
Costa Rica policy was which government would guarantee stability in the area
and be less inclined to meddle in the internal affairs of its neighbors. He recognized that Figueres was anticommunist, but his decision was calculated more
to follow the immediate concerns of the United States, his most important ally,
who could ensure his continuation in office. Although Washington viewed the
Soviet Union and new radical groups as potentially disruptive forces in Central
American politics, it was not as yet prepared to intervene directly on any one
side, as this conflict had not spilled over into other Central American states.[97]

Adhering to the United States's anticommunist stance in 1948, and supporting its security interests in the Western Hemisphere, reflected Carías's
commitment to a close alliance with Washington. Since the economic and political crises in the 1930s helped Carías reach the presidency, loans, financial assistance, and material help to build an infrastructure were essential. The stability of his regime made U.S. interests there secure. His antifascism and
anti-Marxism linked him to North America's World War II goals and Cold war
diplomacy.[98] Only Washington could provide Carías the resources to achieve
his objectives. He felt the simultaneity of his presidential terms with Franklin
Roosevelt created a special kind of relationship during World War II. Later, se-

95. Honduran Minister, Costa Rica [to Foreign Minister, Tegucigalpa], 28 April 1948, Correspondencia Diplomática Recibida, 1947–1948, no. 186.

96. La Época, 24 August 1948, 1.

97. Dispatch, U.S. legation, Tegucigalpa, to Department of State, 28 May 1945, Confidential
U.S. Diplomatic Post Records, reel 41, 771. See also Marcia Orlander, "Costa Rica in 1948: Cold War
or Local War?" The Americas: A Quarterly Review of Inter-American Cultural History, Vol. 52 No. 4, (April
1996): 483 n.64.

98. Mensaje, 1941, 5 December 1941, 219; President Franklin Roosevelt, Washington, DC to President Tiburcio Carías, Honduras, 30 March 1933, Cartas autográficas, 1932–1933, Ministerio de Relaciones Exteriores, Archivo, Palacio de los Ministerios.

curity issues were focused on the creation of an anticommunist alliance in the Western Hemisphere. On the sixteen occasions Carías delivered his annual message to congress he reaffirmed his friendship with Washington. He made no excuses and gave no apologies for this association. Its meaning was clear and its benefits self-evident. He called his administration and plans for economic recovery "El New Deal Hondureño."[99]

Before taking office in March 1933, Carías assembled his cabinet and leaders of congress at the U.S. legation in Tegucigalpa and gave Washington's envoy, Julian Lay, an outline of his forthcoming inaugural address. It was a blueprint for maintaining close relations with Washington from then on. Typically, his statement was brief and to the point. He told his hosts he would first establish peace in Honduras, tackle the economic and fiscal crisis, and pay off the internal and foreign debt;[100] he said he would also promote good relations with all his neighbors. The president made good on the promise in 1933 when he accepted Washington's proposed demarcation boundary line with Guatemala.[101]

The United States was preoccupied with defeating Augusto César Sandino militarily in Nicaragua and supervising presidential elections there in the early 1930s. Carías successfully convinced the Yankees that his Liberal adversaries in Honduras were Sandino sympathizers who wished, he said, "to Sandinize all of Central America."[102] He pointed out that his political rival, Ángel Zúñiga Huete, often linked him with "the regions dictators, Ubico, Hernández Martínez, Somoza, and Franklin Roosevelt's good neighbor policy."[103] Leaving nothing to chance, he made the U.S. president an honorary Honduran citizen and declared the Fourth of July a national holiday.[104]

When Washington briefly held to a position of neutrality as Hitler expanded his forces in Europe in the early 1930s, Carías followed suit. He refused to allow all belligerent warships from entering Honduran ports.[105] But following

99. La Época, 12 November 1934, 3.

100. Diario Comercial, 3 May 1933, 3.

101. Dispatch, U.S. legation, Tegucigalpa, to Department of State, 8 August 1933, Confidential U.S. Diplomatic Post Records, reel 7, 503, 20.

102. Dispatch, U.S. legation, Tegucigalpa, to Department of State, 6 December 1932, Confidential U.S. Diplomatic Post Records, reel 5, 526, 534.

103. La Época, 19 November 1938, 1.

104. Boletín del Congreso Nacional Legislativo, 30 January 1942, 44. Franklin Roosevelt was made an honorary Honduran citizen.

105. La Época, 16 November 1936, 3.

Franklin Roosevelt's efforts to aid England unofficially with Lend-Lease in January 1941, Carías's controlled press observed that "the present policy of neutrality favors the aggressor and ought to be changed."[106] Moving along with Washington's shift on the neutrality issue, he saw the economic and financial benefits to be gained by supporting the United States. Undersecretary of State Sumner Welles, in September 1939, assured Latin American foreign ministers in Panama that Washington was prepared to assist them economically and financially, bolstering democracies in the Western Hemisphere against Axis aggression.[107] Carías joined the Pan-American Financial and Economic Consultative Committee created by the foreign ministers. Its purpose was to show where financial assistance could be utilized to strengthen their economies for regional defense.[108]

When Germany invaded France in June 1940, Washington made plans for a continental alliance. Two U.S. officers, Major Clayton C. Jerome and Captain Maxwell Taylor (who could read and write Spanish, and was later commander of the 82nd Airborne Division in England and commander of U.S. forces in Korea in 1953), traveling in civilian attire, visited Carías and his minister of war, Juan Manuel Gálvez. The North Americans received assurances from Honduras that they would accept whatever military and naval equipment Washington sent for strategic operations in the area.[109] Carías offered territorial waters, railroads, airfields, and port facilities and assured them the use of docks and equipment owned by United Fruit Company.[110]

In subsequent conversations with U.S. military personnel, Carías allowed U.S. patrol boats in Honduran territorial waters and the construction of a naval base in Amapala, in the Gulf of Fonseca.[111] In addition, Honduran aviation services provided photos and reconnaissance services.[112] Honduran cities, ports, and harbors such as Tegucigalpa, Amapala, Puerto Cortés, Tela, La

106. La Época, 22 September 1941, 1.

107. La Época, 25 September 1939, 3.

108. La Época, 20 November, 3.

109. Dispatch, Department of State to U.S. legation, Tegucigalpa, Confidential U.S. Diplomatic Post Records, Honduras 1935–1940, reel 21, 226.

110. U.S. legation, Tegucigalpa, to Department of State, Confidential U.S. Diplomatic Post Records, reel 21, 230.

111. Major Clayton Jerome, U.S. legation, Tegucigalpa, to Captain R. S. Renshaw, UNS, Director of War Plans, Office Chief of Naval Operations, Department of Navy, 4 September 1940, Confidential U.S. Diplomatic Post Records, reel 21, 249.

112. Ibid., 3.

Ceiba, Puerto Castillo, and San Pedro Sula were designated, in the liaison team's words, "to receive technical supplies for defense for continued use by the United States and Honduran Armed Forces."[113] Of lasting significance for Carías, however, was the creation of a "permanent liaison system" of U.S. and Honduran military officers to plan for the war effort.[114] The Hondurans stressed, and Washington agreed to, the need to have military equipment in place for immediate use.[115] Eight months later, in May 1941, arms and ammunition valuing $1.3 million were made available to Honduras. If at any time Carías could not pay for military equipment, Washington was willing to ship the materials directly to him anyway.[116]

Colonel Walter Mayer of the U.S. Army was assigned directly to Carías's office as a liaison between the U.S. legation and the president to facilitate the military supply shipments and work with the Honduran army.[117] The colonel offered the accurate observation that in 1941 the Honduran military "was merely a force of scattered militias, commanded by squabbly generals." "It could," he said, "barely defend the government even from internal unrest."[118]

U.S. diplomats in Tegucigalpa were aware of Carías's deep reservation against arming militias. They cautioned Washington on the need for a large-scale military buildup, "given," as one diplomat said, "the fact that all Hondurans, except the president, can be considered revolutionists. We would not want them trained using molotov cocktails and hand grenades as attempts at revolution might be made."[119]

President Carías declared war on the Axis powers on December 8th, 1941, one day after the Japanese bombed Pearl Harbor. He also announced a state of

---

113. Ibid.

114. Ibid. A permanent liaison system was established between the War Department and Honduras.

115. Ibid.

116. Legation (Washington, DC) to Ministro Salvador Aguirre, Ministerio de Relaciones, Honduras, 16 May 1941, 2. Honduras promised to give unlimited help in the war effort. The United States would facilitate cooperation by making available to the Honduran government $1.3 million worth of arms and munitions.

117. Dispatch, Colonel Walter Mayer (attaché to the office of President Tiburcio Carías) to U.S. Minister John Erwin (Tegucigalpa), 24 June 1941, Confidential U.S. Diplomatic Post Records, reel 24, 576.

118. Ibid.

119. "Memorandum," Blanton Winslip, InterAmerican Defense Board, 13 November 1942, Confidential U.S. Diplomatic Post Records, reel 31, 478.

siege, enlarging his constitutional powers. This was to last until January 1946, two years short of the end of his term. Then he bragged that Honduras had the troops available to send to the battlefield.[120] His liaison officer, Colonel Mayer, assured Washington he did not.[121]

Carías offered the United States the opportunity to build a fueling station at Amapala and an air base on El Tigre Island, both off the southern Pacific coast.[122] The proposal also provided sites for air bases if needed at Puerto Castilla on the north coast.[123] Washington declined the first offer but sent a small navy detachment to the Caribbean port. It remained there until August 1943. Honduran airplanes were made available for reconnaissance in the Caribbean against German U-boats.[124] The United States felt that these sites were not critical to the defense of the Panama Canal. Although inside a defense perimeter, a strategic triangle, Honduras was not to provide key military locations in the war's efforts. The line was drawn from Alaska to Hawaii on to Panamá. Cuban bases at the northern point of the Atlantic began the defense chain south to the western side of the Isthmus, then east to a U.S. base in Trinidad, along the Antilles through Puerto Rico, the Dominican Republic, and Haiti. Approaches to the canal were to be defended with an air base in Costa Rica and a naval station in Venezuela. Western defense lanes to the isthmus would have military bases in Costa Rica, El Salvador, Guatemala, and Nicaragua. Southern access to Panama would have installations in Colombia, Perú, and Ecuador's Galapagos Island.[125]

In his annual messages during the war, Carías painted a picture of heroism and daring by the country's pilots on patrols and boats in the North African invasion in 1943.[126] There were probably damaged merchant vessels and Hon-

120. Mensaje, 1945, 5 December 1945, 294–295; and Boletín del Congreso Nacional Legislativo, 23 February 1946, Biblioteca y Archivos Nacionales.

121. Dispatch, U.S. legation, Tegucigalpa, to Department of State, Confidential U.S. Diplomatic Post Records, reel 31, 478.

122. Stokes, Honduras, 7.

123. Dispatch, Sumner Welles (Asst. Secretary of State), to Department of State, 30 January 1941, Confidential U.S. Diplomatic Post Records, reel 25, 155. Honduras allowed the United States to use a naval base at Puerto Castilla on the north coast.

124. Mensaje, 5 December 1943, 253.

125. "Memorandum," General Staff, War Department, 27 May 1942, Confidential U.S. Diplomatic Post Records, reel 29, 631; J. Lloyd Mecham, The United States and InterAmerican Security (Austin: University of Texas Press, 1961), 219.

126. Mensaje, 5 December 1943, 25.

duran casualties on board these ships. Three, El Tela, El Castilla, and El Comayagua, were sunk in the Atlantic by German U-boats.[127] United Fruit Company's ships also suffered; Miraflores disappeared off La Ceiba en route to the
United States, La Ceiba was sunk, and the Amapala en route to La Ceiba from
New Orleans was fired upon. The captain subsequently abandoned ship.[128]

The lack of any large-scale commitment in troops or strategic sites did not
diminish Carías's total support to the war effort. La Época published all of President Roosevelt's wartime speeches. When El Cronista, sympathetic to the Axis
powers, tried to print rebuttals, Carías threatened to censor it.[129] In contrast to
Guatemala, there were few German nationals or naturalized citizens in Honduras. Yet those few who lived in the country when World War II broke out, approximately 510, owned a considerable amount of property, shipping, and real
estate interests.[130]

Germans from the ports of Bremen and Hamburg came to Honduras in the
1870s during the era of expanding mining and banana interests. The immigration law of 1866 encouraged foreigners as part of the effort to bolster trade.
Most regional commerce moved along the west coast of Central America,
stretching from California to Valparaiso, Chile. Amapala, on the island of El
Tigre in the Bay of Fonseca, became a major trade area linking central and
southern Honduras (Department of Choluteca) to this seagoing trade lane and
with Europe as well. Southern Honduras, including Amapala, was a major
commercial distribution point where around 1887 some 6,000 foreigners
resided. They were mainly engaged in the import/export business. Of this
number, only forty-three were Germans; most were Guatemalans and Salvado-
rans, some Yankees.[131] The Germans maintained ties with commercial houses
in Hamburg and Bremen. The bulk of their merchandise trade was distilled alcohol, bricks, coffee, and leather goods. The Hamburg Pacific Steamship Company was the major carrier of these imports and exports to and from Honduras.[132] Familiar names like Kohncke, Siercke, and Rossner then and well

127. La Prensa Extra (Tegucigalpa), 24 December 1969. The paper reported three Honduran ships
sunk: El Comayagua, El Tela, and El Castilla.

128. Karnes, Tropical Enterprise, 216–17.

129. Dispatch, U.S. legation, Tegucigalpa, to Department of State, 27 January 1941, Confidential
U.S. Diplomatic Post Records, reel 22, 865.

130. Karnes, Tropical Enterprise, 53.

131. Mario Argueta, Los alemanes en Honduras (Tegucigalpa: Editorial Millenium, 1992), 11.

132. Ibid., 13.

into the twentieth century were major entrepreneurs in this part of the country. The Siercke and Kohncke commercial financial interests were wide and diverse. The former employed about five hundred people in their forty-two business establishments, mainly in southern Honduras. They imported wares and merchandise, chinaware, silk, hardware, tools, and liquor, and exported gold, coffee, cheeses, horses, and mules. They made loans for collateral, and held haciendas and property in towns and cities stretching from Amapala to Tegucigalpa. In the city of Choluteca they gave money for the construction of local schools, casinos, and bridges, and built a theater. From time to time they loaned money to the town for special projects.[133]

The Kohncke and Rossner families, also concentrated in Choluteca, focused more on shipping. In 1913 they owned twelve boats and sea-going vessels (from six to thirty tons) that operated in the Bay of Fonseca. They both leased and administered property and, like the Sierckes, loaned money with interest.[134] Numbers belie the considerable influence these German immigrants wielded. In 1917 when the United States entered World War I, there were only twenty-six German merchants total in Amapala, Choluteca, and Tegucigalpa.[135] Pressured by Washington to intern Germans and confiscate their property during World War I, Honduras refused, fearing that costs for paying claims would be enormous.[136] Yet in the interwar era, German imports had declined to 4 percent of total import values, down from 11 percent before 1914.[137] The Siercke, Kohncke, and Rossner shipping, trading, merchandising, and mortgage loan businesses dropped considerably.[138] During this period, these entrepreneurs diversified their commercial and trading activities. They even expanded in some areas, like exporting skins, corn beef, even snake hides. These three German entrepreneurial houses bought 44 percent of the Honduran coffee crop for export in 1938 and 69 percent in 1939.

Washington believed that Carías's opponents, particularly Zúñiga Huete, were being assisted by German agents. Moreover, the United States felt anti-Carías propaganda operations were run by a Baron von Terman, Germany's

---

133. Segisfredo Infante et al., *Los alemanes en el sur, 1900–1947* (Tegucigalpa: Editorial Universitaria, 1993), 60.

134. Ibid., 22.

135. Ibid., 27–29.

136. Argueta, *Los alemanes*, 25–26.

137. Euraque, "Industrialists and Merchants," 124.

138. Argueta, *Los alemanes*, 38.

ambassador in Argentina.[139] As he had in 1936, Carías worked the security issue in his favor. Like Sandino in the 1930s, he said the Nazis were working with his enemies. Washington readily conceded that while the regime could not be considered democratic, it was accepted by most people and governed without bayonets.[140]

Regardless of the extent of German commercial interests, and they were large, Carías was happy to accommodate Washington. On July 11, 1939, the president issued a decree expelling anyone from the country who acts, he said, "with interest against Honduras . . . a government which is republican, democratic, and representative [sic]."[141] The newspaper announcement added that "the decree demonstrates continued solidarity [with the United States]."[142]

The 1940 inter-American conference held in Cuba decreed that European colonies in the Americas could not be turned over to Germany after the invasion of France. The no-transfer principle was added to the 1823 Monroe Doctrine. Carías promptly seized German property. He declared Christian Zinsser, the German chargé d'affaires, persona non grata and deported him and Chilean colonel Manuel Hormazabal. The latter was revising military manuals and was considered a pro-Nazi propagandist. Carías closed the Italian consulate in La Ceiba[143] and its cultural center in Tegucigalpa, Casa de los Italianos. Then he ordered his Investigation Unit of the National Police to begin a surveillance of all aliens, and ordered all Japanese to be imprisoned.[144] There was only one Honduran of Japanese extraction, Juan Ivata Iranoga, who lived in the Department of Cortés. Authorities could not agree as to whether he should be incarcerated.[145] Washington's black list of German properties to be confiscated in-

139. Dispatch, U.S. legation, Tegucigalpa, to Department of State, 27 January 1941, Confidential U.S. Diplomatic Post Records, reel 24, 381.

140. Dispatch, U.S. legation, Tegucigalpa, to Department of State, 7 April 1942, Confidential U.S. Diplomatic Post Records, reel 29, 722.

141. La Época, 11 July 1939, 3.

142. La Época, 3.

143. Dispatch, U.S. legation, Tegucigalpa, to Department of State, 8 July 1941, Confidential U.S. Diplomatic Post Records, reel 24, 328; Ministerio Legación Italiana, Guatemala to Salvador Aguirre, Ministro de Relaciones Exteriores, Honduras, 8 November 1940, Correspondencia Diplomática Recibida de la Legación de Italia, 1940–1941.

144. "U.S. and Honduras Military Staff Conversations on Hemisphere Defense," Tegucigalpa, 6 September 1940, Confidential U.S. Diplomatic Post Records, reel 21, 285.

145. Telegramas Recibidas del Departamento de Cortés desde enero a junio del año de 1944, Vol. 32, Biblioteca de Telegrama, Biblioteca y Archivos Nacionales.

cluded the largest three commercial establishments, Siercke, Kohncke, and Rossner. No one in these families was expelled. They employed several hundred Hondurans and had close ties with the country's political leadership.[146] However, their properties were seized and placed under state control in the Ministry of Hacienda. Some were later sold to Carías's cronies. Others did not fare as well. Of the 510 Germans residing in the country, fifty-three were deported.[147]

Total assets of Francisco Siercke in 1941 reached 7.25 million lempiras. Public sales and auctions of merchandise, furniture, machines, and tools brought 542,745.21 lempiras. Urbano Quesada, a Carías loyalist and minister of hacienda, crédito público, y comercio, was the principal beneficiary of the auctions.[148] Quesada acquired 55 percent of Siercke's beer distillery, Cervecería Tegucigalpa, at a public sale.[149] The Sierckes did not recover their property after the war. At one point, Francisco, who once headed the considerable family resources, asked the government for 200 lempiras as "necessary personal expenses."[150] The family's property in Nicaragua was returned in 1954. Although they never recovered their business in Honduras, they remained in Choluteca throughout the war and after.

The several inter-American conferences held from 1933 on through the war dealt with the hemisphere's defense against the Axis powers and with economic recovery. Carías sent representatives to all meetings with instructions for paying special attention to matters. Beginning in 1943, he devoted an entire section of his annual message on foreign policy to financial and technical conferences.[151] By 1944 his government had received $300,000 for health and sanitary projects.[152] These funds were received under a U.S. plan to work on economic problems bolstering Western-style democracies. Carías was anxious to reduce his country's external debt, so he created the Honduran Committee on Post-War Problems.[153] Its purpose was to find ways to expand and diversify exports and

146. Segisfredo et al., *Los alemanes en el sur*, 54, 90.

147. Ibid., 54.

148. Ibid., 95.

149. Ibid.

150. Ibid., 93.

151. *Mensaje*, 5 December 1943, 250.

152. *Memoria del Congreso Nacional, 1942–1943*, Ministerio de Relaciones Exteriores, Biblioteca y Archivos Nacionales, 156–158.

153. *Boletín del Congreso Nacional Legislativo*, 2 April 1946, 16.

promote commerce and trade. Last, he wanted loans from the International Monetary Fund and the International Bank for Reconstruction and Development. Both were established at the Bretton Woods meeting in July 1944.[154] In effect, he placed Honduras's financial recovery, fiscal stability, and military security on the U.S. postwar recovery program. His continued loyalty to Washington also assured economic help with military assistance during the cold war.

The delivery of armaments from the United States during and after World War II for Western Hemisphere defense served Carías well. Funds and supplies helped build the country's infrastructure and reduced unemployment. Lend-lease offered the first largesse in military supplies in 1942 with rifles and ammunition.[155] Carías's son Gonzalo, Honduran consul in New York City in 1941, purchased approximately 150,000 rounds of ammunition from Remington Arms Company in Bridgeport, Connecticut.[156] A year earlier, Carías deposited $20,460 in the National City Bank in Manhattan for arms purchases.[157] By 1946, the country received defense materiel under the term of a lend-lease agreement in February 1942 worth at total of $362,118.17. The bulk of the equipment went to the air force. He continued to reject outright any plans to build up a professionally trained army. He did not want to build an institution of this kind, particularly if segments of a new military force were to be deployed anywhere outside of Tegucigalpa.[158]

Yet Carías in fact changed the structure of his military forces during World War II, establishing a close liaison with U.S. Army, Army Air Force, and Navy personnel.[159] Local militias were merged, trained, and directed from the na-

154. Memoria, 1944–1945, Ministerio de Relaciones Exteriores, Archivo, Palacio de los Ministerios, 3–4.

155. U.S. minister [to Honduran Foreign Minister], 16 July 1942, Correspondencia Recibida de la Legación de los Estados Unidos de Norteamérica en Honduras durante el año económico de 1942–1943.

156. Armando Flores, Ministro de Hacienda, to Antonio Bermúdez, Ministro de Relaciones Exteriores, Correspondencia Recibida de la Secretaria de Hacienda y Crédito Pública, 23 September 1935; Honduran Foreign Minister to Honduran Minister, Correspondencia Enviada -a la Legación de Honduras en Washington durante el año económico de 1940–1941, 17 January 1941, vol. 30; April 1941, 1–2.

157. Acuerdo No. 484, 27 May 1939, Acuerdos de la Oficina Mayor, Ministerio de Guerra, Ministerio de Guerra, Archivo, Palacio de los Ministerios.

158. Dispatch, U.S. Secretary of State to Foreign Minister, Honduras, "Confidential": "to date $367,118.17 has been spent on the purchase of arms through 1946. $180,311.13 spent on the air force. $69,890.95 on the army." Correspondencia Diplomática Recibida de Varias Cancillerias, 1947–1948, 11 August 1947, Archivos, Comisión de Frontera y Soberania, Comyaguela.

159. Memorias de guerra, marina, y aviación, 1941–1942, Biblioteca y Archivos Nacionales, 4–5.

tional level, but Carías insisted they remain as before in departments and municipalities.[160] Officer training emphasized command structure, obedience, and loyalty to the state as a professional institution. The aviation school headed by a North American gave the air force a new mission. It would operate for the first time outside Honduran territory with anti-submarine reconnaissance training flights with the U.S. Army Air Force in the Caribbean.[161]

The number of army recruits increased in 1942–43, and departmental militias received infantry training assisted by U.S. military personnel. The old "Special Expeditionary Force" led by Carías's loyalists of civil war days was enlarged. Its officers and enlisted personnel became professionals (and later formed the nucleus of a national army).[162] The president established an annual "Day of the Soldier" to instill a new sense of loyalty to the nation.[163] Therefore, by 1945, as World War II drew to a close, Honduras had a U.S.-trained Light Regimental Combat Team with 122 officers, three warrant officers, and 2,588 enlisted men. In addition, it had one light infantry regiment, a field artillery battalion, and engineer and quartermaster companies.[164]

Four years later, and one year after Carías left office, his successor, Juan Gálvez, mentioned the significance of these evolutionary changes in the Honduran military. For the first time a chief executive used the term "professional army." He said, "We no longer speak of militias and their stations in departments but the Basic Arms School in the capital under direction of officers from Ft. Benning, Georgia."[165] The air force extended its anti-submarine reconnaissance in the Caribbean to joint training operations with the United States in Panamá, Jamaica, and Trinidad.[166] It retained its own tactical functions but also was designated as a transport service for the new army.[167]

Although Carías was always cautious modernizing and professionalizing militias, the creation of an officer corps was based on significant developments in his regime during the 1940s. An attempted coup d'état in 1943 and the deaths

160. Ibid., 103.
161. Ibid., 9–11.
162. Ibid., 3.
163. Ibid., 5.
164. Memorandum, U.S. Military Attaché, U.S. embassy (Tegucigalpa) to U.S. ambassador, 3 July 1945, Confidential U.S. Diplomatic Post Records, reel 42, 576.
165. *Memorias de guerra, marina, y aviación, 1941–1942*, Biblioteca y Archivos Nacionales, 5.
166. Ibid., 6.
167. Ibid., 10–12, 14.

of longtime loyalists as local militia commanders reduced his sense of security. His nephew Calixto, who was his eyes and ears on military affairs, died in July 1944. Two of his friends, "generals of the mountains," veterans of numerous civil wars, Francisco Martínez Funes and José López, commander in San Pedro Sula, died in 1943 and 1944 respectively.[168] A mutiny in the San Francisco army headquarters in Tegucigalpa forced Carías to change commands there. A nephew of the ever-faithful Carlos Sanabria was believed to be involved in the uprising. The president took no chances and removed his longtime ally as comandante de armas in Trujillo on the north coast.[169]

In July 1944, his old friend General Justo Rufino Solís, the comandante de armas in La Ceiba, considered a bid for the presidency when, as he hoped, Carías would step down in 1949. Solís was actively making contact with Liberal Party figures in the northern departments. When the anti-Carías San Pedro Sula demonstration took place the same month, Solís criticized the military forces there for acting too carelessly by shooting dissidents. The general suggested that in the wake of changing regimes in Guatemala and El Salvador, Carías should call elections in Honduras sooner than 1948, the year his term was to end. Solís's brief sojourn into national politics was short-lived. Carías wanted a first-hand report on the July San Pedro Sula demonstration from him, so the president sent a plane to pick him up for the trip to Tegucigalpa. After Solís's briefing, he returned to the airport for the return flight to his post, but there was no plane available for him. From then on, Solís's militias were no longer reinforced with arms or supplies from outside his jurisdiction.[170] This incident showed a break in the old alliance of veteran caudillos, and it worried Carías.[171]

The July 1944 demonstrations in Tegucigalpa and San Pedro Sula were warnings that security needed tightening. The U.S. military attaché observed that "the loosely organized bands of local militias needed to be re-organized."[172] Consequently, Carías for the first time named a "head of the army" a

---

168. El Cronista, 18 June 1943, 3.

169. "Political and Economic Forces Report," 24 April 1944, Confidential U.S. Diplomatic Post Records, reel 38, 462.

170. U.S. vice consul, La Ceiba, to U.S. legation, Tegucigalpa, 6 July 1944, Confidential U.S. Diplomatic Post Records, reel 38, 712.

171. El Ciudadano (San Pedro Sula), 31 August 1948, 1–2. See an account of Solís's political activities in Consejo supremo del Partido Liberal: panorama político de Honduras (Tegucigalpa, 1948), Doc. No. 438, 6; Gálvez Barnes interview, 8 November 1987.

172. "Military Intelligence Report, Morale and Loyalty," 6 November 1944, Confidential U.S. Diplomatic Post Records, reel 3, 627.

longtime loyalist, Juan B. Chávez. The same age as the president, he had fought with Carías in military campaigns beginning in 1908 all the way through the 1932 War of Traitors.[173] Under Chávez, military service was made compulsory and police contingents were added to fuerzas extraordinarias (now made into permanent standing units). Appointments to command Chávez's forces came from the pool of officers located in the capital, not departments as before. Carías explained his reasons for enlarging the army as a necessary step to prevent the return of the age of civil wars and revolts.[174] He also faced numerous incursions from Honduran exiles in Guatemala and El Salvador after Presidents Ubico and Hernández Martínez fell in 1944.

In 1946, a U.S. military mission visited Tegucigalpa, and a special session of Congress was convened to greet the guests. Plutarco Muñoz, the president of the legislature, gave the welcoming address. He offered effusive praise for the Honduran military forces. Under Carías, he said, "it would again go to war on the side of the United States, this time, against the Communist octopus." At this point, the U.S. minister in attendance observed that "politically, the Nazis have gone [and] the Communists have not yet arrived." Anti-Marxism as a continuing Western Hemisphere security issue in the postwar era was the centerpiece of Carías's new relationship with Washington. This strategy would continue to bolster his political position and enhance the power of the state as the Axis threat had done in the 1930s and 1940s. The Attaché Office made "stability reports" beginning on November 6, 1944. They always referred to communist influence in Honduras coming from México's labor leader Vicente Lombardo Toledano and supported by the USSR. In many ways Carías fulfilled his primary foreign policy goals in Central America and in relations with Washington. He tied his regime's security goals almost exclusively to the United States. But the victory of the Allied powers in time attributed to the loosening of the dictator's alliance in Central America. This in turn emboldened Carías's enemies at home and abroad. Their successes and failings would be measured on the president's capacity to resist them and accommodate them.[175]

173. La Época, 17 June 1944, 3.

174. Mensaje, December 1944, 272–73.

175. "Weekly Reports," U.S. Military Attaché Office, U.S. embassy (Tegucigalpa), Military Intelligence Division Report, Confidential U.S. Diplomatic Post Records, reel 38, 627.

9

Encierro, Entierro, Destierro
The Opposition

Unlike other movements in Central America and the Caribbean against dictators in the mid-1940s, the opposition to the Carías regime was ineffective. Without a cohesive ruling class and with the Liberal Party broken into factions at home and abroad, Carías easily outmaneuvered his adversaries. His political skills as a decades-old veteran in local and National Party organizations made him a unique foe, a master of his house. Carías astutely measured the strengths of his enemies, both inside and outside Honduras. He also played on Washington's fears of communism and became one of that country's patrons fighting Marxism in the post–World War II era. He managed to stay the course when many of his fellow dictators fell.

On May 28, 1944, three hundred women dressed in mourning led by Emma Bonilla, daughter of the late president Policarpo Bonilla; María Marta Zúñiga, daughter of exiled opposition leader Ángel Zúñiga Huete; and the prizewinning poet Argentina Díaz paraded past Carías's presidential palace shouting "*encierro, entierro, destierro*" ("jail, burial, exile"). They demanded the release of political prisoners.[1] Later that same day, a demonstration of about 2,500 people marched and called on Carías to end incarceration, killing, and exile of the regime's opponents; give women the right to vote; allow a free press; and permit exiles to return home. Placards called for his resignation. How, the protestors asked, could this dictatorship continue as a member of the community of free nations?[2] On July 4, a large gathering of professionals, doctors, lawyers, and engineers presented Carías a signed petition calling for him to resign.

The president's response to these pleas reflected the way his regime largely dealt with the opposition. He brushed off the demonstration, dismissing it as an

1. *El Ciudadano*, 21 July 1948, 1; Bonilla de Larios interview, 18 November 1987.
2. Elpidio Mejía, *4 de Julio 1944*, 143.

"outburst of women new to politics,"[3] and adopted the tactic of accommodation. He listened to their demands, then incarcerated or exiled its most extreme activists. Carías also agreed to allow the demonstration to take place on July 4, a national holiday in Honduras which he had decreed a few years before in an effort to ingratiate himself with the United States. The marchers were allowed to parade by his residence, not the military barracks, thereby avoiding a confrontation and possible armed conflict. The crowd passed the chief executive's home and walked to the city's main plaza where it called for him to step down.

As the demonstration continued downtown, Carías, in an effort to diffuse the protest, received a committee of approximately seventy people who represented the multitude. After the members presented their views, Marta Carías, the president's daughter, joined them on the balcony of the residence to greet the crowd below. While this strategy of conciliation unfolded before the public, government troops were posted at the residences of several Liberal Party leaders, students from the National University were jailed, and sixteen people fled to the Salvadoran and Mexican embassies.[4]

Washington's response to the demonstration was typical throughout the Carías era. It instructed its military and diplomatic staff not to engage in any activity supporting the demonstration. The embassy had long since conveyed its unqualified support for the regime.[5] The U.S. ambassador, when given flowers by María Marta Zúñiga at the chancery door, refused to appear before the crowd outside to thank her, not wanting to show any support for the opposition.[6] The episode reflected but a sector of the Honduran opposition and how it operated against Carías. Some grasped the chance to speak to the president personally and persuade him to accept changes they demanded. Others who persisted in their public outcry in the central plaza felt the oppression of the regime with imprisonment or exile. Carías listened, used force if necessary, and incarcerated his adversaries if they continued their protests.

3. *Informe*, Ministerio de Gobernación, 1944–45, Archivo, Palacio de los Ministerios, 284.

4. U.S. Military Attaché Report to the U.S. legation, Tegucigalpa, 4 July 1944, Confidential U.S. Diplomatic Post Records, reel 38, 503. The United States reported 100 students jailed, thirteen people fleeing to the embassy of El Salvador, and three to the Mexican embassy; Dispatch, U.S. legation to State Department, 6 July 1944, Confidential U.S. Diplomatic Post Records, reel 38, 134.

5. Instructions to Lt. Col. Harold White (Chief, Honduran Air Force), and Major Malcolm Stewart (Director, Honduran School of Aviation), Office of Military Attachés, dispatch, U.S. legation to Department of State, 10 July 1944, Confidential U.S. Diplomatic Post Records, reel 38, 222.

6. Dispatch, U.S. legation to Department of State, 7 July 1944, "Political Demonstration," Confidential U.S. Diplomatic Post Records, reel 38, 146.

The Carías government was indisputably a dictatorship. However, as mentioned before, it was not as cruel and oppressive as the Ubico, Trujillo, and Hernández Martínez regimes in Guatemala, the Dominican Republic, and El Salvador; nor was it as personally greedy for financial gain as Anastasio Somoza's in Nicaragua. Repression existed, but it did so more through intimidation, which by any standard of assessment is hard to gauge. Documentation was scarce, gossip pervasive, and critics saw examples of abuse everywhere. Apologists for the regime called specific cases rumor. As one observed, "Intimidation is largely in the mind of the person intimidated, it is extremely difficult to find unambiguous examples of it."[7] Its application under Carías involved different types of coercion. The regime applied a wide range of punishments such as exile, press censorship, and jail. It utilized a security system to intimidate Liberal opponents and National Party dissidents as well. If political opposition moved from simple rhetoric to organized activism at home or invasion from abroad, then punishment ranged from a guard placed at one's home to imprisonment for days or, in some cases, years. More often than not, incarceration ended when the crisis ended.

Carías did not take unusual security precautions as he went about his tasks as chief executive. He never carried arms, nor was he protected by a police guard. However, he seldom walked the streets of Tegucigalpa as a president *en camisa* ("in shirt sleeves"), more often traveling about in an armed car with a driver.[8] He always made reference in speeches to his accessibility and the public's warm response to his presence.[9]

Members of the Liberal Party, his chief opposition, could remain in the country provided they did not actively organize to oust him. Their efforts to mount campaigns in election years were almost always frustrated by lack of finances and organization. Many of the party's leaders went into exile when they were unable to stop Carías's extension of power in 1936.[10] The National Party made legal opposition almost impossible. Liberals who remained in Honduras experienced imprisonment or house arrest, depending upon the extent to which they criticized the regime. If they stayed out of politics altogether, they could pursue professional interests and remain in the country with little or

7. Howard Wiggins, *The Ruler's Imperative* (New York: Columbia University Press, 1969), 161.

8. Prats interview, and 21 July 1987; Ayes interview, 5 November 1987.

9. *Mensaje, 1937–1945*, 5 December 1943, 265.

10. Charles Ameringer, *The Democratic Left in Exile: The Anti-Dictatorial Struggle in the Caribbean, 1945–1959* (Coral Gables: University of Florida Press, 1974), 49.

no harassment. If an opponent of the regime, a Liberal or Nationalist, was exiled, that person's family was allowed to remain at home. Yet they were watched and their activities reported by *orejas* ("ears"—spies). On occasion, when the exiled relative openly criticized the government or, worse, participated in an invasion to overthrow the regime, the family was placed under house arrest.[11] For example, Ángel Zúñiga Huete left Honduras after his electoral defeat to Carías in 1932. He failed on several occasions to return home, but when he criticized the regime from abroad, his brother, Manuel, who remained in Honduras, endured harassment and house arrest.[12] Generally, the harsher punishments, like detention, imprisonment, or execution, were handed out by departmental military commanders or local political chieftains. Carías was never personally associated with these capricious and violent penalties meted out in local jurisdictions.[13] Intimidation was applied in subtle ways. For example, lawyers and doctors found that the number of their clients and patients declined or ended altogether when they participated in any anti-government activity. Merchants and shopkeepers experienced a dramatic loss of business.[14]

Carías cooperated closely with his neighbors, Presidents Ubico, Hernández Martínez, and Somoza, to end armed incursions and organized opposition in their countries. For example, for years he detained and placed under house arrest longtime Somoza critic Toribio Tijerino of Nicaragua.[15] Carías was conscious of and cultivated the image of a conciliator. Stressing order and peace, he frequently issued statements calling for exiles to return home. If they sent a telegram agreeing to do so, he published it and offered to provide air transportation for the flight back. However, he emphasized that reconciliation with the regime meant accepting his time-honored theme of peace and order. This meant in effect ending resistance to his rule.[16]

Two prisons, the Central Penitentiary in Tegucigalpa and the Castillo de

11. Guerrero interview, 23 October 1985.

12. Interview with José Reina Valenzuela, Liberal Party leader and close associate of Ángel Zúñiga Huete, Tegucigalpa, 11 March 1987; Dispatch, U.S. Military Attaché report to the U.S. embassy, Tegucigalpa, 17 September 1945, Confidential U.S. Diplomatic Post Records, reel 42, 38. The dispatch gives an account of Carías's decision not to incarcerate members of Ángel Zúñiga Huete's family, particularly his brother, Manuel Guillermo Zúñiga Huete.

13. Valenzuela interview, 11 March 1987; Zúñiga Cáceres interview, 14 August 1987.

14. Dispatch, 17 September 1945, 38.

15. U.S. Military Attaché report to U.S. embassy, Tegucigalpa, "Activities of Nicaraguans in Honduras," 3 October 1944, Confidential U.S. Diplomatic Post Records, reel 38, 598.

16. *La Época*, 6 June 1943, 1; *New York Times*, 22 May 1936.

Omoa in the Department of Cortés on the north coast, were major detention centers. Both, particularly the second, carried an aura of mystery and fear. Castillo de Omoa housed many political prisoners and was for some time under the complete jurisdiction of local authorities. As Carías assumed authority over municipalities like Puerto Cortés and Omoa, local detention centers came under his government's supervision.[17] Generally, however, jails throughout the country were filled with political dissidents and criminals incarcerated by local authority rather than from Carías's dictates.[18] The Central Penitentiary mostly held people judged guilty of sedition and treason.[19]

Indisputably, Carlos Sanabria, the comandante de armas of Atlántida, was considered the most brutal dispenser of justice in the Carías regime. Sanabria's detentions and executions were viewed more as responses to offenses against his authority. But Carías concurred, never once criticizing these actions. Challenging Sanabria's or Carías's authority brought swift judgment, jail, and death.[20] One of Honduras's leading literary critics and journalists, Arturo Martínez Galindo, a relentless opponent of the Carías regime, was assassinated by Sanabria's henchmen. He was once a codirector of *Revista Ariel* with the writer Froylán Turcios. He founded, directed, and edited several newspapers, among them *Renovación, El Ciudadano,* and *El Norte.* His *Breve Análisis del Momento Político Hondureño* was a biting indictment of the government from 1936 to 1939, the period following continuismo. Carías exiled him several times for a particular treatise and attacks on the government. Galindo persisted, condemning the dictatorship at home and abroad.[21]

People who were suspected of being members of the illegal Communist Party were summarily imprisoned. Manuel Calix Herrera, head of the Liga Sindical del Norte and a Marxist, died in Castillo de Omoa. Juan Pablo Wainright, a labor leader, fled Honduras, but he was captured in Guatemala and Jorge Ubico ordered him shot.[22]

17. *Memoria,* Ministerio de Gobernación, 1935–36, Archivo, Palacio de los Ministerios, 59.

18. *Acuerdo* (EM) No. 538, 4 May 1936, Ministerio de Guerra, Marina y Aviación, January–August 1936, Archivo, Palacio de los Ministerios.

19. *Informe,* Ministerio de Gobernación, Penitencia Central, 1944–1945, Archivo, Palacio de los Ministerios, 279–80.

20. *La Tribuna,* 17 February 1947, no. 12, 2.

21. Louisa Benneton de Galindo (widow of Arturo Martínez Galindo), interview, Tegucigalpa, 5 May 1987.

22. Salomón Sanabria, *La cárcel y mis carceleros* (México: Talleres del Editorial JUS, 1952), 32. Frequently, people who spoke out before audiences were ignored by the regime; even Ruben Rodríguez,

Only one newspaper, *La Época*, was allowed to publish throughout the Carías era. It was run by a longtime loyalist, Fernando Zepeda Durón. It acted as the official mouthpiece of the dictator. Less fortunate were newspapers that criticized the government even mildly. *El Cronista* in Tegucigalpa, once a Fascist journal, underwent an abrupt turnaround during World War II, proposing elections and the restoration of democracy. One of its writers, Alfredo Trejo Castillo, wrote a series of articles urging Honduras to join the victorious Allies politically by restoring democracy. The writer included the names of lawyers and priests who were asking for the release of political prisoners.[23] Castillo bravely and foolishly unleashed a torrent of criticism on Carías, calling him *el delincuente político* ("the delinquent politician").[24] For his criticism he was exiled and *El Cronista* was closed in June 1943. From El Salvador, Trejo became a major organizer of the armed resistance to the regime.[25]

Other journalists and editors of newspapers were detained, imprisoned, or exiled for their criticism of or organized opposition to the government. J. Antonio Peraza, once a National Party member and director of San Pedro Sula's *El Heraldo*, escalated his indictment of Carías after the presidential term was extended in 1936, and again in 1943. For his unceasing editorial barrages he was first jailed, then released and exiled. Like the exiled Alfredo Trejo Castillo in El Salvador, he became a leader of Honduran exiles in Guatemala.[26] The list goes on. Antonio Castillo Vegas, editor of *El Ciudadano* in Tegucigalpa, was jailed for two years. The paper was closed.[27] *El Espectador* in La Ceiba was shut down November 30, 1935. Its editor, Adolfo Miraldá, went into exile.[28] Manuel Barahona, director of *El Norte* in San Pedro Sula, was briefly imprisoned. His paper was forced to change its staff and editorial view. It ended all political reporting and became merely a news tabloid.[29]

---

a Communist Party leader in La Ceiba, was allowed to address rallies. Vice-Consul Wimberly Coerr to U.S. embassy, Tegucigalpa, 2 December 1941, "Report, Political Activities in La Ceiba."

23. *El Cronista*, 29 May 1943, 3.

24. *El Cronista*, 3 June 1943, 3.

25. Amilcar Gómez, Guatemala, to Alfredo Trejo Castillo, El Salvador, 21 May 1946, Amilcar Gómez Robelo Papers, San Pedro Sula, 175–76.

26. José Antonio Peraza (director, *El Heraldo*) to Amilcar Gómez, Guatemala, 7 May 1945, Amilcar Gómez Robelo Papers. Peraza, a National Party member who became a Carías critic, was briefly jailed and later exiled.

27. *El Ciudadano*, 30 November 1935, 1.

28. *El Espectador* (La Ceiba), 30 November 1935, 1; Zúñiga Huete, *El desastre de una dictadura*, 24.

29. *El Norte* (Atlantida), December 1944; U.S. consul, Puerto Cortés, to U.S. embassy, Teguci-

Several well-known writers, essayists, and journalists suffered repeated harassment, jail, and exile. Among the better known were Ismael Mejía Deras,
Ernesto Matamoros Lucha, Guillermo Bustillo Reina, José Castro, Alfonso
Guillén Zelaya, the historian Rafael Heliodoro Valle, and writer Froylán Turcios.[30] This massive exodus reflected the dictatorial nature of the Carías
regime and its refusal to entertain criticism. Yet brutality, torture, and abuse
were absent against relatives of critics who remained in Honduras and remained silent.[31]

Oftentimes during and after the Carías dictatorship, poems appeared in
Honduras critical of the regime. A few were blunt and frank about their targets,
others more subtle and stinging. But curiously, the language in works published abroad and in Honduras was directed more at the president's henchmen
and only, if at all, in oblique fashion against the president himself.

Biting attacks were also leveled at local political and military chieftains like
Carlos Sanabria of the northern department of Atlántida. Others, like Plutarco
Muñoz, president of the legislature; Lowell Yerex, the pilot, arms carrier, and
bombardier; and Carlos Izaguirre, Carías's "jack of all trades," deal maker, and
essayist, were targets of sarcastic treatises.

SELECTED FLAWS

Sanabria did not like the heat in Trujillo
those temperatures did not suit him
they would melt his eyeglasses
and had him drinking water like a fish
he kept writing letters asking for a replacement
asking for repellents against snakes and mosquitoes
which daily attacked him in that no man's land
in that land where the Spaniards always shipwrecked
and where palm trees grew old just like his hands

---

galpa, "Political Review of Puerto Cortés," 26 February 1944, Confidential U.S. Post Records, reel
38, 757.

30. El Crónico (Tegucigalpa), 10 July 1943, 3; 11 July 1943, 1.

31. This view is reflected in the statements of several Carías's critics to the author. Among them
are José Antonio Barahona Ortega, conspirator in the Presidential Honor Guard coup attempt; and
José Reina Valenzuela, Oscar Guerrero, and Liana Zúñiga de Cáceres, leading members of the department's Liberal Party governing directorate.

just like the name of his daughters grew old
those daughters who yawned and cut flowers
when he got off the car
when he came back full of fever
or just to rest in silence
because after all it was not easy to keep order
among those peasants
who would not let themselves be shot
and who sprung from the sea like fish[32]

RAIN OF FISH
to Roberto Sosa

Plutarco Muñoz hated fish
especially those which rained in incredible amounts
during election times
this made the people forget about the congressmen
like himself
who had conquered barbarism and old habits
conquered malaria
and even conquered the scorched hills where one could hardly breathe
especially in Yoro
where those strange things happened
such as one fish falling just like that
on any common day
and ruining his oratory
or making the people close the doors
worrying about the end of the world
one had to fight against those fish
that ruined everything with their scales
one had to take away the people and the superstitious matrons
who saw him as the man
who brought bad luck
one had to sprinkle salt/rosewater/or decrees
just like those which he himself signed in Congress
in those times
when the fish filled the homes with music[33]

32. Jose González, *Poemas del Cariato* (Tegucigalpa: Editorial Guaymuras, SA, 1984), 31–32.
33. Ibid., 33–34.

THE LAST FLIGHT OF LOWELL YEREX

lowell yerex came from New Zealand
but he became a Honduran the rough way
he learnt how to chew tobacco
and to inhale the coarse smoke it produced
he was impressed
with the khaki color of those times and by the fashion of carrying a pistol
    under the belt
he was impressed to such extent that just a few weeks later
he was wearing a hat like the commanders
he spoke like them
and he was respected
we shall never forget he fought for Carías in 1932
when nobody believed that aeroplanes existed
(the same ones that overflew El Sauce[34]
throwing smoke and scalding water on the troops)
or that he founded TACA
to bring liquor and arms
and gunpowder and bronze for the busts sculpted at that time
and also the machines to open the mouths of the mines
that was Lowell Yerex's last flight
after that he used to have his picture taken
and listen to the band
on Sundays and other holy days[35]

Overall, Carías felt secure in power all during his tenure as president, though less so, perhaps, before the 1940s. Yet throughout his term, patterns of repression or a lessening of control reflected the times when he felt threatened either inside the country or from abroad. He exercised vast, almost unlimited, executive powers from 1939 to 1946 after decreeing a state of siege. The Foreign Residents Act (1939) also gave him authority to prohibit organized political activity. Although directed to people "of German or Italian extraction,"[36] the law was enforced to include all "subversive groups."[37]

34. The name of an unidentified town. Many villages and towns were called "El Sauce" because they were built near willow trees (sauce).

35. González, Poemas del Cariato, 21–22.

36. El Cronista, 9 June 1943, 1. See also Organo de la Asociación Nacional de Cronistas, Año II, No. 18, 30 June 1939, 34.

37. Ibid.

Carías was harsh on critics and dissidents in 1933, 1936, and 1944, when his position was less tenable. During the War of Traitors (1931–33), the intractable rebel leader General Justo Umaña was chased west into Guatemala and shot by the cooperative Ubico government. Liberal partisans were summarily imprisoned, shot, or forced out of the country. But when Carías was securely installed as president and his allies were in full control of departments, he allowed forty-seven rebels to return to Honduras from Nicaragua. They were permitted to live in Amapala and would not have to stand trial for their insurrection. A major holdout was Justo Umaña, who continued armed resistance. He attacked a military post in El Progreso in the Department of Yoro on February 14, 1936. Francisco Martínez Funes, Carías's longtime ally, defeated him there. The opposition remained deeply divided, principally over tactics, military, and propaganda campaigns. Some Liberals landed from Belize, others from Guatemala and El Salvador. Ángel Zúñiga Huete felt totally frustrated when trying to control these separate forces. He had no plans to mount a military campaign to oust Carías. He focused all his attention on keeping warring factions united. He wanted to use the ballot box to end the president's rule.[38]

In 1936 when continuismo was affirmed, Carías canceled elections, closed newspapers, and imprisoned and exiled editors. It became noticeably difficult, if not impossible, for Liberals to run for congress and municipal government posts from then on.[39] Several National Party leaders and members of congress, such as Ramiro Carvajal, Mariano Bertrand Anduray, and Venancio Callejas (grandfather of President Rafael Leonardo Callejas, 1988–1994), who objected to the chief executive's extended term without an election, were exiled. Venancio Callejas openly broke with Carías over the issue of the leadership of the National Party. Callejas objected to Carías holding the candidacy of the party for president and serving as head of the party as well. Callejas had been selected as the National Party candidate for vice-president, but after Carías continued his term, Callejas's wife and children went into exile.[40] Yet none of them abandoned the party. In exile, however, mostly in Costa Rica, they led other dissi-

---

38. *Tegucigalpa*, 26 May 1933, 1; *Memorias, Ministerios de Gobernación 1936–1937*, 11; Ángel Zúñiga Huete, Guatemala, to Froylán Turcios, Rome, 26 February 1936, Nora Landa Blanco Trochez Papers, Tegucigalpa; Ángel Zúñiga Huete, Guatemala, to Froylán Turcios, Rome, 23 August 1933, Trochez Papers.

39. Zúñiga Huete to Turcios, 23 October 1940. Ángel Zúñiga Huete wanted Liberals in Honduras to run for congress in the fall elections in 1934.

40. *El Pueblo*, 25 February 1932, 1, 8; Bonilla, *Continuísmo y dictadura*, 14.

dents in efforts to criticize the Carías regime in newspapers or participated in military campaigns to invade Honduras. Elements of the Liberal Party, despairing of any chance for electing candidates to congress and limiting Carías's 1932 term, fled to Nicaragua and El Salvador with National Party partisans of Venancio Callejas. Ángel Zúñiga Huete and Venancio Callejas agreed to a pact in 1936 whereby Rafael Medina Raudales, minister of fomento under the Mejía Colindres administration, would become president should Carías be ousted. There was little chance that these political leaders could enact the plan, as Callejas was in Costa Rica and Ángel Zúñiga Huete in Mexico City.[41]

From late 1936 to 1940, members of the opposition, if not openly critical of the regime, were not intimidated, detained, or imprisoned. Carías was clearly confident of his control. But as World War II progressed and an Allied victory seemed probable, the Carías dictatorship, like its neighbors in Guatemala and El Salvador, felt the pressures for reform from a new and burgeoning middle sector. Citizens of San Pedro Sula were especially critical of the political dictatorship in the capital. This north-central metropolis witnessed the growth of a commercial class, people who in turn looked for greater participation in government. Dictatorships, as allies of Western democracies, became glaring embarrassments, anomalies up against the commitment of the Atlantic Charter and its call for defeat of the Axis regimes. A coup attempt led by Liberal Party figures and General Salvador Cisneros in mid-October 1940 was quickly put down. The general was "retired." "Thankfully," the U.S. legation said, "arrests were carried out quietly . . . there is no popular support for this."[42]

In November 1943, a second coup occurred. This one was more serious because it involved members of the president's Honor Guard along with Liberal Party members. The plan was to go into effect on November 21. Conspirators included eighty people, a few guard members, some from headquarters, and general staff of the army, several of whom had military training in México, Guatemala, and the United States. Many were Liberal "volunteers" and others National Party dissidents, among them José Callejas, brother of Venancio Callejas. The civilian component was under the direction of Emilio Gómez Ro-

41. *Memoria de Gobernación, 1935–1936*, 84. By 1942, the Liberal Party no longer ran candidates for congress. U.S. Minister Lay to the Department of State, 9 October 1942, Confidential U.S. Diplomatic Post Records, reel 29, 64, microfilm. Policarpo Callejas (son of Venancio Callejas), interview, Tegucigalpa, 28 November 1987.

42. U.S. legation to Department of State, 22 October 1940, Confidential U.S. Diplomatic Post Records, reel 21, 370.

belo, a journalist and prominent Liberal. The operation was led by the commander of the Honor Guard, Captain Jorge Ribas Montes, a twenty-three-year-old graduate of the military school in Guatemala.

The plan was doomed from the start. There was no coordination between the volunteers, guardsmen, and general staff headquarters. Nor was anyone delegated to assume executive power had the operation succeeded. One member of the Honor Guard, José Barahona Ortega, said the operation was betrayed by an informer in the guard whom he called "a leper, a vampire," Mario Sosa Navarro.[43]

The coup attempt was significant because its leaders, especially the military officers, were frustrated with Carías's unwillingness to form a professional army. Along with Liberal and National Party dissidents, they wanted to place a cadre of army leaders in the center of political opposition to the regime. This coup attempt marked the first time Honduran officers (all trained abroad) linked their political interests with civilians.[44]

The coup failed and the plotters were dismissed from the presidential Honor Guard and imprisoned for two years. Barahona Ortega was held in solitary confinement for eleven months.[45] Ribas Montes was condemned to death but instead spent two and a half years in prison. He then left Honduras for Costa Rica to form a Liberation Army. He was joined by four others: Miguel Francisco Morazán, a descendant of President Francisco Morazán; Francisco Sánchez Reyes ("El Indio"); Alfredo Mejía Lara; and Mario Sosa Navarro.[46] Again relieved that Carías had survived a second coup attempt, the U.S. legation held on to the need for stability rather than reform. It noted that, "at age 67, the President is still in good health-holding on. His death would result in total

43. José Antonio Barahona Ortega (member of the Presidential Honor Guard and conspirator to kill Carías), interview, Armenia, Department of Francisco Morazán, 28 November 1987. Barahona Ortega's motive was simply that Carías had stayed in power too long; only death could remove him. No more than twenty-five or thirty people were involved. Plotters had counted on 300 people to assist in the military takeover.

44. "The Conspiracy Plotted against Tiburcio Carías Andino," El Heraldo (Tegucigalpa), 7 March 1997, 2–3. This article was written as a letter to the editor by a conspirator, Marco Tulio Mendieta.

45. Ibid. Barahona said he and his cohorts were optimistic that their plans could be carried out with the support of public opinion, as presidents Ubico of Guatemala and Hernández Martínez of El Salvador had been ousted.

46. Ameringer, The Democratic Left in Exile, 62.

chaos."[47] Curiously, plot members liked Carías and admired his valor and strengths as a politician, but they felt he had been president for too long. They were grateful for the peace and order he had given Honduras. Now, they asked, what about freedom?

Confidently, Carías held municipal elections in November of the same year. His National Party was in full control of electoral machinery and elected all their candidates with a total of 88,725 votes.[48] The hapless Liberals received 1,228 votes. Carías praised "the near unanimous vote" and accepted an extended third term to 1949. His loyalists in congress made him Fundador de la Paz de Honduras y Benemérito de la Patria ("Founder of Honduran Peace and Benefactor of the Country").[49]

Carías's control of Honduras with a little less than a 1.25 million people seemed secure. Coups aborted and rigged elections confirmed his total control. Yet in 1944, general strikes in Guatemala and El Salvador brought down Jorge Ubico and Maximiliano Hernández Martínez. Carías faced more demonstrations and a strike by university students demanding press and political freedom, elections, and the ouster of the president. Students in the School of Medicine and Engineering quit classes and refused to sign a Declaration of Allegiance to Carías as the heads of the school had demanded. Store owners called for a general strike but failed to generate widespread support. In response to the protests, the government released forty prisoners.[50] On July 6 in San Pedro Sula and in La Ceiba, marchers passed by the offices of United Fruit Company, taunting chants at the Yankee enterprise. Marches celebrating U.S. independence on July 4 were staged as a protest to Carías's regime. Six hundred people marched in front of the United Fruit Company manager's office in La Ceiba. The government ordered all soldiers and police off the street to avoid any confrontations. Carías decided to allow the marchers to proceed without interference.[51]

47. "The Conspiracy," 2–3. Plotters were also anxious to stop an alleged Carías succession plan whereby his son Gonzalo would succeed him.

48. U.S. legation to Department of State, 30 November 1943, Confidential U.S. Diplomatic Post Records, reel 33, 841. National Party candidates for municipal posts polled a total of 88,725 votes, the Liberals a mere 1,228.

49. Carías called the victory "almost unanimous"; Mensaje, 5 December 1944, 272.

50. U.S. embassy, Tegucigalpa, to Department of State, 6 July 1944, Confidential U.S. Diplomatic Post Records, reel 38, 110.

51. U.S. consulate, La Ceiba, to U.S. embassy, Tegucigalpa, 6 July 1944, Confidential U.S. Diplomatic Post Records, reel 38, 12.

Suddenly the Carías regime and those of his neighbors came under siege. In El Salvador, Hernández Martínez stepped down on May 9, and a handbill carried into Honduras in late May or early June 1944 said, "I have just felt and struggled in the prodigious Revolution that freed the people of El Salvador. . . . This glorious and magnificent act of our Salvadoran brothers should serve as an example and encouragement to you, oppressed people of Honduras. . . . Women of Honduras: imitate the women of Cuscatlan who in this struggle has been the most heroic and self-denying. Students, professionals, workers, working people in general, let us prepare ourselves for the peaceful strike which is the only action that can overthrow the tyrant of tyrants, Tiburcio Carías Andino."[52]

Students, teachers, professionals, lawyers, and doctors in Guatemala began a general strike. Students in Nicaragua demonstrated against Somoza, carrying signs that read, "The Students of Nicaragua are with the Democratic Students of Central America," "We Shall Sustain Democracy in Central America, Cost What It May," "The Students Persecuted by Ubico Call for Vengeance," and "The Students of Honduras Will Put Down Carías."[53]

Following his usual method, the Honduran president moved with caution and efficiency, avoiding a direct confrontation with demonstrations in the cities. In fact, he ordered troops off the streets in Tegucigalpa and San Pedro Sula.[54] At the same time, however, he had his National Police and departmental military commanders detain and imprison people, specifically the opposition's major leaders. On the orders of jefes políticos many people were jailed, some released. Most cases of imprisonment were reported in San Pedro Sula, the center of protest in the northern part of the country. The U.S. embassy had a list of imprisoned protesters. Six were released in June 1945; sixteen others remained in custody.[55] Carías strengthened garrisons and dispatched his closest allies, old "generals of the mountain," to key port cities to prevent the shipment of arms into the country. He strengthened military garrisons along the El Salvadoran border near Amapala. From El Salvador, exiles called for

52. Patricia Parkman, *Nonviolent Insurrection in El Salvador: The Fall of Maximiliano Hernández Martínez* (Tucson: University of Arizona Press, 1988), 1.

53. Ibid., 2.

54. U.S. consulate, La Ceiba, to U.S. embassy, Tegucigalpa, 17 August 1944, Confidential U.S. Diplomatic Post Records, reel 38, 582. Some protesters were jailed but then released.

55. U.S. embassy, Tegucigalpa, to Department of State, 29 June 1945, Confidential U.S. Diplomatic Post Records, reel 41, 1050.

Carías's ouster just as had happened to Hernández Martínez.[56] Modesto Amador was assigned to the southern port of Amapala. On the north coast, Rufino Solis was dispatched to La Ceiba, Rafael Ponce to Puerto Castilla, Fermín Boquín to Puerto Cortés, and Eduardo Rosales to Tela.[57] As a precautionary measure, troops were sent to the Guatemalan and El Salvadoran frontiers and were prepared to take cross-border action if deemed necessary. These troops, numbering 485 in all, mostly from units stationed in departments contiguous to El Salvador and Guatemala and a few troops stationed in Tegucigalpa, were called "strike forces."[58]

Prominent women, among them Emma Bonilla de Larios, daughter of the Liberal Party leader Policarpo Bonilla, witnessed the march on July 4, 1944, in Tegucigalpa. Marchers walked to the central park. Most of the protesters were women, students, and children. They distributed a leaflet saying, "Carías resign." Emma Bonilla recalled that the government ordered the troops off the streets, deliberately avoiding any confrontation.

Counter-demonstrations supporting Carías went as scheduled on July 10, but in San Pedro Sula several people were killed and wounded on July 6. The demonstration in San Pedro Sula, numbering approximately a thousand people, called for the release of political prisoners, freedom of the press, civil rights, and the end of the dictatorial rule. Carías ordered the withdrawal of military personnel, as he had done in La Ceiba and Tegucigalpa. He allowed the marchers in San Pedro Sula to parade along the Avenida Comercio (also known as Avenida Tercera), one block from the police station. Protesters and local officials agreed that no speeches were to be given either at the rally or at the end of the demonstration. Several of Carías's advisers wanted him to send troops to the city, where antigovernment sentiment was considered the strongest. Instead, he sent Juan Manuel Gálvez, minister of war, navy, and aviation, to monitor events. He had lived in San Pedro Sula, knew the area, and was therefore expected to soothe leaders he knew. According to Robert Gálvez Barnes, son of Juan Manuel Gálvez, his father flew to San Pedro Sula and decided to allow the July 4 march to proceed on Calle Comercio but prohibited the making of speeches.

56. U.S. legation, Tegucigalpa, to Department of State, 2 August 1944, Confidential U.S. Diplomatic Post Records, reel 38, 1.

57. *Correspondencias recibidas de la Secretaria de Guerra, Marina y Aviación*, 1944–1945, Archivo, Palacio de los Ministerios, 87.

58. Memo, U.S. embassy, Confidential U.S. Diplomatic Post Records, reel 38, 36.

Colonel Ángel Funes, commander of the Central Plaza, observed the march while carrying a .45 pistol. By chance he encountered an old rival, Alejandro Irias, once governor of Olancho. Shots were exchanged, either between them or their partisans. At that moment, José Antonio Peraza, a member of the November 1943 plot and now a demonstration organizer, mounted the balcony in the plaza ordering the crowd to disperse. Policemen nearby, believing the ban on speeches had been violated, and hearing shots, opened fire. One round hit a soldier; then firing began. Several were shot, some wounded, and others fled. Accounts of the number of casualties vary from 20 deaths to 144. [59]

The San Pedro Sula march of July 6 had been organized by prominent political leaders, mostly Liberals. Among them were Oscar Guerrero, Graciela Bográn, Amilcar Gómez Robelo, and José Antonio Peraza. Most of these people escaped to private homes and eventually fled to El Salvador or Guatemala. They had no funds, army, or prominent leader. Exiles in these different countries never merged their efforts. The Carías forces had deeply divided the opposition— what was left of it—at home and abroad.[60] The consequences were enormous, as it was the first time the Carías government had openly confronted a civilian opposition. But accounts of the dead and wounded brought to full attention the oppressive rule of Carías all over the Americas. His longtime efforts to maintain a low profile as a dictator were shattered.

The San Pedro Sula massacre became an international episode. Exile groups in Guatemala, El Salvador, Costa Rica, and México publicized accounts of it in full. To counter the widespread coverage and outrage over the carnage, Carías sent his own press releases to capitals of Central American states, Mexico City, Washington, and consulates in New York City, San Francisco, New Orleans, Havana, and Panama City.[61] The smoldering discontent among Hondurans, contained by the shrewd and wily Carías for so long, erupted full-blown throughout the hemisphere.

The president survived these demonstrations because they were separate, held in two cities and not linked politically or strategically. Dissidents, Liberals, and many Nationalists in Honduras lacked the means and wherewithal to oust Carías. A general strike, although planned, never materialized. Even though

59. Gálvez Barnes interview, 30 October 1987.

60. Bonilla de Larios interview, 26 November 1987; Guerrero interview, 16 October 1987.

61. Military Intelligence Report, "Servicio Internacional de Prensa," U.S. embassy, Tegucigalpa, to Department of State, 22 September 1944, Confidential U.S. Diplomatic Post Records, reel 38, 593.

exiles from El Salvador crossed the border into Honduras in October and captured the town of San Marcos, the incursion was not coordinated with dissidents inside the country.[62] In April 1945, Carías's opponents in Guatemala raided the western town of Copán, but that too failed to work with other opponents of the regime at home.[63]

In 1937, people opposed to continuismo had founded the Asociación Revolucionaria (Revolutionary Association) in San Pedro Sula. But those who fled the country bickered over its leadership. The first exile organization was formed in 1937, the Asociación Revolucionaria Hondureña; another was formed in 1944 in Guatemala, Frente Democrático Revolucionario Hondureño (FDRH). In 1946, the Partido Democrático Revolucionario Hondureño (PDRH) was organized in Tegucigalpa and San Pedro Sula, combining the above two parties.[64] Later in Guatemala and El Salvador, Honduran exiles established the Partido Democrático Revolucionario de Hondureño (Honduran Revolutionary Democratic Party). The organization was a radical wing of the Liberal Party established in San Pedro Sula in 1946. It was not associated with the FDRH, which was made up of traditional Liberals exiled by Carías after the San Pedro demonstrations in 1944.[65] In 1947, three years after the demonstrations, the two groups merged and officially became the Partido Democrático Revolucionario. It had directorates in San Pedro Sula and Tegucigalpa, yet for practical purposes they operated independently of each other after 1946. The FDRH central committee remained in Guatemala City with committees in Costa Rica, El Salvador, and Mexico City. The exiles promised to join the PDRH later. Generally, members of this loosely tied opposition were from the country's small middle sector—lawyers, doctors, schoolteachers, merchants, engineers, and students. Many of its members refused to recognize Ángel Zúñiga Huete as their leader.[66]

Like the Democratic left in other Central American and Caribbean states in the 1940s, the PDRH condemned caudillo politics, including both Liberals and Nationalists.[67] As a democratic socialist party, it took the Peruvian Victor Raúl

---

62. Oscar Guerrero estimates that there were anywhere from 3,000 to 5,000 exiles. Guerrero interview, 16 October 1987.

63. Leonard, *The United States in Central America*, 115.

64. *Vanguardia Revolucionaria* (San Pedro Sula), 13 December 1947, 1.

65. Euraque, *Reinterpreting the Banana Republic*, 42.

66. "Memorandum," Frente Democrático Revolucionario Hondureño, n.d., Amilcar Gómez Robelo Papers, 99.

67. PLN: National Liberation Party in Costa Rica; PR: Revolutionary Party in Guatemala; AD:

Haya de la Torre's APRA (American Popular Revolutionary Alliance) as its model. Its platform resembled the radical reformist liberalism of President Juan José Arévalo of Guatemala and José "Pepe" Figueres of Costa Rica in the late 1940s and early 1950s. PDRH members greatly admired their fellow countryman Froylán Turcios, and his journal *Ariel* for its efforts in the 1920s to emphasize Honduran cultural, political, and economic independence.[68] The party newspaper, *Vanguardia Revolucionaria*, was founded in 1945 and published clandestinely in San Pedro Sula until 1954. It never successfully linked the widely scattered opposition groups in Honduras with the exiles in the rest of Central America and México. The paper frequently published transcripts of radio broadcasts by exiles from their Radio Mitin in Guatemala.[69] Marcos Carías Reyes, the president's nephew and a strong advocate of Honduran cultural nationalism, founded the *Vanguardia Nacionalista* (1946–1949) to counteract *Vanguardia Revolucionaria*.[70]

More than organizational difficulties plagued the opposition forces in the mid-1940s. The PRDH condemned both Liberals and Nationalists for engaging in civil wars and backing the Carías dictatorship. Many rejected Ángel Zúñiga Huete's leadership as well. As the caudillo of the Liberals, in fact once a close friend and collaborator of Carías at the turn of the century, Ángel Zúñiga Huete was labeled a relic of the past, a product of the old politics of personalism.[71] He was desperate to establish himself firmly as the leader of Honduran exiles and pressured others in Guatemala, El Salvador, and Costa Rica to follow his lead and bring down Carías. He called for the general strike of 1944. In letters and personal visits to Guatemala City from México, Zúñiga Huete admitted flaws in his leadership as an organizer and mediator but appealed to Hondurans' patriotism and his experience to unite them.

Democratic Action in Venezuela; PDR: Democratic Revolutionary Party in the Dominican Republic; Populist Party in Puerto Rico led by Muñoz Marin.

68. *Vanguardia Revolucionaria*, 17 June 1946, 3–4.

69. *Vanguardia Revolucionaria* published broadcasts from the exile-run Radio Mitin in Guatemala. *Vanguardia Revolucionaria*, 23 August 1947, 1.

70. *Vanguardia Revolucionaria*, founded in 1945, was published weekly and distributed clandestinely until it was seized in October. Carías also asked a close associate, Francisco Martínez, to begin a newspaper to counter the *Vanguardia*. He did so from 1946 to 1949 and called it *Vanguardia Nacionalista*. Francisco Martínez, interview, Tegucigalpa, 19 October 1987.

71. Many Liberals requested Ángel Zúñiga Huete's leadership. They did so to avoid a caudillo with a strong hand in party matters like Tiburcio Carías. "En memoria ante la tumba," Amilcar Gómez Robelo Papers, 348.

The 1944 exiles were a generation younger than Zúñiga Huete. Having failed to bring down the dictator in the 1944 demonstration, they wanted to use force. Needing funds and arms, the Guatemalan-based group urged Zúñiga Huete to act; "we cannot wait indefinitely," said one. Zúñiga Huete struggled to unite Liberal exile groups in México, Guatemala, and El Salvador, but he had lost contact with many of these exiles since the 1932 elections. These separate groups had their own leaders, yet all lacked funds. They felt Zúñiga Huete was too cautious, lacking a political agenda and a strategy for ousting Carías, either by force, which seemed unlikely, or the ballot box. One member put it bluntly to the Liberal chieftain: "You have little influence here [in Guatemala] or in El Salvador."[72] Specifically, the younger exiles denounced a 1936 Ángel Zúñiga Huete–Venancio Callejas (Nationalist) pact to field a ticket to run against Carías in 1943 as old politics. While not casting the Liberals out of their organization, figures like Amilcar Gómez Robelo and Antonio Peraza, veterans of the San Pedro Sula debacle now in Guatemala, refused to accept Zúñiga Huete's leadership. They asked instead that collective decisions be made. Honduran exiles in El Salvador and Costa Rica were less impatient with Zúñiga Huete. They simply deplored the poor regional organization of exiled Liberals and urged him alone to take command of all groups.[73]

Yet Carías's enemies abroad realized that Ángel Zúñiga Huete remained the best known and most popular anti-carísta. They knew he was important to their efforts to topple the dictatorship,[74] but they refused to abide by his decisions and directives. Zúñiga Huete traveled from México to Guatemala and El Salvador in late fall of 1944 to try to organize the exile groups under his leadership. He viewed his greatest challenge as merging pre- and post-1944 exiles. He wrote an open letter to all exiles proclaiming that there was such thing as Zúñigahuetismo. "I am a simple Liberal Party soldier," he said. He disavowed any plans to be candidate for any post in a popular election.[75]

---

72. Amilcar Gómez, Guatemala, to Ángel Zúñiga Huete, México, 9 October 1944, copy, Amilcar Gómez Robelo Papers, 3.

73. The Honduran exiles in El Salvador formed El Comite Liberal Democrático de Honduras. Amilcar Gómez Robelo Papers.

74. The PDH tried to create an overall unification plan for exiles in México, Guatemala, and El Salvador. José Antonio Peraza, Finca California in Guatemala, to Amilcar Gómez, Guatemala City, 10 June 1946, Amilcar Gómez Robelo Papers, 136–37.

75. Ángel Zúñiga Huete, México, to Amilcar Gómez, Guatemala, 18 October 1944, Amilcar Gómez Robelo Papers, 2.

The young exiles were not convinced. To them, Zúñiga Huete did not press hard enough against the dictatorship. They felt he lacked the tenacity, the fire, to win militarily. He relied too heavily, they said, on the vain hope that when free elections were held, if ever, he would run and win. Their impressions were correct. Once in a letter to Froylán Turcios in Mexico City, he said, "I have no plans to return to Honduras. They [militant exile groups] say that victory is for those who suffer and wait. I chose the path of Don Quixote. . . . I do not reject my political romanticism."[76] He depended entirely on Liberal leaders inside Honduras to plan an uprising. He wanted Liberals in San Pedro Sula to act first, seizing the city's military installation; then he, with other exiles from Guatemala, would invade.[77]

Exiles in Guatemala hoped for military support from the newly reformed Guatemalan government to invade Honduras. They asked Captain Jacobo Arbenz of the Guatemalan army to help them. Carías was actually aware of the deep divisions within the opposition. In May 1945 he released some political prisoners in an effort to show his magnanimity.[78] Jacobo Arbenz, finding that the Honduran exile activity made relations with Tegucigalpa unpleasant, forced Ángel Zúñiga Huete out of the country.[79]

Hondurans in El Salvador were more willing to accept Zúñiga Huete's leadership. The Nationalist Venancio Callejas selected a Liberal, Rafael Medina Raudales, as his candidate for provisional president in the event Carías fell. They also mounted a propaganda campaign asking the United States for help in their cause. Two hundred rebel forces attacked San Marcos de Ocotepeque, twelve miles into Honduras from the El Salvadoran border.[80] "Why," they asked in one article, "did Washington support Carías with planes to kill his own people trying to establish a democracy?"[81]

Venancio Callejas and former president Vicente Mejía Colindres (1928–32)

76. Ángel Zúñiga Huete, Guatemala, to Froylán Turcios, Rome, 9 January 1945, Trochez Papers.

77. Ángel Zúñiga Huete, Guatemala, to Antonio López and Carlos Perdomo (Liberal leaders in San Pedro Sula), n.d., Confidential U.S. Diplomatic Post Records, reel 38, 305.

78. Boletín (Guatemala), 18 December 1944, Amilcar Gómez Robelo Papers, No. 302.

79. U.S. embassy, Tegucigalpa, to Department of State, 21 May 1945, Confidential U.S. Diplomatic Post Records, reel 12, 200.

80. U.S. embassy, Mexico City, to Department of State, 17 August 1944, copy to U.S. embassy, Tegucigalpa, Confidential U.S. Diplomatic Post Records, reel 38, 2.

81. Rebel forces also criticized Carías and the Roosevelt administration. They attacked the U.S. president for his support of the dictatorship. In an open letter from México, Honduran exiles there published a directive by the "Union Patriotica Centro-Americana" attacking the Somoza regime in Nicaragua, Carías, and U.S. ambassadors to both governments. The letter is dated 27 December

were in Costa Rica in 1945. Ángel Zúñiga Huete believed that since the former remained opposed to Carías and Liberal exiles were cooperating with their counterparts in Honduras, an electoral victory someday was possible. Both Callejas and Mejía Colindres devoted their time publishing articles in San José attacking Carías's dictatorship. Often the Carías press included responses to criticism from Honduran exiles. Venancio Callejas's articles in *La Tribuna* (Costa Rica) were answered in *La Época*. Neither Callejas nor Mejía Colindres actively participated in organized exile movements. Through letters intercepted by the U.S. Embassy in El Salvador, Carías learned, to his relief and satisfaction, that the successor government to Maximiliano Hernández Martínez was giving no help to the exiles. Exiles in El Salvador did not expect help from the government. Even though a longtime dictator had been ousted, they reported, "El Salvador is run by the army . . . [they] are the Lords of the House."[82]

Honduran intellectuals like Froylán Turcios in Costa Rica and Rafael Heliodoro Valle in México also distanced themselves from the exile movement. Valle initially made several attempts to solicit the help of President Juan José Arévalo in Guatemala and lobby U.S. senators in Washington.[83] But Valle recognized the PDRH only as a movement to oust Carías, not a party to replace the Liberals.[84] At one point, leaders of the FDRH wanted Valle to become its standard-bearer, replacing the ineffective Ángel Zúñiga Huete. They felt Carías would be hard-pressed to oppose the revered historian. They also hoped Washington might find his candidacy acceptable.[85] Valle made several well-publicized trips to Central American capitals calling for an end to dictatorships. He even wrote articles in the *Vanguardia Revolucionaria*.[86]

1943 and enclosed in Dispatch, U.S. embassy, Tegucigalpa, to Department of State, 7 January 1944, Confidential U.S. Diplomatic Post Records, reel 38, 794. The U.S. legation in Tegucigalpa speculated that communists might be members of the group; see reel 38, 794.

82. Dr. José Callejas, San Salvador, to his wife, Tegucigalpa, n.d., Confidential U.S. Diplomatic Post Records, reel 38, 339.

83. The writer Rafael Heliodoro Valle reported to Amilcar Gómez that U.S. senators had expressed an interest in aiding groups to oust Carías. Rafael Heliodoro Valle, Washington, DC, to Amilcar Gómez, Guatemala, 4 February 1946, Amilcar Gómez Robelo Papers.

84. Rafael Valle joined the Frente Democrático Revolucionario Hondureño. Valle, Washington, DC, to Amilcar Gómez, Guatemala, 30 June 1945, Amilcar Gómez Robelo Papers.

85. Exiles liked having Valle join them; they believed he was a creditable person. Amilcar Gómez, Guatemala, to Rafael Valle, Washington, D.C., 30 November 1945, Amilcar Gómez Robelo Papers.

86. Rafael Heliodoro Valle wrote articles in *Vanguardia*, 14 August 1946, 1; 20 September 1946, 2; 9 October 1946, 1. Valle also published articles of a literary nature in *Tegucigalpa* in 1946–47.

Visiting Honduras in May 1946 to assess the political situation, Valle was invited to visit Carías.[87] After the meeting, he told exiles in Guatemala that the president had offered all of them the chance to return home. Despairing of obtaining any material help after this offer, exiles bemoaned that Valle had been duped by the dictator. They concluded that his excessive idealism and his naiveté made him an unlikely opposition figure. Their only hope was free elections. Prospects for a military campaign were also fast receding.[88] Despite Valle's misgivings about the Carías dictatorship, he wanted to see the two-party system continue, not be weakened or encumbered by new political groups. Actually, his involvement in politics as a Liberal extended back to the era of President Policarpo Bonilla at the turn of the century. Members of his family were close associates of party stalwarts like Ramón Reyes, Alberto Membreño, and Ramón Rosa. He considered Bonilla his patron, and even received a pension from him when studying abroad in México. Later, after returning to Honduras, he frequently praised him for his leadership as a main architect of the party's renovation, a courageous person with a program and a vision for the nation.[89]

The Carías-Valle meeting in the spring of 1945 marked a turning point in the latter's participation in the FDRH. He concluded that since there was no unity in the exile movement, opposition to Carías was futile. He felt that if a plebiscite were held, the president would likely win. Valle, once an outspoken critic of Carías, appeared to be convinced of the chief executive's willingness to release political prisoners, welcome exiles, and hold elections. Washington diplomats in Tegucigalpa were elated that the popular literary figure was accepting the Carías regime. His words, "The choice is not between Carías and democracy, rather between Carías and chaos," were glumly received by exiles.[90]

A story widely circulated in newspapers giving an account of Valle's conversation with the president reached Carías's critics outside Honduras in Central

87. Valle met Carías in Tegucigalpa in January 1948. With elections planned and Carías not running, Valle endorsed the plan to elect a new president and vice-president. *La Época*, 29 January 1948, 1.

88. Valle's meeting with Carías was met with cautious hope: "We have to believe in el Maestro Valle because he is a just man and never has he said anything dishonorable." Valle had reported to the exiles that Carías would allow dissidents to return home. José Antonio Peraza, Guatemala, to Amilcar Gómez, Guatemala, 17 May 1948, Amilcar Gómez Robelo Papers.

89. Rafael Heliodoro Valle, "Bonilla El Procer: Esquema para una biografía," in Ismael Mejía Deras, *Policarpo Bonilla: Apuntes Biográficos* (México: Imprenta Mundial, 1936), xxxvii–xli.

90. U.S. embassy, Tegucigalpa, to Department of State, 7 May 1945, Confidential U.S. Diplomatic Post Records, reel 141, 1022, 1055.

America. According to the story Valle had said, "I can't leave Honduras without a souvenir since I am a tourist." When Carías asked him what he wanted, he replied, "Three political prisoners." He then listed their names, and Carías turned them over to him.[91]

In 1947, Valle endorsed the candidacy of Juan Manuel Gálvez, Carías's chosen successor for president. He was certain fair elections would take place. Moreover, he believed his longtime friend Gálvez could win and be a democratic chief executive. For his endorsement of the Carías regime in its remaining year, Valle was awarded an honorary degree from the Universidad Central de Honduras[92] and made special representative of Honduras to the inauguration of Carlos Prio Socarrás of Cuba in 1948.[93]

Valle's departure from the FDRH left its leaders demoralized. They openly condemned his betrayal.[94] He was expelled from the organization in December 1947. His rewards from the dictator continued, however. He was made Honduran ambassador to Washington. There he pursued his literary interests at the Hispanic Foundation in the Library of Congress and established the Ateneo Americano, where renowned Latin American historians and writers published their works.[95]

Froylán Turcios, indisputably the preeminent Honduran intellectual of his day, remained in Costa Rica. Much to the disappointment of exiles, he did not become engaged in the movement abroad. In fact, Turcios said he was not in Costa Rica for political reasons but only for his health and to run a bookstore. Left demoralized by his disinterest in criticizing the Carías regime, he said, "I am free to return to Honduras anytime with absolute security."[96] Like Valle, he succumbed to the lure of the Cariato. At the initiative of Fernando Zepeda Durón, director of _La Época_ and a member of congress, Turcios was granted a lifetime pension "for literary services granted the country."[97]

91. Celeo Murillo Soto, _Un hondureño y una actitud política (en busca) de la concordia_ (Tegucigalpa: Talleras Tipográficos Nacionales, 1948), 46.

92. A degree of honoris causa in philosophy was bestowed on Rafael Valle on 1 July 1948. _La Época_, 17 August 1948, 1.

93. _La Época_, 21 October 1948, 3.

94. _Vanguardia Revolucionaria_, 6 May 1948, 3.

95. Oscar Acosta, _Rafael Heliodoro Valle: vida y obra_ (Rome: Instituto Italo-Latino-Americano, 1981), 91.

96. _Revista del Archivo y Biblioteca Nacional_, December 1943, 322–32.

97. _Tegucigalpa_, 18 February 1940, 1, outlines a proposal to give Froylán Turcios a lifetime pension; it was granted at 2,000 lempiras monthly.

Both Valle and Turcios chose reconciliation—not combat to resolve the issue of dictatorship. Their positions devastated morale among exiles abroad.
Their actions can be explained in part by the fact that they were of the generation of the 1920s and 1930s, which witnessed civil wars, the politics of the machete, and they deplored those early days. The FDRH misjudged the two men's
political instincts and temperament when it hoped they would adhere to the
organization's call for militarily liquidating both the Liberal and National
Parties.[98] Froylán Turcios earlier broke with the Nicaraguan Augusto César
Sandino on that very issue. The rebel wanted to begin a new political movement
outside the traditional two-party system. More compelling and convincing to
Valle was the fact that he saw an opportunity to end the Carías rule when the
president said in December 1944, "I will leave office when the Honduran people
choose my successor."[99] Typically Carías, the phrasing was deliberately vague.
It was not a resignation or a promise to step down when his term ended in 1949.
Yet it was an opening, a crack in the dictatorial system. Some pounced on it.
Valle did. He felt any further commitment to war or casting aside the country's
two parties was foolish.

The Honduran opposition in exile remained hopelessly divided with
groups located in Guatemala, El Salvador, Costa Rica, and México. The Liberal
Party was later merged into a democratic left in the 1950s under the leadership
of President Ramón Villeda Morales (1957–63),[100] but this took place after
Carías left office. Generational problems may have been at the root of the
problem too. The younger political activists, most from the new and small
middle class, were veterans of the San Pedro Sula massacre. They rejected outright the leadership of both the National and Liberal Parties. The PDRH reflected their views on contemporary politics. This group was democratic, so-
cialist-reformist, and wanted elections and constitutional government, not
dictatorship and Honduras's politics of combat. Antonio Peraza, the young
journalist and FDRH leader in Guatemala, made the most accurate and telling
observation on the effectiveness of Carías's opponents abroad in March 1946
when he said, "The only good we can do as émigrés is return to Honduras and

98. José Antonio Peraza, Guatemala, to Amilcar Gómez, Guatemala, 7 July 1945, Amilcar
Gómez Robelo Papers.

99. *Mensaje*, December 1944, 289. Carías said, "I will leave office when the Honduran people
choose my successor."

100. Ameringer, *The Democratic Left in Exile*, 49.

fight on the side of our friends in a civil-political campaign they now are waging."[101]

The antidictatorial movement in Honduras was the weakest in Central America. The Honduran elite was not a well-organized sociopolitical element. Moreover, the young Liberal veterans of the 1944 demonstrations rejected the leadership of Ángel Zúñiga Huete, the titular head of the party. With the PDRH they attempted to create a new, progressive group outside both political parties but failed. Even the National Party showed signs of internal dissent with the establishment of the National Reformist Movement (MNR). Like the PDRH, it challenged Carías. But Honduras had no institutionalized and professional military caste from which opposition to the dictatorship could emerge in the 1940s as in Guatemala and El Salvador.

Ironic, but maybe an advantage for Carías, was the fact that modernization and economic recovery came to Honduras well after its neighbors. Coffee was a relatively new and small industry as a cash crop in the postwar era. Carías's government started to gain economic strength as the Ubico and Hernández Martínez regimes declined in productivity, leaving a growing middle class—which Honduras lacked—angry and frustrated. In 1948, per capita gross domestic product in Honduras was still less than the pre–World War II peak. The growth of banana exports was negative, and cotton production had little or no effect on trade receipts. The country's manufacturing base was the weakest in Central America. It lacked large cities, which were centers of social and economic change. Only 10 percent of the Honduran population of 1.4 million in the late 1940s lived in communities over 10,000 people. Tegucigalpa had 72,000, San Pedro Sula, 21,000.[102]

U.S. diplomatic relations with Carías were correct and formal, yet they lacked closeness. One historian described these ties as "officially not supporting his regime . . . but unofficially . . . less deplorable than Anastasio Somoza in Nicaragua and Rafael Trujillo in the Dominican Republic."[103] Washington accepted his stewardship because the country was peaceful, fiscally responsible, and had no unemployment—a nation where most people seemed to accept a benevolent dictatorship. Some U.S. diplomats viewed the caudillo as "a great

101. José Antonio Peraza, Guatemala, to Amilcar Gómez, Guatemala, 16 May 1946, Amilcar Gómez Robelo Papers.

102. Dunkerley, *Power in the Isthmus*, 525.

103. Leonard, *The United States in Central America*, 109.

Honduran patriot, entirely without ambitions beyond his own frontier."[104] The Department of State correctly concluded that Carías could not be ousted violently because the opposition was too divided. Diplomats in Tegucigalpa were certain that he would complete his term. They also stressed the need for a peaceful transition to his successor, a factor banana company officials pressed on them. Leading National Party candidates like Minister of Defense Juan Manuel Gálvez and Vice-President Abraham Williams, both considered possible successors, were viewed as trustworthy moderates, people not expected to upset the political landscape.

Carías survived exile invasions, assassination attempts, aborted coups, and demonstrations. These events drew adverse attention to his dictatorship and the anomaly it posed in a world undergoing rapid change and democratization. Former president Mejía Colindres once called Carías the "Juan Domingo Perón of Honduras." He was not that, but his regime, still intact, was grounded in the old school of Latin American dictatorships begun in the 1930s. He was a veteran of forty-eight years in politics, thirty-four of them before he became president in 1933. He outmaneuvered his adversaries in the late 1940s as he had in the past.

The year 1944, a watershed year in caudillo politics in Central America, was another test of Carías's wiliness, and he dealt with it effectively. He applied force, offered mediation, and enticed his would-be adversaries home by offering them pensions and perks. Thus, opponents in Honduras and abroad could not agree on how to oust him. They were separated by geography, ideology, and tactical distances, and Carías took each faction on, one at a time, and dealt them all a psychological blow by promising to step down. He frustrated some by not saying when, but others were satisfied enough to end their war and wait for a turn at the ballot box. He was a dictator who set the pace and calculated the timing for change. These were his moves, not theirs. He would step down, but not leave politics. Assessing Carías's stewardship, taking measure of the man as they knew him, diplomats in Tegucigalpa, like U.S. ambassador John Erwin, felt the president could do no wrong. The Yankee diplomat offered, at one point, a sweeping and rather dramatic historical analogy:

> As Latin American dictators go, President Carías is fairly good, far better than most, perhaps less enlightened than some. His record should be viewed in perspective. . . . When he assumed office, he was faced with substantially the same

104. Ibid., 110.

problem met and overcome by James I in Scotland and Cardinal Richelieu in France—the establishment and maintenance of order. James I (1394–1437) smashed the semi-independent chiefs (MacDonalds, Mackintoshes, Gordons, and even Douglasses were never the same again); Richelieu (1585–1642) smashed the feudal power of the Rohans and Montmorencys; and Carías smashed the guerilla [sic] generals. James and Richelieu are often arbitrary, and there are occasional cases of personal injustice, but, by and large, the system is fairly sound; like his great predecessors, President Carías will leave his country more civilized and otherwise better off than he found it eleven years ago.[105]

105. U.S. ambassador John Erwin to Department of State, 18 August 1944, Confidential U.S. Diplomatic Post Records, reel 38, 147.

10

Stepping Down but Not Out

"Tiburcio Carías must be allowed to finish his term" read pro-government signs in the July 4 and July 6, 1944, demonstrations.[1] These hastily made National Party placards conveyed the chief executive's unannounced plan for stepping down in 1949. In 1944, the year of upheaval in Central America and unrest in Honduras, Carías declared, "I will step down when the Honduran people choose my successor."[2] He later disavowed any personal ambition for remaining president beyond his term. Then, in 1945, he declared that he would turn his office over on June 1, 1949, to the person elected.[3] In 1944 Jorge Ubico of Guatemala and Maximiliano Hernández Martínez of El Salvador had announced that they would extend their terms. Carías moved from a very vague position in 1944 to a specific plan by 1945. But his shift reflected the inexorable course of events domestically and internationally that was forcing his hand. He chose to control political events by making the National Party his vehicle for orchestrating a change, in effect selecting his successor and ensuring that he would retain a large measure of power.

In December 1945, Carías communicated to the U.S. legation in Tegucigalpa his specific political agenda for the future. His plan had five stages: hold fair elections in 1948, allow more freedom of the press, release political prisoners (the U.S. embassy had a list of 170 of them), end the state of siege declared in 1941, and last, when his term ended in 1948, step down.[4] The steps added up to a long-term strategy of remaining in control of the National Party.

Carías was a realist and a pragmatist; he knew that his presidency was

---

1. U.S. consulate, Puerto Cortés, to U.S. embassy, Tegucigalpa, 15 July 1944, Confidential U.S. Diplomatic Post Records, reel 38, 214.

2. *Mensaje, Segunda Parte*, 1937–1945, Biblioteca y Archivos Nacionales, 5 December 1944, 289.

3. *Mensaje, Segunda Parte*, 1945, 294.

4. U.S. embassy, Tegucigalpa, to Department of State, 1 December 1945, Confidential U.S. Diplomatic Post Records, reel 41, 1112.

spent. His time was up, but a role in Honduran politics did not have to end when he left office.[5] He was aware that the Allied victory in 1945 made dictatorships a cruel anomaly in the Western Hemisphere, making extended rule difficult, inevitably failing. Demonstrations in the country's two largest cities were an indication that new economic, political, and social forces were emerging. Several of his closest friends debated ways to persuade him to step down,[6] but they had to find a way for him to remain influential politically—at least to stand aside, said one, "for the moment."[7]

Carías accepted the fact that if he remained in office by extending his term in 1944, serious unrest would result. Calling for elections would avoid the instability and civil wars he so well remembered.[8] He gave an interview at this time which conveyed his thinking on the need for an orderly succession. He did not say whom he supported but first described the kind of president he wanted: "someone who can balance political and social forces in the country, a moderate."[9] Keen observers, even critics like the historian Rafael Heliodoro Valle, predicted that Carías would look for the stability he so long cherished by having Juan Manuel Gálvez, the minister of war, navy, and aviation, succeed him.[10] Prophetic comments, but not the force that propelled him toward his decision.

The ever-faithful and discreet Carlos Izaguirre, at Carías's request, sounded out the U.S. ambassador on the issue of continuismo after 1949.[11] The president's emissary received a simple but cryptic reply from the Yankee diplomat: "Carías has been a fine President. We are in an era of change, dictatorships are unpopular. A peaceful transition is needed, an appropriate opening is required, democratization. Carías has been supported by the U.S. since 1932. He will be backed to the end of his term in 1949. The process can be successful with the appropriate choice of a successor."[12]

Views expressed by influential officials from the banana companies reinforced the envoy's comments. Walter Turnbull, manager of United Fruit, and

---

5. Lucas Paredes, El hombre del puro (Tegucigalpa: Imprenta Honduras, 1973), 32.

6. Ibid.

7. Ibid., 50.

8. Ibid., 27–28.

9. Ibid., 28.

10. Rafael Heliodoro Valle, Mexico City, to Amilcar Gómez Robelo, Guatemala, 11 July 1946, Amilcar Gómez Robelo Papers, 126.

11. Pérez Cadalso interview, 1 December 1987.

12. Minister John Erwin, Tegucigalpa, to Department of State, 23 August 1946, National Archives, Record Group 59, File 815.W-8–2346.

the company's president, Samuel Zemurray, felt Carías's time had come to an end. Both wanted a new strongman who had popular support. They wanted a peaceful change and a candidate who would not provoke bloodshed and stir up old animosities. Zemurray and Turnbull believed elections would prevent confrontation and violence. "Prevent another Guatemala, pick Juan Manuel Gálvez," they said; this would ensure a peaceful transition to a new era.[13] But the Carías government had suggested that an effort be made to reduce the country's total dependence on the Standard Fruit Company's Banco Atlántico. This gave the banana companies cause to shift their earlier unequivocal political endorsements to a more sympathetic candidate.

Other factors weighed heavily on Carías's decision to step down. The old guard, the generals of the mountains, the veterans of many civil wars who became military commanders of departments, were dying off. General Martínez Funes; Carías's nephew and troubleshooter, Calixto Carías; and José Chepe López all passed away in 1943–44.[14] Only three members in congress from 1945–48 were allies in the formation of the National Party in 1919.[15] The aborted coup in 1943 left the president shaken. Its organizers had come from the ranks of his closest security forces; some were members of the National Party. While they admired Carías personally, several felt he had deserted the party's democratic principles when he established a dictatorship.[16] The loss of support among members prompted Carías to pay close attention to the party's activities. Properly supervised and controlled, it could guarantee the election of his chosen successor. It would also allow him to hold on to power levers after leaving office. Municipal elections in the fall of 1945 gave Carías a hefty victory and a message. But the numbers of total votes were down, as the Nationalists received 77,226 out of 85,036. However, more important than being democratic, said Washington, was the fact that "they were orderly."[17]

13. Mejía interview, 9 September 1987. Walter Turnbull, general manager of the United Fruit Company, was a close friend of Mejía. The latter said, in the interview, that Turnbull had urged Carías to select Juan Manuel Gálvez as his successor.

14. Justo Rufino Solís became the head of a dissident National Party faction, the Authentic National Party. It allied with Ángel Zúñiga Huete. El Ciudadano, 11 June 1948, 3.

15. By 1945, only three members of the congress were old Carías associates whose careers stretched back to the 1920s and 1930s. They were Plutarco Muñoz from the Department of Yoro, Rodolfo Velásquez Hernández from Intibucá, and Alvaro Suazo from La Paz. Boletín del Congreso Nacional Legislative, 1945–1948, 5, Biblioteca y Archivos Nacionales.

16. Barahona Ortega interview, 29 November 1987.

17. U.S. embassy, Tegucigalpa, to Department of State, 27 November 1945, Confidential U.S.

If Carías doubted the U.S. position on the extended term issue after the Izaguirre meeting at the embassy, a telling message was delivered on an arms purchase requisition he made in 1946. The Honduran ambassador in Washington asked for six attack trainer planes. His request was unanswered for some time, leading to speculation in the Carías regime that "political considerations," emphasizing its no-extended-term position, were the reason. In time, the State Department turned down the plane purchase request, as well as one for arms and ammunition. This rejection did not mean Carías had fallen out of favor with the United States, but from Washington's response, Tegucigalpa understood that a once open-ended arms procurement policy associated with political incumbency was over.[18]

Many factors, personal and political, convinced Carías to step down in 1949. Political unrest, signs of division in his own party, and pressure from banana company executives and U.S. diplomats in Tegucigalpa all influenced his decision. But his wife's poor health and her insistence that he retire in 1949 may have been the most compelling factors. Doña Elena, unprepossessing, always shunning the limelight, had strong feelings on many issues but never expressed her opinion in public. This time, keeping her own counsel as usual, she urged her husband to step down.[19] There had always been speculation that Mrs. Carías wanted him to leave office in 1943, but if he had, then he would have had to turn over the office to his vice-president, Abraham Williams, whom he did not entirely trust; nor would United Fruit Company likely have accepted him as the new president. Williams had, from time to time, criticized the companies for their labor policies.[20] Doña Elena also encouraged her husband to choose Juan Manuel Gálvez as a successor. She greatly admired the minister of war for his personal integrity and loyalty to her husband.[21]

Diplomatic Post Records, reel 41, 1110. Of 85,036 votes cast in the municipal elections, the National Party received 77,226. This dispatch observed, "[These] elections appear to have been orderly."

18. Chief, Central American/Caribbean Division, 28 May 1946, National Archives, Record Group 59, 815.248/5–2486.

19. Mrs. Carías had been in ailing health. In fact, back in 1944 during the antigovernment demonstrations, her reactions to the criticisms leveled at her husband worsened her physical condition. Concern for his wife's health and dislike of the course of events compelled Carías to send her out of the country in a TACA Lockheed plane to Costa Rica.

20. Mejía interview, 18 September 1987.

21. Military Intelligence Report, U.S. embassy, July 1944, Confidential U.S. Diplomatic Post Records, reel 32, 528.

Carías had many other reasons to support Juan Manuel Gálvez. By experience, temperament, and character, Gálvez was his ideal successor. Also, Williams might have prevented Carías from maintaining a dominant role in the National Party after leaving office, as Williams was more interested in managing it than Gálvez was. Therefore, by placing the minister of war at the head of the ticket, Carías could run the party.

Williams had already begun a dissident movement in the National Party called the *nacional reformista*. Never really active politically, Williams's main interest was engineering. However, having been vice-president for Carías's entire presidency, he felt that his number-two post entitled him to succeed the president. His faction was made up of a younger generation of mostly professionals and entrepreneurs who wanted to broaden the party's base to include representation from the urban middle class. When Williams resigned his cabinet post as minister of government in 1946, many believed it was a step in an effort to win the presidency in 1948.[22] Yet the fruit companies did not support his higher aspirations. They remembered that years back, he had called for restrictions in their land purchases for expanded banana products and railroad construction along the north coast.[23] Confrontational and prone to argue with the president, Williams could not be expected to honor any influence Carías might want to exert after leaving office. Some party leaders and longtime Carías loyalists always believed that Williams, like Venancio Callejas, had objections to the president holding on to the party leadership, diminishing its role, after 1936. Several of these critics went into exile; others remained at home, silent and disgruntled. Williams in the mid-1940s appealed to this group who wanted to remove Carías from office and National Party leadership as well.[24]

Even-tempered, called the conciliator, never confrontational, Juan Manuel Gálvez actually had been groomed for the presidency for some time as one of the earlier members of the National Party; his chief interest was practicing law, not acting as a party regular. Moreover, his loyalty to the president was tested in the bitter political electoral losses in 1924 and 1928. Gálvez remained minister of war, navy, and aviation (later air force) from 1932 to 1949. As a lawyer and civilian, he could be trusted not to build a military-political power base. A proven administrator, meticulous in his work habits like Carías, and a political

22. *Tegucigalpa*, 5 January 1947, 1.

23. Richard Lapper and James Painter, *Honduras: State for Sale* (London: Latin American Business, 1985), 30.

24. Cáceres Lara interview, 3 July 1987.

moderate, Gálvez was not one to make changes abruptly. He was a consensus builder and could be expected to guide, not promote, the social transformation of society.[25]

By nature not a power broker, Gálvez lacked the visceral instincts to seize and destroy his adversaries. He had no desire to be the National Party leader after becoming president, leaving this position open for Carías. He would be content carrying out his duties as chief executive, not to be a partisan leader for National Party interests. Put simply, it was not likely that Juan Manuel Gálvez would have challenged Carías politically after the president left office. In a revealing and singularly candid way, Carías assessed Gálvez's qualities and the pragmatic reasons why he chose him: "Juan Manuel Gálvez is the most honored man in my government. I can entrust the power of this office to him in order to soften the harshness produced by my long stay in the presidency."[26] Carías kept his promises to the U.S. legation by ending the state of siege in 1946.[27] He let several political prisoners free,[28] and he allowed three newspapers to reopen, one in San Pedro Sula and two in Tegucigalpa. This meant that publications like the Liberal Party mouthpiece, El Ciudadano in San Pedro Sula, could now attack the regime, and, as expected, they did so with relish.[29]

Central to Carías's decision to step down in 1949 was his intention to turn his full attention to politics and quickly take firm hold of the National Party. From his position as president of the central committee, he could oversee Juan Manuel Gálvez's nomination, manage the election, and remain a major political figure in the country. He knew the party organization needed restructuring, as telegrams poured in during the early months of 1948 urging a reorganization of its committees at the departmental and municipal levels. The old guard was feuding with new, younger members.[30] A few years earlier, without revealing the source of its creation, Carías authorized the establishment of a new paper, Honduras Nueva. The journal was published by Tomás Quiñonez, chief of the Tegucigalpa city council. Quiñonez also printed the slavishly pro-Carías news-

---

25. Paredes, El hombre del puro, 58.

26. Ibid., 14–15.

27. The siege ended on 21 January 1946.

28. Vanguardia Revolucionaria, 14 December 1946, 1, 4.

29. El Ciudadano, a liberal newspaper, reappeared in June 1948. Its editor, Antonio Castillo Vega, had been imprisoned on 30 November 1935 for three years.

30. Telegramas recibidos del Departamento de Francisco Morazán de mayo 1943 a junio 1944, 7 December 1943, Biblioteca de Telegramas, Biblioteca y Archivos Nacionales.

paper *La Época*. The journal was to deemphasize the personal cult of the president in order to deflect criticism of Carías and turn attention to the National Party, whose principles and organization provided substance and goals for the regime. Equally important, the paper was to encourage Carías's return to a party he helped found and from where he could continue to exert an influence on public affairs after 1949. As ex-president, Carías planned to select candidates for congress, the Supreme Court, and numerous departmental and municipal posts throughout the country.[31]

In late 1947 and early 1948, Carías began reorganizing local committees and lining up support for Juan Manuel Gálvez. This activity marked his move back into direct control of the Nationalists, just the kind of work he enjoyed.[32] A National Party youth organization was created under the Movimiento Vanguardia,[33] delegates to the national convention were named, and Radio Honduras Nacional gave accounts of party rallies and the convention.[34] As proof that the president and his generation were still in charge of affairs, Plutarco Muñoz, a Carías ally since the 1920s and still president of the congress, presided over the political conclave that nominated Juan Manuel Gálvez for president on February 20, 1948. Julio Lozano Díaz, who had held numerous cabinet posts under Carías, was selected as vice-president. Just as he had planned, Carías was named director of the party's central committee. The transition process had begun.

Carías's last speech as president before the delegates was typically brief and simple. He did not draw on the memories of those present with elections won and lost, or mention military campaigns he had led. The address sounded exactly the same as his 1933 inaugural speech and the fourteen annual messages given since then—flat, bland, and devoid of elaborate rhetoric. He merely called for peace and order to continue, the two goals he felt had been achieved in Honduras under his rule.[35]

The 1948 presidential campaign marked a new era in Honduran politics, the year Carías stepped down after a fifteen-year rule. Popular organizations reflecting the interest of new economic and social groups appeared. Divisions

---

31. U.S. embassy, Tegucigalpa, to Department of State, 17 August 1949, Confidential U.S. Diplomatic Post Records, reel 38, 16; Williams interview, 18 November 1987.

32. *La Época*, 5 January 1948, 3.

33. Ibid.

34. Ibid.

35.*La Época*, 9 May 1948, 3.

within each of the traditional parties emerged. The Partido Democrático Revolucionario Hondureño (PDRH), which was composed of political dissidents residing in Honduras and headquartered in San Pedro Sula, lacked a leader, a central figure to direct a campaign against the well-entrenched Nationalists. Its newspaper, *Vanguardia Revolucionaria*, rejoiced that no one person dominated the PDRH as Carías did the National Party. It was a party of issues, it said, not caudillos. But therein lay its weakness.[36] Some of its members wanted Ángel Zúñiga Huete elected president. Others insisted that all exiles residing in Guatemala, El Salvador, Costa Rica, and México meet to select someone else, a new face. But dissident Liberals and the PDRH could not organize the far-flung exiles into a coherent organization. Two people, Graciela Bográn and Antonio Peraza, both journalists and organizers of the San Pedro Sula demonstration in July 1944 and leaders of the PDRH, failed to organize an effective opposition to the Nationalists. Bográn stayed at the PDRH headquarters in Honduras, the latter in Guatemala, trying to bring all exiles together. Their lukewarm support of Ángel Zúñiga Huete, with no viable candidate to replace him, gave the National Party campaign easy access to the presidency.[37]

Broadcasting from Guatemala on La Voz de las Américas, PDRH members ridiculed Ángel Zúñiga Huete as a doomed presidential contender.[38] The radio and newspaper *Vanguardia Revolucionaria* called for the union of workers and campesinos against the tyrannical Carías regime.[39] Rhetoric far outdistanced organization on the part of PDRH and anti-Zúñiga partisans, but this division further weakened the traditional Liberal Party leaders' chances of winning the election.

Ángel Zúñiga Huete, the old Liberal standard-bearer and Carías's opponent in 1932, returned to Honduras in March and was met by a large crowd of followers at the Tegucigalpa's Toncontín airport.[40] This was his first visit home in fifteen years. The party ticket, the same nominated in 1932, was announced at a convention on May 16, as grass roots organizations were barely evident. Harassed and intimidated for years with no leadership, the Liberal Party in 1948 was a paper institution. When party members were listed in the several departments, they were called "opponents of the Carías regime," not Liberal stal-

---

36. *Vanguardia Revolucionaria*, 2 August 1947, 1; 16 October 1947, 4.
37. *Vanguardia Revolucionaria*, 6 May 1948, 1, 4.
38. *Vanguardia Revolucionaria*, 25 September 1948, 1.
39. *Vanguardia Revolucionaria*, 23 May 1948, 1.
40. Accounts give three separate months: January, February, and March.

warts.[41] The party platform closely resembled its rival's; as someone observed, it was like "a warmed over sixteen-year-old dish."[42]

Ángel Zúñiga Huete began a "whistle stop" campaign by airplane. An excellent orator, he flew about the country filling his speeches with local anecdotes. He was a good entertainer, more amusing than taken seriously, but he simply could not rely on an organized party working on his behalf. He was further challenged by a new populist figure, Modesto Rodas Alvarado. A student leader at the National University, Rodas pressed Ángel Zúñiga Huete to take a stronger stand against the Carías government. The young Liberal called for the president's resignation to ensure a fair election, freedom of all political prisoners, free press, and respect for human rights.[43] Ángel Zúñiga Huete adopted Rodas's proposal, calling for Carías to step down before the election.[44] Although there was no chance of this idea taking hold, Ángel Zúñiga Huete, undaunted, continued his whirlwind campaign attacking Carías for detaining and harassing his followers. He wrote several articles on the doctrines and principles of Liberalism for his party's newspaper. Always the intellectual, he was more concerned about defining his party's principles than campaigning for election.[45]

PDRH members, mostly in San Pedro Sula, refused to work for Ángel Zúñiga Huete, but they admired "his long fight against the Carías tyranny as patriotic . . . heroic."[46] They saw no hope for his victory. In fact, exiles in Guatemala urged him to leave Honduras and called on Liberals and other dissidents to abstain from voting.[47] Loyalists in Honduras wanted party followers to vote but, in the event fraud took place, to resort to violence and oust Carías from power.[48] Later, in his *Autobiografía*, Ángel Zúñiga Huete described his party's plan for an armed uprising. The project was to disrupt all communications, use guerrilla forces against the powerful government air force, and, with National Party dissidents abroad like Mariano Bertrand Anduray, obtain arms for the

41. El Ciudadano, 28 August 1948, 5.

42. Leonard, The United States in Central America, 121.

43. El Ciudadano, 11 June 1948, 2.

44. El Ciudadano, 21 September 1948, 1, 6.

45. El Ciudadano, 1 July 1948, 5.

46. José Antonio Peraza, Cuba, to Amilcar Gómez Robelo, Guatemala, 7 June 1948, Amilcar Gómez Robelo Papers, 32–33.

47. "Resolución," n.d., Amilcar Gómez Robelo Papers, 34.

48. El Ciudadano, 7 September 1948, 3.

rebels.[49] At some point, plans for the insurrection may have reached the government. Anduray was assassinated and Ángel Zúñiga Huete fled to the Chilean embassy, fearing for his life.[50] His vice-presidential running mate, Francisco Paredes Fajardo, wanted to resign from the ticket, saying, "I'm 68 years old, I'm too old [for this] campaign."[51] In 1947, before returning to Honduras, Ángel Zúñiga Huete had made several attempts in Washington to persuade the Department of State to condemn the dictatorship and call for free elections. His pleas were turned away with the comment that the United States would not interfere in the country's internal affairs.[52]

By contrast, Juan Manuel Gálvez's campaign for the presidency was a model of organization. It had money, a favorable press, radio, and, of course, the National Party apparatus run by Carías—in effect, the unlimited resources of the dictatorship. Juan Manuel Gálvez never left Tegucigalpa. Carías ran the campaign for him throughout the country at departmental and municipal levels. All Gálvez had to do was to convey in his persona the symbol of the Nationalists' campaign and its traditional message of peace, order, and now, in 1948, continuity, which appealed to Washington and the fruit companies. Government-backed press attacks on Ángel Zúñiga Huete were unmerciful. Without Carías as a candidate, tongue-in-cheek editorials appeared in several papers attacking the Liberal as a "friend of Ubico" and a political figure "who suffered from 'presidentitis,'" or painfully, but true, "a professional political vagabond."[53]

Carías made full use of Rafael Heliodoro Valle's political peace with his regime. While not pressing for the distinguished historian and literary figure to participate actively in the campaign, his mere presence in Tegucigalpa was good propaganda. Valle attended numerous noncontroversial symposia on topics such as "The Contemporary Mexican Novel" and spoke on radio discussing the merits of Honduran writers. Carías appeared in photos with him. It was pure theater. Hundreds of telegrams praising the historian poured in to Fernando Zepeda Durón's paper, La Época, from all over the country. The editor, also a member of congress, had that body unanimously pass a resolution proposing an Honorary Doctor of Laws bestowed on Valle.[54] There were pub-

49. Ángel Zúñiga Huete, Autobiografía (Comyaguela: Imprenta Cultura, 1970), 58.
50. Ángel Zúñiga Huete later returned from exile on 20 February 1948.
51. La Época, 2 August 1948, 4.
52. Leonard, The United States in Central America, 121.
53. La Época, 23 August 1948, 1.
54. La Época, 14 January 1948, 1.

lished photos and written accounts of Carías and Juan Manuel Gálvez meeting with the returned exile.[55] Valle visited the headquarters of the Frente de la Juventud Nacionalista (National Youth Party) and in addressing the youngsters said the 1948 presidential campaign was a battle for peace. Insisting he was not endorsing a candidate, the message got across.[56]

In the remaining months of the electoral campaign, Ángel Zúñiga Huete called on Liberals to abstain from voting and left for México.[57] Many of his colleagues, whom the U.S. ambassador said "took the coward's path, took cover," fled to the Chilean, Guatemalan, and Mexican legations. At the same time, Juan Manuel Gálvez displayed a U.S. endorsement by appearing on the front page of La Época with the ambassador.[58] Elections were held on October 10. The results, a foregone conclusion, gave a resounding victory to the minister of war. He received 254,802 out of approximately 300,000 votes cast; Ángel Zúñiga Huete received 210. The others tabulated were blanks or nullified ballots.[59]

The full measure of Carías's power, the party he long controlled and the state he managed, easily delivered the presidency to Juan Manuel Gálvez. The president's plans for stepping down did not leave him out of the political picture. His party was intact, and he dominated it. He could say, as he did with a measure of truth in 1948, "I have known Honduran politics since 1893. I'm the only old politician [of that generation] still standing. I know very well what Hondurans want. I know they don't want to resurrect the past."[60] The peace and order he insisted on maintaining throughout his tenure and with Juan Manuel Gálvez's election probably was what most people wanted. The United States and the banana companies certainly did.

Juan Manuel Gálvez was inaugurated on January 1, 1949, at the National Theater. Carías placed the presidential sash on his shoulders and embraced him. The new president left the ceremonies and plunged into the waiting crowd outside. A sea of humanity followed him to the lobby of the hotel El Só-

---

55. La Época, 15 January 1948, 1.

56. La Época, 21 January, 3; 9 February, 1, 4; 12 February 1947, 1.

57. Vanguardia Revolucionaria, 4 October 1948, 1; "Ángel Zúñiga Huete Admits Defeat," New York Times, 27 July 1944, quoted in a U.S. embassy dispatch, n.d., Confidential U.S. Diplomatic Post Records, reel 38, 312.

58. La Época, 14 September 1948, 1.

59. The 1948 presidential election results were as follows: National Party, 254,802; Liberal Party, 215. La Época, 11 October 1948, 4.

60. La Época, 29 January 1948, 4.

tano in downtown Tegucigalpa, where he held an impromptu press conference. His first informal meeting with reporters conveyed a new era, a sense of
engagement, as the chief executive, "*un presidente en camisa*" as some described
him ("a president in shirt sleeves"), comfortably interacted with people. Calling for national reconciliation, he promised to release political prisoners and
invite all exiles, including Ángel Zúñiga Huete, home. He said a new penal law
would be enacted.[61] The walk, with no guards, from the National Theater to the
hotel and the press conference were dramatic episodes, marking a break in
style and, in some ways, substance with the Carías regime. In time this angered
and disappointed the ex-president. But in the meantime, without ever criticizing his mentor, Juan Manuel Gálvez crafted an administration that both continued and developed policies that began under the former president.

Juan Manuel Gálvez broke tradition by no longer living in the presidential
palace. Instead, he walked each day from home, first to the barbershop for a
shave, then to his office in the president's old residence.[62] On weekends, without advance notice, he boarded a plane and with only a pilot accompanying him
made unexpected stops at construction sites, village fairs, and municipal council meetings around the country. Tireless, in a broad-brimmed hat, he discussed local problems with people. He took the affairs of state with him to all
parts of the country.[63] When visiting communities, he paid his respects to National Party leaders but stayed in the homes of personal friends, even individuals who were known critics of his government. He enjoyed easy conversation
with people and made himself approachable, in an unassuming manner. He
liked the public and they reciprocated.[64]

The new president was a hard worker. He took governing seriously and, like
Carías, paid uncommonly close attention to administrative details. Although
his annual messages to congress still offered a litany of accomplishments like
roads paved and schools constructed, he initiated changes that went beyond
Carías's interests and liking. First, enlarging on his reconciliation policy, he
granted the National University its autonomy, included Liberals in government
posts, and dispatched dissidents to prestigious posts abroad more in the name
of fostering peace than with the goal of placing them in exile. He enacted the
country's first income tax law and created the Faculty of Economic Science at

61. *Tegucigalpa*, n.d.; El Día, 22 May 1948, 3.
62. Gálvez Barnes interview, 30 November 1987.
63. El Día, 29 July 1952, 1.
64. La Tribuna, 19 June 1987, 18.

the National Autonomous University of Honduras (UNAH) to train economists with specialties in banking and developmental economics.[65]

In 1943, Carías had invited a U.S. commission to study the country's monetary and credit policies. Its report recommended the reorganization of the government for more effective management of public finances and proposed that a central bank and a development bank be established.[66] On July 1, 1950, following up on the proposal Carías had shelved, Gálvez created the Central Bank and National Development Bank. The former would make loans to commercial institutions and to the government. It would in effect be the fiscal agent of the state, issuing currency and setting interest rates and requirements against deposits. The second entity, an autonomous state-owned bank, soon issued lines of credit for cotton growers in the south, sugar cultivators, cattle ranchers in the north, and small farmers in the country's highlands. With the National Development Bank, Juan Manuel Gálvez expanded commercial agriculture into meat, coffee, cotton, and food processing. For the first time a Ministry of Agriculture was established. In effect, Juan Manuel Gálvez implemented earlier plans proposed by Carías for a major state role in future international economic development. Continued assistance from the United States and international financial agencies was important in this process.

Juan Manuel Gálvez departed from Carías more in style than in substance, but there were issues besides beginning a modernization process in public policy which divided them. Labor unrest, long simmering in the north coast's banana companies, erupted in 1954. Gálvez demonstrated his interest in improving the condition of workers when he created the office of Labor and Social Security in 1954. Workers in United Fruit's Tela Railroad joined Interamerican Regional Organization of Workers (ORIT), which was affiliated with the AFL-CIO. That May, 25,000 workers at United Fruit and 15,000 at Standard Fruit went on strike, lasting sixty-nine days. Dockers in Puerto Cortés demanded double pay on Sundays; others insisted on better housing conditions and a 72 percent increase in pay. Standard settled with the workers, but United refused. Finally, only a few demands were met, such as a 9 percent pay increase, not 72 percent. Gálvez supported provisions that allowed unions to organize and mandated a minimum wage, paid vacations, and overtime pay. He was more willing than his predecessor to meet certain demands and generally gave more

65. El Día, 21 January 1954, 5.
66. Dunkerley, Power in the Isthmus, 526.

attention to workers' interests. For example, he created a Ministry of Labor in December and when an opponent of his new conciliatory labor policy told him that there was no law permitting a strike, the president noted that neither was there a law that prohibited one.[67]

The president's moderate approach to workers' demands won him plaudits from reformers within his party and elsewhere, but it earned Carías's displeasure. It was not so much that Gálvez was taking steps Carías opposed as the fact that the ex-president was rarely consulted on these matters. Old guard National Party members were also annoyed with the president's independence, but moderates warned, "Don't harm Gálvez, you might get Carías back."[68]

U.S. efforts to topple the leftist government of Jacobo Arbenz in Guatemala in 1954 further strained relations between Carías and his successor. Eliseo Pérez Cadalso, Carlos Izaguirre's secretary, recalls that Colonel Carlos Castillo Armas, backed by Washington, the counter-revolutionary leader in Guatemala, came to Tegucigalpa and asked Gálvez for help. The president, unwilling to involve his regime directly in an invasion from Honduras, sent him to see Carías. Accounts of the assistance are sharply contradictory. The former president, says Pérez Cadalso, promised arms and money,[69] and Gonzálo "Chalo" Luque, one of Carías's loyal followers, supports this account. He claims to have personally shipped arms offered by Carías to Carlos Castillo Armas.[70] Rafael Bardales, a longtime functionary in the National Party, insists that while Carías was sympathetic to Carlos Castillo Armas's campaign, he could do little to help him and was disappointed that his successor had not been more forthright and helpful in the operation. Ultimately, Washington used Honduran territory to launch the movement to topple the Arbenz regime. The differences between the two men on this issue and the labor questions simply added to Carías's frustration that he was unable to exert enough influence on Juan Manuel Gálvez.[71] Yet by careful political maneuvering, guaranteeing that his successor would not

67. Paredes, *Biografía Carías*, 133. See also Victor Meza, *Historia del movimiento obrero Hondureño* (Tegucigalpa: Editorial Guaymuras, 1981); Manuel Posas and Rafael del Cid, *La construcción del sector público y del estado nacional en Honduras, 1876–1979* (Tegucigalpa: Editorial Universitaria Centroamericana, 1981).

68. Pérez Cadalso interview, 1 December 1987.

69. Ibid.; *El Día*, 24 December 1969, 11.

70. Izaguirre interview, 9 April 1987; Luque, *Memorias de un soldado Hondureño*, 2:118.

71. Raúl Barnica (private secretary to Tiburcio Carías, 1954–58; secretary to President Ramón Cruz, 1971–72), Tegucigalpa, 23 November 1987.

disrupt the structure of the Carista state, along with the political ineptness of the opposition, Carías was able to leave office in 1949 with a measure of credibility and little expectation of recrimination by opponents. The former president was not idle in retirement; the National Party became the centerpiece of his political life, and he devoted full time to it, controlling the party apparatus and for some time remaining its most popular leader.[72]

72. Antunez Rivas interview, 10 October 1987.

11

Never Giving Up

Carías left office at a time of profound change in Honduras. The stability he had imposed on the country was continued by his successor Juan Manuel Gálvez, and the National Party fortified the presidential succession. Yet by the early 1950s the viability and strengths of the two traditional parties began to decline. They were weakened by new popular organizations that made demands on an expanding state apparatus the president had established. Middle-class technocrats, lawyers, entrepreneurs, workers, and campesinos created their own movements and forged new factions within the Liberal and National Parties. Even the military began to define its mission in the state. As political polarization escalated, the army and air force became arbiters, even participants jockeying for power.

The underpinning of these political changes was the result of a significant social and economic transformation going on in the 1950s. Migration on a greater scale occurred from rural areas to cities and towns. The landless population grew as sugar and cotton cash crops increased, and cattle raising became important export activities. In 1943 the Honduran population was 1.075 million. By 1950 it had reached approximately 1.4 million. The number of residents in Tegucigalpa and San Pedro Sula jumped from 72,000 and 21,000 to 134,000 and 59,000 respectively. Yet with all these demographic changes, the country had only 40 kilometers of paved and some 2,300 kilometers of unpaved roads. The capital and San Pedro Sula were not linked by a hard-surface road until 1970. Economic growth and a better infrastructure were slow in coming, but the pressures for change grew.

Juan Manuel Gálvez's administration (1949–54) made a political opening, allowing more dissent. It also undertook steps to begin the modernization of the state's fiscal and financial system by creating a National Bank. These changes, political and economic, were widely acclaimed by a younger generation within the two traditional parties. They deplored old-line politicians like

Carías and Ángel Zúñiga Huete, who reached their political maturity in the 1920s and 1930s. The tensions between the new and old forces may have been simply a generational conflict, yet the discord rested on the significant changes emerging in the post–World War II era.

Tiburcio Carías viewed his departure from office in 1949 as merely temporary and devoted all his time out of office to politics.[1] His major interest as head of the National Party was to reassert his leadership at all levels of its organization. His nephew, secretary, and confidant, Marcos Carías Reyes, worked in the mid-1940s to organize and promote the interests of the younger generation of National Party members. Of course, this effort was done in part to strengthen Carías's position. But more serious and dangerous to the ex-president's leadership was a challenge from his former vice-president, more politically ambitious than Gálvez, Abraham Williams. With his own presidential ambitions in mind, but enthusiastic too with the modernizing reforms and conciliatory policies of the Juan Manuel Gálvez administration, he created the National Reformist Movement (MNR) within the National Party.

The MNR had basically two goals. The first was to wrest National Party leadership from Carías, and second, to support and extend the modernizing policies and political reforms of President Juan Manuel Gálvez by bringing younger people into leadership positions in the party. The movement made direct appeals to reformers in both the National and Liberal Parties. It included people who had challenged Ángel Zúñiga Huete's leadership following the July 1944 demonstrations in Tegucigalpa and San Pedro Sula.[2] The MNR wanted to capture the support of new economic and social groups. Taking up the message of women's rights, it called for the political equality for all citizens. Its program urged a labor code, social security legislation, restoring elected officials to municipal governments abolished by Carías in 1940 and the direct election of judges.[3] Last, most controversial, and threatening Carías's leadership, was a proposal to convoke a constituent assembly changing the constitution allowing Juan Manuel Gálvez to extend his term beyond 1954 or to allow him to run for reelection. Both proposals were prohibited by the constitution. Essentially, the MNR wanted to change the National Party from an exclusively Carías organization to a political force, representative of a new and broader

1. Barnica interview, 2 November 1987.

2. *Abraham Williams Calderón: su pensamiento político y sus planes de gobierno* (Tegucigalpa: Talleres Tipográficos Nacionales, 1954), 16–18.

3. El Día, 24 January 1954, 1, 8; 10 February 1954, 1.

constituency. Its platform took a swipe at the former president by referring to several figures, omitting Carías's name, as founders of the party.[4] Basically, the MNR wanted to prevent Carías from capturing the organization's nomination for the 1954 presidential election. It also wanted to continue the political opening and economic modernization plans Juan Manuel Gálvez had begun.[5]

The Carías-Williams split created deep divisions among party members. An old Carías ally, López Piñeda, a recognized intellectual leader of the party who backed him in 1924, wanted to see it focus more on modernization, bringing in younger people, rather than remaining an organization dominated by the former president.[6] Yet Carías, the political organizer, had the votes in congress to prevent reform. His leadership was undamaged as long as a chance existed that Juan Manuel Gálvez would run again or accept an amended constitutional provision extending his term. Party regulars would simply have to choose between a popular reform-minded incumbent president or the founder and head of their party.

Two newspapers, both mouthpieces of the Nationalists, were split on the issue. Bitter denunciations were exchanged between El Día in Tegucigalpa, the MNR paper, and the ever-faithful Carías journal, La Época. El Cronista, closed in 1948 for criticizing the regime but now reopened, called the ex-president "the ogre from Zambrano."[7] One editorial said, "People preferred one death rather than have to live again under the terror of Carías."[8]

Juan Manuel Gálvez remained noncommittal in 1952.[9] He simply did not want to enter the party feud. Admittedly, he was in a difficult position. The MNR was enthusiastically endorsing his policies and urging him on to a second term, but he owed a personal loyalty, and of course his presidency, to Carías.[10] Williams pushed ahead and challenged Carías on the issue of a constitutional amendment extending Juan Manuel Gálvez's term. The die was cast for a major battle among the Nationalists, a feud between two architects of peace and order who governed Honduras for sixteen years.

4. El Día, 2 May 1954, 3; 10 May 1954, 1.

5. Cáceres Lara interview, 23 June 1987; El Día, 24 May 1954, 1. El Día supported the MNR.

6. Raúl Bardales, "El fundador de la paz" (unpublished ms., Tegucigalpa: Bardales Library), 146.

7. El Cronista, 25 October 1954, 1.

8. El Cronista, 11 November 1954, 1.

9. El Día, 25 October 1952, 3.

10. Gálvez Barnes interview, 30 October 1987.

Still in control of the party, Carías was nominated as its candidate for president in February 1954. In his acceptance speech, he castigated members who wanted to split the Nationalist Party and amend the constitution extending Juan Manuel Gálvez's term.[11] The real showdown, the test of leadership and strength between the two rivals, took place in congress in the summer of 1954. There, Williams's MNR followers introduced a proposal calling for a constituent assembly to revise the 1936 constitution extending Juan Manuel Gálvez's term. The bill had virtually no chance of passage. Carías had a firm bloc of legislators and beat back efforts to amend the constitution. On three separate occasions, July 26, July 29, and August 2, National Party deputies voted thirty-three, thirty-two, and thirty-five "no," to Williams's firm eleven votes, "yes."[12]

As the fall, 1954 presidential contest approached, a three-way race took shape. Carías headed the party ticket. Williams decided to run as the MNR candidate when Juan Manuel Gálvez announced he would not run for reelection.[13] Ramón Villeda Morales, successor to Ángel Zúñiga Huete, led the Liberals. But he, too, faced opposition within his party from the younger populist, Modesto Rodas Alvarado. A deadlock seemed likely. Washington suggested that Juan Manuel Gálvez continue as president for one or two more years then allow a constituent assembly to reform the constitution. Elections would be held for his permanent successor. Carías remained firm; he would not accept any suggestions for amending the 1936 constitution.[14]

Actually, Washington feared that if Juan Manuel Gálvez continued in office, political uncertainty, even unrest might result. Its embassy in Tegucigalpa worked feverishly to avoid a constitutional crisis, "which," it said, "would mean a choice of president left to a Carías-dominated supreme court."[15] As a result, Yankee diplomats tried to create a Liberal-MNR ticket of moderate reformists with a broad base of support. The U.S. ambassador gloomily predicted that if a reformist regime did not take shape, "a communist government

11. Ibid.

12. *La Gaceta*, 12 July 1954,1; *Boletín del Congreso Nacional Legislativo*, Biblioteca y Archivos Nacionales, ND 1954.

13. El Día, 1 October 1952, 3.

14. Mejía interview, 9 September 1987.

15. The U.S. embassy reported that the congress having failed to convoke a quorum, the Carías-dominated Supreme Court would decide the matter. U.S. embassy, Tegucigalpa, to Department of State, 24 September 1954, National Archives, Record Group 59, file 715.00/9–2454.

like [the] one in Guatemala [Juan José Arévalo] would emerge."[16] However, Carías held the trump card. If no one received an absolute majority in the election, the next chief executive would by law have to be chosen either by Congress, and failing in that, the Supreme Court, which his partisans dominated.

Elections were held on October 10. Of 400,000 eligible voters, Ramón Villeda Morales, the Liberal candidate, received a large plurality of 121,213 votes, but he lacked a majority by just over 8,000 votes. Carías followed with 77,041, and Williams with 53,041.[17] By law, congress therefore was obliged to elect a chief executive. Thirty-eight votes were needed to obtain a quorum electing a chief executive. Carías's National Party loyalists had twenty-two deputies, MNR twelve, and Liberals twenty-three. A bloc of solid Liberal votes with the MNR still lacked three for the needed quorum.[18] Then, compounding the political problem, Juan Manuel Gálvez resigned prematurely on November 16, claiming poor health. He turned his office over to Vice-President Julio Lozano Díaz. This act probably most typified the political style of Juan Manuel Gálvez. Uncharacteristic for a politician, he was not by nature combative and rather than manipulate the outcome of the crisis, he walked away from it, expecting that his decision would end the crisis.

The sudden turn of events bringing Lozano, a longtime Carías friend and cabinet minister in his government, changed the political equation.[19] While Carías remained a major power broker, his influence had declined. Although out of office and head of his party, he had to contend with other political forces. For example, President Lozano, asserting his independence, dissolved congress and appointed a consultative council with representatives from the Liberal, National, and MNR Parties. It was to write a new constitution, labor code, social security law, and act merely in an advisory capacity to the president.[20] Lozano organized his own political organization, the National Unity Party, with support from MNR's Abraham Williams, and he packed the Liberal leader Villeda Morales off to exile then governed for two years. Carías vigorously opposed Lozano's actions as the chief executive's steps diminished the old veteran's position in the party. When questioned by skeptics why he objected to

16. Ibid.

17. Dunkerley, *Power in the Isthmus*, 528. The vote was as follows: Cariistas, 77,041; MNR Abraham Williams, 53,041; Liberal Party Ramón Villeda 121,213.

18. El Día, 25 November 1954, 6.

19. "Mensaje del jefe del partido nacional, 30 diciembre 1954," in Bardales, "El fundador," 158.

20. El Día, 9 December 1954, 1.

the president's actions when in fact he had extended his own term in 1936, Carías replied, "It is true that I was president of Honduras for sixteen years, but [the] people made me."[21]

In 1956, congressional elections were held, with the president firmly in control of electoral machinery. Feeling locked out of any chance to win legislative seats, Carías urged his followers to abstain from voting. Lozano's party obtained 370,318 votes, Liberals 41,726, and Carías's Nationalists 2,000, but the president's congressional victory was short-lived. For the first time in modern Honduran history the military staged a coup d'état, installing a junta (1956–57) "to save the country from chaos."[22]

In 1952, an officers' training school, the Francisco Morazán Military Academy, had been founded. Two years later, the organic military law was enacted, defining the army's mission in terms of national defense, security, and public order. The supreme paradox of this event was a further decline in Carías's power. He had feared the military for years and deliberately refused to professionalize it. It was only during World War II that he had accepted military equipment, but he rejected assistance and a formal military agreement after the war. Now in 1956 the armed forces bypassed old politicos like Carías and proclaimed themselves the guardians of the nation's security and managers of the political process. The military junta called for elections to a constituent assembly to draw up a new constitution and select a president. Since the National Party remained deeply divided between Carías's old guard and Williams reformers, the Liberals won a resounding victory. The new legislative body in turn elected Ramón Villeda Morales, who took office in December 1957.

By far, the Villeda Morales government (1957–63) was more reformist than any of its predecessors. It enacted a labor code, social security law, and numerous welfare benefits for workers. The president created a civil guard of some 2,500 men to resist rightist militants and elements of the armed forced opposed to his radical policies. Many believed that the 1963 presidential elections offered the chance that a more antimilitary Liberal candidate, Modesto Rodas

21. Matías Funes, Los deliberantes: el poder militar en Honduras (Tegucigalpa: Editorial Guaymuras, 1995), 181.

22. Bardales, "El fundador," 59. Robert Gálvez Barnes served as a member of the government junta from 21 October 1956 to 12 November 1957. He also served as the minister of fomento in the de facto government of Julio Lozano Díaz from 5 December 1954 to 21 October 1956. Gálvez Barnes interview, 2 September 1987; 10 October 1987.

Alvarado, might win. So the military overthrew Villeda Morales ten days before the election.

Although this campaign marked the last time Tiburcio Carías played a role in politics, his chances for becoming his party's standard bearer actually ended with the 1954 election. Although the National Party named Carías its *jefe supremo* ("supreme chief") in February 1960, the conclave created a governing central committee for the first time. His new post was merely honorary. So in May 1963, three years later, he resigned. Yet no one was selected to replace him as the party chief.[23] The division begun in the party during the decade of the 1950s had yet to be healed. In 1963 he wanted his son, Gonzalo, selected as the nominee of the Nationalists, but there was strong support for Juan Manuel Gálvez, still a significant figure in the party. New faces appeared too as prospects for leading the party. Among them were Gabriel Mejía, a prominent businessman and longtime Carías ally who once held the posts of *auditor de las aduanas* ("customs collection," 1936–1939), and *administrador de rentas* ("administrator of revenue") in Cortés (1940–49). He also had been a director of both the Central Bank of Honduras and the National Development Bank in 1956–57. For Mejía's support in the race for the nomination and election, Gonzalo Carías offered him the chance to select three ministers in a future Carías regime.[24] Mejía turned down the offer, feeling he had substantial support for the nomination himself. At the very least he wanted to be a major broker selecting someone else.[25] Mejía controlled a number of delegates that ultimately chose Dr. Ramón Ernesto Cruz, a jurist, as a compromise between Gonzalo Carías and Juan Manuel Gálvez.[26] The Carías family, father and son, remained a powerful force in the party along with Juan Manuel Gálvez and Abraham Williams, but no one could hold it together for an election contest.

Just a few weeks before elections, Oswaldo López Arellano, chief of the armed forces, ousted President Villeda Morales. Tiburcio Carías supported General López Arellano's move when his son Gonzálo's chances for the presidency faded.[27] The general, although never formally affiliated with the Na-

23. El *Día*, 22 May 1963, 1.

24. Gonzalo Carías, Tegucigalpa, to Gabriel Mejía, San Pedro Sula, n.d., Mejía Papers, San Pedro Sula.

25. Gabriel Mejía, San Pedro Sula, to Gonzalo Carías, Tegucigalpa, 29 December 1962, Mejía Papers.

26. El *Día*, 22 May 1963, 3.

27. Antunez Rivas interview, Tegucigalpa, 6 October 1987.

tional Party, managed to merge warring factions of Nationalists into his own following. Two years later, with the party as his political base, Oswaldo López became president (1965–71) and selected Carías's son Tiburcio Jr. as his foreign minister (1965–69).[28]

Although the mantle of National Party leadership passed from Carías's hands, the name remained prominent and respected. He still kept an interest in politics, never giving up. The old guard—people like Roberto Velásquez from Intibucá, who had been in Congress for forty years—created the Partido Popular Progresista (PPP). Essentially it was a group organized to support Carías when he resigned as party chief. He actually remained in the National Party, but these people stayed loyal to him. Personalism remained for them more compelling than politics by committee or turning toward new leadership. Many were bitter at the disloyalty of Juan Manuel Gálvez and Abraham Williams's MNR, especially after Williams challenged Carías's leadership.

The split in the National Party left these old timers with no choice but to do what they had done since the 1920s, organize a new party and follow a leader.[29] When Carías's son Gonzalo became a member of PPP, many believed it was an appropriate and necessary step to keep the family in politics. Even though it formally separated from the Nationalists,[30] the senior Carías remained on the National Party rolls.

The PPP applied for status as an official party in the spring of 1963; it needed 10,000 signatures but acquired approximately 24,000.[31] Most of the names came from Tegucigalpa and western Honduras. None were from San Pedro Sula or the north coast. They were from the old guard, in the nation's political capital. The PPP platform offered all the general platitudes expected of a modern party. It supported a free, secret ballot; separation of powers; and freedom of thought, religion, and property. But it had some of the elements of the Ibero-American political culture, too, perhaps like (Juan Perón's) Justicialista Party in Argentina, calling for the balance of social, economic and political forces by a state with vast powers, "to give direction, supervision in private economic activity . . . and integrate society at all levels . . . to prevent an

28. *La Prensa*, 24 December 1969, 5.

29. Interview with Luis M. Coello Ramos (director of the PPP), Tegucigalpa, 3 March 1987; Barnica interview, 2 November 1987.

30. Coello Ramos and Barnica interviews; *El Diario*, 13 June 1963, 1.

31. *Ideario del Partido Popular Progresista de Honduras* (Tegucigalpa), n.d., 13–15.

unequal distribution of wealth . . . and to insure harmony between capital and labor."[32]

Party leaders and authors of the platform were close friends of Carías, like family members and his business manager.[33] Luis Coello Ramos, a PPP organizer, said it was founded to end *sectarismo* ("factionalism"), which had created political instability in days past, especially at the turn of the century when Honduran politics was almost exclusively, but not entirely, personalist. Confident, boastful, and proud, Coello Ramos proclaimed, "Have faith in me; I will bring *Cariismo* to power the way Tiburcio Carías did in 1932."[34] The PPP was Honduran politics come full circle during the career of Carías, who helped found the National Party in the 1920s because of sectarismo by the Bonillas, Manuel, and Policarpo.

Carías spent the last years of his life in a large stucco home in the center of Tegucigalpa. Every Thursday until the day he died, he sat in the foyer of his residence before the open front door and welcomed people. For twenty years after he left office, as before, he adhered to a strict and rigid daily schedule. Party stalwarts young and old continued to call on him for advice, which of course was flattering. Close associates and critics alike, like Juan Manuel Gálvez and Abraham Williams, visited him.[35]

Carías spent a good part of his time overseeing the management of haciendas outside Tegucigalpa: El Berrinche, a 120-*manzana* experimental farm that exported fruit, and El Espinal, 26 kilometers north of the capital, where cattle and sugarcane were produced. At Villa Elena, coffee beans and an assortment of flowers and plants were grown.[36] When his wife Doña Elena died in 1958, he rarely left the city to visit these country places.

All during his retirement years and even after his death, newspapers celebrated him on March 15, his birthday, with messages proclaiming "El Día de La Paz y Dar Gracias a Dios" ("A Day of Thanksgiving and Thanks to God").[37]

32. Ibid.

33. Barnica interview, 2 November 1987.

34. *La Tribuna*, 13 May 1987, 46. Coello Ramos interview, 2 July 1987.

35. *El Cronista*, 10 May 1963, 1.

36. Elias Lizardo (Carías's business manager), interview, Tegucigalpa, 3 December 1987. Carías's haciendas were El Berrinche, an experimental farm of 120 manzanas (1 manzana = 1.57 acres), which exported fruits, and El Espinal, also an experimental crop farm of 200 manzanas, located 200 miles north of Tegucigalpa. His third hacienda, Villa Elena, was just outside Tegucigalpa.

37. Ibid.

During the last years of his life and continuing to the present day, events in his career have been remembered with memorials, poems, songs, and calls for his return to restore order and peace.[38] His death on December 23, 1969, at age 93, evoked a flood of tributes.[39] Newspapers chronicled every milestone in his career. His dictatorship was portrayed by loyalists as an epoch providing peace, whereas his critics scoffed at the tributes. As expected, nostalgia set in, especially by the old-time National Party leaders. All segments of the press, even the most critical, referred only to his iron-hand rule, rarely singling out its harshness. Politicians across the political spectrum attended his funeral but, interestingly, no military officials appeared. This institution never considered him an enthusiastic sponsor. Even today, Carías is not remembered by the Honduran armed forces on special occasions commemorating military holidays. Nor is his picture displayed at armed forces posts. Maneuvers undertaken since his death have never been named after him. The funeral ceremonies recalled only a political leader.[40]

The funeral seemed to memorialize the end of an era rather than the death of a tyrant. Eulogies referred to his rectitude, discipline, and sense of purpose. The irony of all this is that his political contemporaries, Central American dictators long gone like Maximiliano Hernández Martínez, Anastasio Somoza, and Rafael Trujillo, had by comparison suffered worse fates. Jorge Ubico, Fulgenio Batista, and Marcos Pérez Jiménez of Venezuela were expelled. Most dictators in South America in the post–World War II era, unlike Carías, did not have majestic funerals in countries where they governed. Their contemporaries were not able to move about in their countries or abroad freely, independently, and exerting the influence in party politics as Tiburcio Carías had done after he left office. But, after all, their political careers were unalike, as they were different types of caudillos, although coming generally from the same Ibero-American culture.

38. La Tribuna, 9 February 1987, 1, 70.
39. El Día, 25 December 1969, 24; La Prensa, 24 December 1969.
40. Funes, Los deliberantes, 315.

Conclusion

Carías's rise to power came from the confluence of three developments: a world economic crisis, the growth of U.S. economic interests in banana production, and constant civil wars. From these conditions, he created political stability and stayed in office by extending his terms. Economic and fiscal reforms with centralization of administration were his chief preoccupations.

After leaving office in 1949, Tiburcio Carías defended himself from critics who accused him of being a dictator. He told them, in Don Quixote style, "It is true I was President of Honduras for sixteen years, but that was because the people made me." Essentially, he viewed his stewardship as the embodiment of the public will, what they needed and wanted, what they could not give themselves: peace and order. He considered his regime in the 1930s and 1940s as a restoration of the late nineteenth century's liberal age of progress, growth, and modernization. More precisely, he believed his government marked the reinstatement of the stability and order the Liberal Party had briefly given Honduras in the 1880s and 1890s.

His chief message, justifying his extended term of office in 1936, was the need to keep order and maintain peace at home and cordial ties to neighbors and the United States so that progress and development would take place. Stability promised development and progress for a generation who had known nothing but civil war and chronic upheaval in the early twentieth century. Carías considered himself an instrument for making changes for a broad spectrum of citizens: "The people made me serve. I am the embodiment of their interest," he said.

There were two periods in Carías's public life. The first was the age of personalism, the politics of combat that dominated much of Honduran history to the 1930s. Carías altered the political culture in the next phase of his career in 1933 as president by stabilizing and centralizing administration with his dictatorial rule and continuation of the caudillo style of politics, with his name fully imbedded in all aspects of Honduran political life. Like his predecessors, he reached the presidency through elections and civil war, but he changed the rules of the political game. He did not cast aside local chieftains, friends of his for decades and politicians like himself, but controlled them unlike any president had done before.

The Cariato was a unique period existing between the age of civil wars in the 1920s and the emerging modern state at the end of World War II. It was also part of a larger sweep of Honduran history that stretched from the 1870s to the end of Carías's term in 1949, a time that witnessed the rise of agrarian capitalism and foreign economic domination of the nation's resources. Carías laid the foundation for the growth of modern capitalism and development, expanding the state's role in society. Government institutions were transformed from mere paper entities to well-managed agencies. Ministerial functions were consolidated and integrated; the power of regional, departmental, and municipal government was reduced or eliminated altogether; and authority for the first time flowed out of Tegucigalpa, the country's political center, rather than from regional and local political chieftains.

Carías began again in 1932 what his fellow Liberals at the turn of the century had started, namely the modernization of the state. He did so by imposing his rule, centralizing fiscal procedures, laying out territorial boundaries, and controlling them. He created security forces to impose law and gave the country a constitution in 1936, a legal framework and document for his extended rule. He also introduced a new curriculum in his public educational system.

But Carías undertook major steps to modernize the state, not society. Honduran people for the most part were not transformed by social and economic reforms under his rule. Paradoxically, Carías largely made his regime obsolete by his own handiwork. New forces such as the middle sectors and the military were entering the political process toward the end of his sixteen-year term. Yet much remained unchanged when he left office in 1949. Seventy-eight percent of the 1.4 million people lived in rural areas, and only 40 kilometers of paved and 2,300 kilometers of unpaved roads existed. Neither hard-surface highway nor railroad linked San Pedro Sula in the north with Tegucigalpa in the south.

Honduras was really a nation of small villages in the 1930s and 1940s—less than 10 percent of its people lived in cities over 10,000. Yet while governing was relatively simple, distance made administering the remote villages almost impossible. Citizens moved within a limited sphere, and local politicians could dominate their lives easily. Tegucigalpa in 1949 had 72,400 inhabitants. It was a modestly sized provincial town. San Pedro Sula with 21,000 was barely that. Carías therefore did not have to manage a vast, diverse, and complex society. Yet he had to grapple with political anarchy, fiscal chaos, and economic collapse when he assumed office in 1933.

Carías's personal demeanor and public persona evoked awe and respect, not love. He was never accused personally of committing crimes, though major injustices were done on his behalf. Exile and internment were inflicted on political enemies. Yet their families were not visited with these punishments. He governed with a strong hand, but in a benevolent, paternalistic style. He did so largely through the National Party, which he dominated before he became president. He had obtained political prominence long before exercising power as a chief executive. As one of its earliest members, he shaped the party's organization in the 1920s. Through it he made lifelong friends and collaborators throughout Honduras. He was secure in these relationships, based on the old caudillo clientelistic tradition. When he assumed office in 1933, he was assured of their loyalty. For serving their interests and imposing limits on their power, he dispensed largesse and patronage. A brutal, oppressive police state as existed in other Central American and Caribbean countries was not necessary to guarantee his personal authority and security of the nation.

The National Party was his creation, and he disciplined and administered it from Tegucigalpa. He mobilized its rank and file when needed. From its far-flung committees, scattered throughout the country, proclamations poured in promoting his program, his birthday, and continuismo in 1936 and again in 1943. Its ancillary organizations extended to every social group in Honduras. State employment, patronage, and the party apparatus were integrated. Factionalism rarely emerged, as political dissidents were exiled, muzzled, or imprisoned. They could return home if they did not criticize the dictator. No groups within the party seized leadership during Carías's presidency, but when he left office in 1949, the discipline and slavish support for him eroded. He was challenged by a reformist element in 1954, but even then he trounced his opponent and remained a dominant force. The National Party's durability is attested to by the fact that it has remained a major political force to this day.

Its longevity began because Carías displayed some of his best political skills handling local leaders, something none of his predecessors could do. He allowed the "lords of his house," as they called themselves, vast authority. But in turn, he limited their capacity to extend a domain beyond their regions. Political chiefs and military commanders, both appointed by Carías, were oftentimes rivals. Militias were maintained only at the local level, led by corporals and sergeants. An air force began in the 1920s with bush pilots (some later founders of major airlines) who were contracted out by Carías to deploy arms and logistical support to the regime.

The air force, the telegraph system, and lucrative government contracts kept the "Lords of the Carías House" content and sovereign in their jurisdiction. Time and change forced Carías to shift his divide-and-rule strategy. The old guard, veterans of political contests in the 1920s and 1930s, began to die out, and a failed coup in 1943 forced him to professionalize the militias. Obligatory military service in local units began in 1935.

Carías tied his government to an Allied victory against fascism, then the cold war against the Soviet Union. As these two conflicts went on, he accepted material support from the United States but converted this help to strengthening his internal control, securing Honduras's borders, and building an infrastructure of roads, bridges, and dams.

The change in the army's status during World War II marked the beginning of its crucial role in Honduran politics, which remains to this day. The 1956 military coup ousting President Julio Lozano established the political independence of the armed forces, particularly the air force. Furthermore, a new constitution in the same year limited the power of the chief executive by permitting him to issue orders to the military only through the armed forces, not independently as commander in chief. Article 325 of that constitution gave the military commander the right to disobey a president's order if in the view of the armed forces it was unconstitutional.

Carías in effect began to make the clientelistic tradition of the caudillo state obsolete by professionalizing the armed forces. After he broke the cycle of civil wars and ended revolts and unrest that plagued Honduras for the first thirty years of the twentieth century, the stability he created was imposed on the political system. It did not emerge from a consensus of competing political groups, nor under a legal document dividing power equally and rationally among branches of government. Rather, the peace he achieved was done by a personalistic style of administration.

The Cariato lacked a systematic ideology, a body of principles. It was more a process, capably managed by individuals and loyal associates. The order was shaken in 1944 as World War II drew to a close. The Allied victory of democracies made the Carías dictatorship an anomaly like those of his neighbors in Guatemala and El Salvador. He became an endangered species like the presidents in those nations, Jorge Ubico and Maximiliano Hernández Martínez. In 1944 both these men announced plans to stay in power but were ousted. Reluctantly, Carías planned for a successor after Washington and the banana companies assured him of their support only through the end of his term. They wanted a smooth transition to take place, guaranteeing order, so the president gave the nod of support to his trusted ally and minister, Juan Manuel Gálvez.

Carías retained leadership in the National Party beyond his term. It remained the foundation of his public life until 1963. His control of the party apparatus from 1949 to 1963 gives as much evidence of political acumen and effectiveness as a leader as his sixteen years in office do. Although out of power in 1954, he obtained a greater number of popular votes for president than his party competitors, but this was his last victory. Inevitably, his influence declined, and he could not pass leadership to his son Gonzalo as the nominee for president in 1963, even though he controlled most of the delegates at the party convention. However, admirers remained loyal to him even though power slipped away. The Popular Progressive Party (PPP), founded in 1963 by Carías along with his son, enrolled many veterans of civil wars and political campaigns in the 1920s and 1930s. Like their patron, they too never gave up.

Carías's success dealing with neighbors, all dictators with the exception of Costa Rica, was a testament to his diplomatic skill. Their relationships were reciprocal and purely pragmatic. For different reasons they needed him in power. Although a conservative, he worked for the same solutions to problems that faced them. In the 1930s every dictator in Central America faced porous borders on all frontiers with political dissidents seeking their overthrow. Close cooperation among his fellow dictator presidents was important to end the flow of political opponents moving back and forth. Regional order and stability were important to all of them.

Carías followed the same economic and fiscal policies as Ubico, Somoza, and Hernández Martínez. Ubico needed an ally in his regional power play against El Salvador. El Salvador needed Carías to break out of its diplomatic isolation imposed by Washington after the 1931 Hernández Martínez coup. Carías the pragmatist never let conservative ideology interfere with the immediate needs of Honduras, Central America's most geographically central state.

Carías gave Honduras order but not progress. The brief democratic interlude under Miguel Paz Barahona was short lived (1924–28). The banana industry, the basic staple and singularly the largest export for Honduras, declined during the Carías era and the healthy trade surplus in 1925–26 had disappeared by 1937. World depression forced major fruit companies, Standard and United, to cut production. Floods in 1934 and the sigatoka disease all but devastated the banana crop. World War II further reduced production as Washington requisitioned banana company boats. Exports in 1942–43 were only 10 percent of the 1929–30 high. In 1943, gross domestic product per head was 36 percent of its 1930 peak.

Many government officials in the Carías regime, the president included, were longtime associates of the banana companies. Juan Manuel Gálvez, minister of war, and Plutarco Muñoz, president of congress, were banana company lawyers. The producers obtained lucrative concessions with rail lines for plantation expansion. In turn, Carías received hundreds of thousands of dollars for his political campaigns and the financing of government operations.

The Honduran fiscal crisis occupied most of Carías's attention while in office. He paid far more attention to this matter than to economic development. His approach to the collapse of the economy was to focus exclusively on income and expenditure matters. The centerpiece of his annual messages to congress was assessing the extent to which government expenditures were met by revenues. He grappled with this issue using draconian measures. He received loans from United and Standard Fruit Companies, introduced exchange controls and tariffs in 1934, and concluded a bilateral trade agreement with Washington in the same year (for political reasons). These steps actually destroyed what restrictions on imports may have accomplished by way of promoting the development of local industry for revenue. Yet Carías reduced the domestic debt and obtained a fiscal balance in 1937 and held it from then on.

He made significant strides building the country's infrastructure. Under him, Honduras had the best internal air transport system in Central America, and U.S. strategic interests built an inter-American highway running along the country's south coast. U.S. engineers also constructed a road link around Lake Yojoa, connecting Tegucigalpa to the railway and north coast ports.

Carías's political acumen was tested in 1944, when dictatorships fell in Central America. He survived demands for his ouster by simply letting his detractors know he was legally finishing his term in 1949. His orderly exit and smooth transition of power relieved Washington and banana companies. They, too, wanted him to end his term and provide for a successor, guaranteeing stability. Carías also outlasted his fellow dictators because his opposition was divided and weak. Liberals split their allegiance between the exiled Ángel Zúñiga

Huete, who failed to organize an effective opposition, and new radical groups like the Honduran Revolutionary Democratic Party (PDRH).

Under Carías, Honduras was transformed from a state of chronic civil war and fiscal chaos to a stable political system, but it was an enforced peace. The dictator provided the opening for reconciliation with enemies and modernization by choosing Juan Manuel Gálvez as his successor. Economic development after 1949 became a prime interest of the central government when Juan Manuel Gálvez created both a Central Bank and Development Bank in 1950, and new interest groups like labor were given attention with the creation of an office of Labor and Social Security affairs. A Ministry of Labor was established in 1954.

Carías also left many issues unresolved. The multinationals, particularly banana companies, remained the sole financial backbone of the Honduran government. They did almost nothing to contribute to the nation's revenue. These vast enterprises stayed completely in the hands of Yankee managers with almost total control of the Honduran external trade. Virtually the entire infrastructure of the nation, such as railroad, commercial establishments, and air transport systems, remained under their control. In 1951, United and Standard Fruit companies produced 91 percent of all tax revenue from income and profits in the country. They produced 48.6 million lempiras of gross national product when Honduras's operating budget was 50 million lempiras. Although government was administered better than ever before under Carías, the nation-state was not an independent, fully sovereign entity. In effect, Carías institutionalized the essential features of the country's economic, social, and political elements begun in the early years of his political career. Honduras remained wholly dependent financially on the U.S. banana companies and subservient to U.S. policies in Central America, and it retained the features of authoritarian rule.

The dictator remained active in retirement for twenty years, still visible and influential in National Party affairs until 1963, six years before his death. He left office without personal or bitter legacies, retiring gracefully, forever maintaining a paternalistic image, sitting in the front hall of his downtown residence receiving all kinds of petitioners. As always, he remained more respected than loved, more detached than emotionally engaged with people. These qualities, however, preserved his reputation during the dictatorship and after. Asked on one occasion what his plans for retirement were, he responded, "avoid alcohol and maintain constant physical activity," a typical Carías rejoinder. Prudence and discipline were the pillars of his charisma. They were purposefully crafted to make him different, set apart from his contemporaries. He never wavered from the singular objective of creating order and maintaining peace in the country. He offered no guidelines, no plans for governing a state undergoing change. He was neither a thinker nor a visionary. He was foremost a veteran of the politics of machetismo ("combat"), a tradition and practice he wanted to end in fixed presidential terms. He was proud that his regime ended civil wars and that good administration began under his imposed peace. Above all, Carías was wedded to his time. That was his strength. It was also his weakness.

Bibliography

BOOKS AND MANUSCRIPTS

Abraham Williams Calderón: su pensamiento político y sus planes de gobierno. Publicaciones del Movimiento Nacional Reformista. Tegucigalpa: Talleres Tipográficos Nacionales, 1954.

Acosta, Oscar. *Rafael Heliodoro Valle: vida y obra.* Rome: Instituto Italo-Latino-Americano, 1981.

Ameringer, Charles. *The Democratic Left in Exile: The Anti-Dictatorial Struggle in the Caribbean, 1945–1959.* Coral Gables: University of Florida Press, 1974.

Anderson, Thomas P. *The War of the Dispossessed: Honduras and El Salvador, 1969.* Lincoln: University of Nebraska Press, 1981.

Argueta, Mario. *Los alemanes en Honduras.* Tegucigalpa: Centro de Documentación de Honduras, 1992.

———. *Bananos y política: Samuel Zemurray y la Cuyamel Fruit Company.* Tegucigalpa: Editorial Guaymuras, 1989.

———. *Tiburcio Carías: anatomía de una época, 1923–1948.* Tegucigalpa: Editorial Guaymuras, 1989.

Aro Sanso, Ismael Mejía Deras. *Policarpo Bonilla: apuntes biográficos.* México: Imprenta Mundial, 1936.

Barahona, Ramón. *Carías: el caudillo de Zambrano, 1938–1948.* San Pedro Sula: Graficentro Editores, 1988.

Bardales Bueso, Rafael. *Biografía del Profesor Rodolfo Velásquez.* Tegucigalpa: Imprenta Cettna, 1985.

———. "El fundador de la paz." Unpublished manuscript. Tegucigalpa: Bardales Library.

———. *Historia del Partido Nacional.* Honduras: Sericopias Editores; Tegucigalpa: Bardales Library, 1980.

———. "El Partido Nacional en la historia." Unpublished manuscript. Tegucigalpa: Bardales Library.

Becerra, Longino. *Evolución historica de Honduras.* Tegucigalpa: Editorial Baktun, 1983.

Bethel, Leslie, ed. *History of Latin America since 1930: Central America and the Caribbean.* Cambridge: Cambridge University Press, 1990.

Bonilla, Emma. *Continuísmo y dictadura.* Comayaguela: Litográfica Comayaguela, 1989.

Bulmer-Thomas, Victor. *The Political Economy of Central America since 1920*. Cambridge: Cambridge University Press, 1987.

Carías Andino, Tiburcio. "Informe del Gobernador." In *Mensaje del President Miguel Dávila*. Tegucigalpa: Imprenta Nacional, 1907.

———. *Mensaje, President Miguel Paz Barahona*. Tegucigalpa: Litografía Nacional, 1928.

Carías Reyes, Marcos. *Consideraciones sobre aspectos históricos y sociales de Honduras*. Tegucigalpa: Imprenta Calderón, 1942.

———. *La Heredad*. Tegucigalpa: Tipo-Litográficos Ariston, 1945.

Castañeda, Gustavo S. *El Congreso de 1924*. Comayaguela: Empresa "La Sol," 1925.

Checchi, Vincent, et al. *Honduras: A Problem in Economic Development*. New York: Twentieth Century Fund, 1959.

Cisneros, Abel Villacorta. *Reseña história del Partido Nacional de Honduras*. Tegucigalpa: Publicaciones del Comité Central del Partido Nacional de Honduras, 1966.

Coello, Antonio, ed. *Anuario Estadístico Comercial de los Departamentos de Tegucigalpa, Cortés, y Atlantida*. Tegucigalpa: Tallares Tipográfica Nacionales, 1935.

Davies, R. E. G. *Airlines of South America*. Washington, DC: Smithsonian Institution, 1986.

Díaz Chavez, Filander. *Carías: el último caudillo frutero*. Tegucigalpa: Editorial Guaymuras, 1982.

Dosal, Paul. *Doing Business with the Dictators: A Political History of the United Fruit Co. in Guatemala, 1899–1994*. Wilmington: Scholarly Resources, 1993.

Dunkerley, James. *The Long War: Dictatorship and Revolution in El Salvador*. London: Verso, 1982.

———. *Power in the Isthmus: A Political History of Modern Central America*. New York: Verso, 1988.

Durón, Romulo E. *Bosquejo histórico de Honduras*. Tegucigalpa: Ministerio de Educación Pública, 1956.

Editorial de la Universidad de Costa Rica, 1995.

Ellsworth, Harry A. *One Hundred Eighty Landings of United States Marines, 1800–1934*. Washington, D.C.: Historical Section, Headquarters, U.S. Marine Corps, 1934.

Elpidio Mejía, Romualdo. *4 de Julio 1944*. Tegucigalpa: Talleres Tipográficos Aristan, 1945.

Euraque, Darío. *Reinterpreting the Banana Republic: Region and State in Honduras, 1870–1972*. Chapel Hill: University of North Carolina Press, 1996.

Funes, Matías. *Los deliberantes: el poder militar en Honduras*. Tegucigalpa: Editorial Guaymuras, 1995.

Gálvez: un presidente en mangas de camisa: breves relatos sobre alugnas obras administrativas y viajes presidenciales del Doctor Juan Manuel Gálvez. Tegucigalpa: Talleres Ariston, Tip-Litográficos, 1952.

González, José. *Poemas del Cariato*. Tegucigalpa: Editorial Guaymuras, SA, 1984.

González y Contreras, G. *Un pueblo y un hombre: Honduras y el general Carías*. Tegucigalpa: Imprenta la Democracia, 1934.

———. *El último caudillo.* Mexico City: Costa Amic, 1946.

Grieb, Kenneth J. *Guatemalan Caudillo: The Regime of Jorge Ubico, Guatemala, 1931–1944.* Athens: Ohio University Press, 1979.

Grimaldi, Antonio. *Biografía del Dr. Celeo Arias.* Tegucigalpa: Tipográficos Nacional, 1931.

Guatama, Fonseca Zúñiga. *Cuatro ensayos sobre la realidad política de Honduras.* Tegucigalpa: Universidad Nacional Autonoma de Honduras, Editorial Universitaria, 1984.

Hamill, Hugh M. *Caudillos: Dictators in Spanish America.* Norman: University of Oklahoma Press, 1992.

Inestroza, Jesús. *Génesis y soluciones de las escuelas militares del ejército, 1831–1837.* Tegucigalpa: Talleres de Paz, 1990.

Infante, Segisfredo, et al. *Los alemanes en el sur, 1900–1947.* Tegucigalpa: Editorial Universitaria, Universidad Nacional Autónoma de Honduras, Junio, 1993.

Izaguirre, Carlos. *Bajo el chubasco: novela de carácter política-social premiada en concurso nacional.* Tegucigalpa: n.p., n.d.

———. *Readaptaciones y cambios.* Tegucigalpa: Imprenta Calderón, 1936.

Karnes, Thomas L. *The Failure of Union: Central America, 1824–1960.* Chapel Hill: University of North Carolina Press, 1961.

———. *Tropical Enterprise: Standard Fruit and Steamship Company in Latin America.* Baton Rouge: Louisiana State University Press, 1978.

Kepner, Charles, and Jay Soothill. *The Banana Empire: A Case Study of Economic Imperialism.* New York: Vanguard, 1935.

Krehm, William. *Democracies and Tyrannies in the Caribbean.* Westport, CT: Lawrence, Hill, 1984.

Lagos, Agustín. *Los Pioneros: conversaciones con Doña Rosario S. de Ferrari.* Tegucigalpa: Imprenta Calderón, 1983.

Lainfiesta, Margot. *Cámara lenta.* Tegucigalpa: Talleres Tipográficos Nacionales, [1935].

———. *Honduras comienza hoy.* Tegucigalpa: Tipográficos Nacional, 1937.

———. *El renacimiento de una nación.* Tegucigalpa: Imprenta Calderón, 1936.

Lapper, Richard, and James Painter. *Honduras: State for Sale.* London: Latin American Business, 1985.

Lara Cerrato, Fausto, ed. *Aspectos culturales de Honduras.* Tegucigalpa: Imprenta Ariel, 1951.

Leonard, Thomas M. *The United States in Central America, 1944–1949: Perceptions of Political Dynamics.* Tuscaloosa: University of Alabama Press, 1984.

Lewis, Paul. *Paraguay under Stroessner.* Chapel Hill: University of North Carolina Press, 1980.

López Piñeda, Julián. *Algunos escritos.* Vol. 1. Tegucigalpa: Talleres Tipográficos Calderón, 1956.

———. *La reforma constitutional.* Paris: Ediciones Estrella, 1936.

Luque, Gonzálo Chalo. *Memorias de un Sanpedrano.* Vols. 1–2. San Pedro Sula: Los Modernos Talleres de Empresora Hondureña, 1980.

———. *Memorias de un soldado Hondureño*. San Pedro Sula: Los Modernos Talleres de Empresora Hondureña, 1980.

———. *Las Revoluciones en Honduras*. San Pedro Sula: Tallares Tipo-Litográficos de Central Impresora, 1982.

Martínez Funes, Gerado. *Viajando por el istmo a través de Honduras, recopilación de impresiones y de ideas de una vista a vuelo de pájaro*. Tegucigalpa: n.p., 1941.

Mecham, J. Lloyd. *The United States and InterAmerican Security*. Austin: University of Texas Press, 1961.

Mejía, Romauldo Elpidio. *4 de Julio 1944*. Tegucigalpa: Talleres Tipográficos Aristan, 1945.

Mejía Moreno, Luís. *El calvario de los demagogos*. Tegucigalpa: Talleres Tipográficos Nacionales, 1939.

———. *El calvario de un pueblo o un doble error constitucional*. Tegucigalpa: Talleres Tipográficos Nacionales, 1937.

Meza, Victor. *Historia del movimiento obrero Hondureño*. Tegucigalpa: Editorial Guaymuras, 1981.

———. *Política y sociedad en Honduras*. Tegucigalpa: Editorial Guaymuras, 1981.

Morris, James A. *Honduras: Caudillo Politics and Military Rulers*. Boulder: Westview Press, 1984.

Murillo Soto, Celeo. *Un hondureño y una actitud política (en busea) de la concordia*. Tegucigalpa: Talleras Tipográficos Nacionales, 1948.

Pagoaga, Rail Arturo. *Carlos Izaguirre y su multiple actividad mental*. Tegucigalpa: Imprenta Soto, 1947.

———. *Honduras y sus gobernantes*. Tegucigalpa: Imprenta Soto, 1979.

Paredes, Lucas. *Biografía del Dr. y General Tiburcio Carías Andino*. Tegucigalpa: Tipolitografía Ariston, 1938.

———. *El hombre del puro*. Tegucigalpa: Imprenta Honduras, 1973.

———. *Liberalismo y nacionalismo: transfugismo político*. Tegucigalpa: Imprenta Honduras, 1963.

Parkman, Patricia. *Nonviolent Insurrection in El Salvador: The Fall of Maximiliano Hernández Martínez*. Tucson: University of Arizona Press, 1988.

Posas, Manuel, and Rafael del Cid. *La construcción del sector público y del estado nacional en Honduras, 1876–1979*. Ciudad Universitaria Rodrigo Facio, Costa Rica: Editorial Universitaria Centroamericana, 1981.

Proclamas que dirigen a sus correligionarios el jefe Policarpo P. Bonilla y vice jefe Manuel M. Bonilla del Partido Liberal. Tegucigalpa: Tipográfica Nacional, 1894.

Rivas, Pedro. *Límites entre Honduras y Nicaragua en el Atlántico: historia cartográfica documentada*. Tegucigalpa: Talleres Tipográficos Nacionales, 1938.

Ruíz, José, and Rogelio Triminio, eds. *Apuntes biográficos: Hondureños e información para el turista*. Tegucigalpa: Imprenta Hernández, 1943.

Sagastumé, Ramón. *Carías: el caudillo de Zambrano, 1938–1948*. San Pedro Sula: Graficentro Editores, 1988.

Sanabria, Salomón. *La cárcel y mis carceleros*. México: Talleres del Editorial JUS, 1952.

Santoveña, Manuel, and Alejandro Novas Gardela. *Hombres y cosas*. Tegucigalpa: Talleres de la Democracia, 1933.

Schoonover, Thomas, and Lester Langley. *The Banana Men: American Mercenaries and Entrepreneurs in Central America, 1880–1995*. Lexington: University Press of Kentucky, 1995.

Stokes, William. *Honduras: An Area Study in Government*. Madison: University of Wisconsin Press, 1950.

Valenzuela, José Reina and Mario Argueta. *Marco Aurelio Soto: reforma liberal de 1876*. Tegucigalpa: Banco Central de Honduras, 1978.

Valle, Rafael Heliodoro. *Historia de las ideas contemporáneas en Centroamérica*. Mexico City: Fondo de Cultura Económica, 1960.

Villacorta Cisneros, Abel. *Reseña histórica del partido nacional de Honduras*. Tegucigalpa: Imprenta Nacional, 1966.

Villars, Rina. *Porque quiero seguir viviendo habla Graciela García*. Tegucigalpa: Editorial Guaymuras, 1991.

Walter, Knut. *The Regime of Anastasio Somoza, 1936–1956*. Chapel Hill: University of North Carolina Press, 1993.

Wiggins, Howard. *The Ruler's Imperative*. New York: Columbia University Press, 1969.

Yerex, David. *Yerex of TACA: A Kiwi Conquistador*. Carterton, New Zealand: Ampersand Publishing, 1985.

Zúñiga Huete, José Ángel. *Autobiografía*. Comayaguela: Imprenta Cultura, 1970.

———. *Un cacicazgo centroamericano*. Mexico City: Imprenta Victoria, 1938.

———. *El desastre de una dictadura*. Kingston, Jamaica: Times Publishing, 1937.

ARTICLES, ESSAYS, AND THESES

Blom, Franz. "La aviación conquista a Honduras." *Revista del Archivo* (Tegucigalpa), Vol. XIV, No. 9 (May 1936).

Bobadilla, Perfecto. "Monografía del Departamento de Cortés." *Revista del Archivo* (Cortés), Vol. XVIII (September 1940).

Brand, Charles. "The Background of Capitalist Underdevelopment: Honduras to 1913." Ph.D. diss., University of Pittsburgh, 1972.

Carías Andino, Tiburcio. "El establecimiento de las máquinas ha mejorado la condición de los obreros." Thesis, Facultad de Leyes, Universidad Nacional de Honduras, November 19, 1898.

Euraque, Darío A. "Industrialists and Merchants in Northern Honduras: The Making of a National Bourgeoisie in Peripheral Capitalism, 1870–1972." Ph.D. diss., University of Wisconsin, 1990.

————. "Los recursos económicos del estado Hondureño, 1830–1970." In Arturo Tara-cena and Jean Piel, eds., *Identidades nacionales y estado Moderno en Centroamérica*. San José, Costa Rica: Editorial de la Universidad de Costa Rica, 1995.

————. "La reforma liberal en Honduras y la hipótesis de la oligarquía ausente, 1870–1930." *Revista de Historia* (San José, Costa Rica) No. 23 (1991): 7–56.

————. "San Pedro Sula, la capital industrial de Honduras: su trayectoria entre Villo-rio Colonia y emporio bananero, 1536–1936." *Mesoamerica* 26 (December 1993): 217–52.

————. "Social, Economic, and Political Aspects of the Carías Dictatorship in Honduras: The Historiography." *Latin American Research Review*, Vol. 29, No. 1 (1994): 238–48.

Fitzgibbon, Russell H. "Continuísmo: The Search for Political Longevity." In Hugh Hamill, ed., *Caudillos: Dictators in Spanish America*. Norman: University of Oklahoma Press, 1992.

Guevara-Escudero, Francisco. "Nineteenth-Century Honduras: A Regional Approach to the Economic History of Central America, 1839–1914." Ph.D. diss., New York University, 1983.

Muñoz, Plutarco. "Mensaje." In *Boletín Legislativo*. Tegucigalpa: Imprenta Nacional, 1946.

Ropp, Steve. "The Honduran Army in the Socio-Political Evolution of the Honduran State." In James A. Morris, ed., *Honduras: Caudillo Politics and Military Rulers*. Boulder: Westview Press, 1984.

Ross, Daniel J. "The Honduran Revolution of 1924 and the American Intervention." Master's thesis, University of Florida, 1969.

Stokes, William. "The Land Laws of Honduras." *Agricultural History*, Vol. 3 (1947): 148–54.

Thompson, Joseph. "An Economic Analysis of Public Expenditure in Honduras, 1875–1950." Ph.D. diss., University of Florida, 1963.

Valladares, Juan B. "Algunos datos sobre la ascendencia del General Tiburcio Carías Andino." *Anales del Archivo Nacional*, No. 8 (August 1970): 66–67.

Valle, Rafael Heliodoro. "La aviación en Honduras." *Honduras Rotaria*, No. 33/34 (April–May 1954).

Wiarda, Howard J., and Michael J. Kryzanek. "Trujillo and the Caudillo Tradition." In Hugh Hamill, ed., *Caudillos: Dictators in Spanish America*. Norman: University of Oklahoma Press, 1992.

Woodward, Ralph Lee. "The Rise and Decline of Liberalism in Central America: Histor-ical Perspectives on the Current Crisis." *Journal of Interamerican Studies and World Affairs*, Vol. 26, No. 3 (August 1984).

NEWSPAPERS AND PERIODICALS

Acuerdos, Ministerio de Fomento, Tegucigalpa, 1934, 1936, 1938.
Acuerdos, Ministerio de Gobernación, Tegucigalpa, 1941.

Acuerdos, Ministerio de Guerra, Estado Mayor, National Archives, Tegucigalpa, 1929, 1932, 1933, 1934, 1935, 1936, 1937, 1939, 1940, 1941, 1942, 1943, 1945–1946, 1947.

Acuerdos, Ministerio de Intendencía, Tegucigalpa, 1936, 1938.

Acuerdos, Ministerio de Mantenimiento del Orden Público, Tegucigalpa, 1933–1934.

La Bandera Liberal, Tegucigalpa, 1907.

Boletín, Guatemala, 1944.

Boletín del Congreso Nacional Legislativo, Tegucigalpa, 1934, 1942, 1946, 1954.

El Ciudadano, San Pedro Sula, Honduras, 1935, 1948.

El Crónico, Tegucigalpa, 1943.

El Cronista, Tegucigalpa, 1915, 1923, 1925, 1926, 1928, 1932, 1936, 1939, 1943, 1954, 1963.

La Cultura: Organo del Institúto Normal de Varones, Tegucigalpa, 1940, 1948.

El Demócrata, Tegucigalpa, 1928.

El Día, Tegucigalpa, 1948, 1949, 1952, 1954, 1963, 1969.

El Diario, Tegucigalpa, 1963.

El Diario Comercial, San Pedro Sula, Honduras, 1933, 1938.

El Economista Hondureño, Tegucigalpa, 1939.

La Época, Tegucigalpa, 1933, 1934, 1935, 1936, 1937, 1938, 1939, 1940, 1941, 1943, 1944, 1948, 1954, 1978.

El Espectador, La Ceiba, Honduras, 1935.

La Gaceta, Tegucigalpa, 1891, 1928, 1935, 1938, 1954.

El Heraldo, Tegucigalpa, 1945, 1982.

Libro de Oro, Tegucigalpa, 1939.

Mensaje, Tegucigalpa, 1911, 1928, 1933, 1934, 1935, 1936, 1937, 1938, 1941, 1943, 1944, 1945, 1946, 1947, 1948.

Mensaje (Segunda Parte), Tegucigalpa, 1937–1945.

El Nacionalista, Tegucigalpa, 1919.

New York Times, 1937.

El Norte, Atlantida, Honduras, 1944.

La Prensa, Tegucigalpa, 1908, 1964, 1969.

El Pueblo, Tegucigalpa, 1932.

Revista, Tegucigalpa, 1969.

Revista del Archivo, Tegucigalpa, 1933, 1940, 1943.

Revista Ariel, Tegucigalpa, 1925.

Revista 15 de Mayo, Tegucigalpa, 1970.

Revista de Policía: Organo de la Institución, Tegucigalpa, 1934, 1935, 1936, 1937, 1941.

Revista Extra, Tegucigalpa, 1970.

Revista de Tegucigalpa, 1942.

Sufragio Libre, Tegucigalpa, 1922, 1923, 1943.

Tegucigalpa, 1927, 1932, 1933, 1937, 1938, 1939, 1940, 1942, 1945, 1947.

La Tribuna, La Ceiba, Honduras, 1947, 1987, 1993.

Vanguardia, Tegucigalpa, 1947.

Vanguardia Revolucionaria: organo del Partido Democrático Hondureño, San Pedro Sula, Honduras, 1946, 1947, 1948.

INTERVIEWS

Rafael Jerez Alvarado (member of the faculty, Instituto Normal Central de Varones 1938–1944). Tegucigalpa, 14 October 1987.

Francisca Paca Antunez Rivas (Carías's private secretary, 1949–1962). Tegucigalpa, 10 October 1987.

Guillermo Ayes (Carías's son-in-law). Tegucigalpa, 5 November 1987.

José Antonio Barahona Ortega (member of the Presidential Honor Guard and conspirator to kill Carías). Armenia, Department of Francisco Morazán, 28 November 1987.

Rafael Bardales Bueso (journalist and longtime political associate of Carías in the National Party). Tegucigalpa, 8 February 1987; 5 March 1987; 24 June 1987; 15 July 1987; 10 August 1987; 13 November 1987.

Raul Barnica (private secretary to Carías, 1954–1958). Tegucigalpa, 2 November 1987.

Louisa Benneton de Galindo (widow of Arturo Martínez Galindo). Tegucigalpa, 5 May 1987.

Luis Bertrand (grandson of President Bertrand, 1911–1912, 1913–1915, 1916–1919). Tegucigalpa, 2 April 1987.

Emma Bonilla de Larios (daughter of President Policarpo Bonilla, 1894–1899). Tegucigalpa, 26 November 1987.

Vicente Cáceres Lara (longtime political associate of Carías in the National Party). Tegucigalpa, 30 September 1987.

Emma Callejas (niece of Venancio Callejas, colleague of Carías in National Party, and critic of the caudillo). Tegucigalpa, April, May, June 1987.

Policarpo Callejas (son of Venancio Callejas). Tegucigalpa, 28 November 1987.

Daisy Carías (daughter-in-law to Tiburcio, married to the president's son Tiburcio). Tegucigalpa, several interviews during April 1987; 6 April 1987.

Jorge Daniel Carías (son of General Calixto Carías, Tiburcio Carías's nephew, and main assistant in dealing with military training and operations in the late 1930s and early 1940s). Tegucigalpa, 3 August 1987.

Colonel Carlos Castillo Cáceres (archivist, Ministry of Defense). Tegucigalpa, 1 September 1987.

Baltazar Vigil Claros. La Esperanza, 26 October 1987.

Luís Coello Ramos (founder of Cariista Party, Popular Progressive Party, 1963, and close associate of Carías). Tegucigalpa, 3 March 1987.

Jorge Fidel Durón (close collaborator of Carías, 1930s–1949). Tegucigalpa, several interviews during January and August 1987, also 18 October 1987; 8 February 1987; 10 August 1987.

Captain Luis Alonso Fiallos (first Honduran recruited by Carías to become a pilot). Cerro de Hule, 21 February 1987.

Juan José Flores (father was an early carísta). San Pedro Sula, 13 September 1987.

Abelardo Fortín (subdirector, Instituto Normal Central de Varones, 1937–44; director, 1944–47, 1951–54). Tegucigalpa, 21 November 1987.

Roberto Gálvez Barnes (member of governing junta, October 1956–November 1957, ambassador to the United States, and son of Carías's minister of war, navy, and air force, 1933–1949, Tegucigalpa, 2 September 1987; 30 October 1987.

Rafael Antonio Alberto García (follower of Gregorio Ferrera). San Pedro Sula, 15 November 1987.

Henry Gilbert (Carías's close friend and dentist). Tegucigalpa, 12 April 1987.

Oscar Guerrero (son of Francisco Guerrero, who became a close friend of Carías as commandante de armas in Atlántida). Tegucigalpa, 23 October 1987.

Dora Henriques (daughter of Benjamín Henriques, "Director of Roads"). Tegucigalpa, 7 May 1987.

Orlando Henriques (son of Benjamín Henriques). Tegucigalpa, 4 August 1987.

Miguel Izaguirre (nephew of Carlos Izaguirre, one of Carías's closest confidants through the 1930s and 1940s). Numerous interviews, Tegucigalpa, spring 1987.

Matilda Izaguirre Tosta de Fiallos (daughter-in-law of Carlos Izaguirre). Tegucigalpa, 3 September 1987.

José María Lagos (Carías's bodyguard, 1937–1939, nicknamed "Lagitos" or "Chemita"). Tegucigalpa, 22 October 1987.

Nora Landa Blanco de Trochez (daughter of Yanuario Landa Blanco, deputy of Cortés during the Carías era). Tegucigalpa, 25 August 1987.

Eliseo Lizardo (Carías's business manager). Tegucigalpa, 3 December 1987.

Gonzálo (Chalo) Luque. San Pedro Sula, spring 1987; 10 September 1987; 14 September 1987.

Francisco Martínez (editor, Vanguardia Nacionalista). Tegucigalpa, 19 October 1987.

Tomás Martínez (commander, mounted police, national police force under Carías, 1933–1949). Tegucigalpa, 9 April 1987; 11 November 1987.

Charlie Matthews (a Carías pilot). Cerro de Hule, 31 May 1987.

E. L. McGinnis (former U.S. consul, La Ceiba, 1930s). Silver Spring, MD, 15 December 1986.

Gabriel Mejía (administrator of tax revenues for Cortés, 1940–1949; father, Benjamín Mejía of San Pedro Sula, was a longtime ally of Carías). San Pedro Sula, 25–26 February 1987; November 1987.

Eliseo Pérez Cadalso (secretary to Carías's adviser and confidant, Carlos Izaguirre). Tegucigalpa, 1 December 1987.

Francisco Prats Vives (married to Carías's niece, María Carías Reyes). Tegucigalpa, 22 July 1987.

Presentación Rivera (Carías's chief telegraph operator, 1945–1949). Tegucigalpa, July 1987.

Isidro Sabio (former member, city council). Trujillo, 26 June 1987.

Francisco Sánchez (former member, city council). El Progreso, 12 September 1987.

Secretary of the Junta Central, interview, Trujillo, Department of Colón, 16 August 1987.

José Reina Valenzuela (Liberal Party leader and close associate of Ángel Zúñiga Huete). Tegucigalpa, 11 March 1987.

Rudolfo Zacarías Velásquez (headed National Party in Intibucá for 48 years). Esperanza, Intibucá, Honduras, 27 October 1987; 27 September 1987.

Vicente Williams Jr. (son of Carías's vice-president, Abraham Williams). Tegucigalpa, 18 November 1987.

Marcos Carías Zapata (son of Marco Carías Reyes, private secretary to President Carías). Tegucigalpa, 17 December 1987.

Liana Zúñiga Caceres. Roatan, 14 August 1987.

PRIVATE LIBRARIES
Rafael Bardales, Tegucigalpa

Album de Recortes

Biblioteca de la Escuela Militar de Aplicación para Oficiales, Tegucigalpa

Nora Landa Blanco de Trochez Papers, Tegucigalpa
Letters from Ángel Zúñiga Huete to Froylán Turcios
Luis Coello Ramos Papers, Tegucigalpa
Aníbal Delgado Fiallos Papers, San Pedro Sula
Letters of Amilcar Gómez Robelo

Roberto Gálvez Barnes Library, Tegucigalpa

Oscar and Queta Guerrero, papers and diaries, Tegucigalpa

Benjamín Henriques Library, property of Rafael Teresero, Tegucigalpa

Gabriel Mejía Papers, San Pedro Sula

Library of Miguel Paz Reyes (archivist, Fuerzas Armadas), Tegucigalpa

Datos cronológicos de la comprar de aviaciones de la Fuerza Aérea de Honduras, 1933–1948
Libro diario de la escuela militar de aviación. Ministerio de Guerra. N.d.
Memoria y anexos de guerra, marina, y avación. Républica de Honduras. N.d.

GOVERNMENT DOCUMENTS
Honduras (Tegucigalpa)

Archivos Comisión de Soberanía y Fronteras, Ministerio de Relaciones Exteriores
Archivos, Escuela Militar de Aplicaciones

Archivos del Palacio de los Ministerios
Archivos Ministerio de Defensa Nacional y Seguridad Pública
Archivos Ministerio de Guerra, Marina, y Aviación, Acuerdos de Mantenimiento del Orden Público, 1933–1935; Acuerdos Estado Mayor, 1936–1947
Archivos del Ministerio de Gobernación, Tesorería
Cartas autográficas, 1920–1939, Vols. XIX–XVIII, Archivos del Ministerio de Relaciones Exteriores

Archivos Ministerio de Educación Pública
Memorias, Libros de Acuerdos del Secretario, 1938–1948

Archivos Ministerio de Hacienda
Acuerdos, Ministerio de Fomento, 1933–48

Archivos Universidad Nacional de Honduras
Expedientes de Licenciatura, 1898–1900

Biblioteca y Archivos Nacionales
Manifiesto, Presidente Dávila
Memorias de Guerra, Marina, y Aviación
Mensaje del Señor Presidente de la Republica, 1933–36

United States

Confidential Post Records. Central America, Honduras, 1930–1945. Paul Kesaris, editor. Frederick, MD: University Publications of the Americas, microfilm, 1985
National Archives of the United States, Washington, DC

Index